Nabil Dajani is Professor of Media Studies at the Department of Social and Behavioral Sciences at the American University of Beirut.

"Nabil Dajani, an authoritative voice on Arab media, provides a much-needed reflection on the situation of Lebanese media. He adeptly guides the readers through the different historical changes of the media in Lebanon, a country that has been characterized by its political and religious fragmentation, which, as Dajani rightly says, represents a condensed model of the situation in the Arab East region. Dajani provides an original analysis of the Lebanese media, particularly the press, drawing attention to the reasons behind the demise of the media institutions leading to further fragmentation of the Lebanese society. In an age of 'fake news', where global and local media institutions are under scrutiny, Dajani postulates that Lebanese citizens lost faith in their media partially due to the media's failure to create the national unity needed to mend the moral damages of the past wars and conflicts."

Noha Mellor, Professor of Media, University of Bedfordshire, UK

"This book demonstrates the importance of the historical narrative of the state of media in Lebanon in understanding how it is shaped today and why. The value of the historical investigation of the Lebanese media and the historical facts that generated from the author's personal encounters and experience as a former member of the journalism community in Lebanon is enormous. The book is a valuable addition to the literature on the media scene in Lebanon and its influencers."

Zahera Harb, Senior Lecturer, Department of Journalism, City, University of London, UK

The Media in Lebanon

Fragmentation and Conflict in the Middle East

Nabil Dajani

I.B. TAURIS

LONDON • NEW YORK • OXFORD • NEW DELHI • SYDNEY

I.B. TAURIS
Bloomsbury Publishing Plc
50 Bedford Square, London, WC1B 3DP, UK
1385 Broadway, New York, NY 10018, USA

BLOOMSBURY, I.B. TAURIS and the I.B. Tauris logo are trademarks of Bloomsbury
Publishing Plc

First published in Great Britain 2019
Reprinted 2019

A catalogue record for this book is available from the British Library.

A catalog record for this book is available from the Library of Congress

ISBN: 978-1-7807-6541-9
ePDF: 978-1-78673-657-4
eBook: 978-1-78672-651-3

Series: Library of Modern Middle East Studies 136

Typeset by Newgen KnowledgeWorks Pvt. Ltd., Chennai, India
Printed and bound in Great Britain

To find out more about our authors and books visit www.bloomsbury.com
and sign up for our newsletters.

To four great mentors:
Fuad Sarrouf,
C.K. Zurayk,
Kamal Salibi, and
Malcolm MacLean

Contents

Illustrations

Unless otherwise stated, all images are part of the author's personal collection.

Figures

Table

Acknowledgments

The idea of writing this book began fermenting in 2000 when a serious health condition furthered the plan to relate my media experience in Lebanon and the Arab region. I started going through my old files of notes, early newspaper clippings and later electronic files. Heavy involvement in academic, administrative and community work, however, kept on deferring efforts on this project. A 2011 contract with then I.B. Tauris Middle East editor Maria Marsh lead to signing a contract to write this book, then continued prodding from I.B. Tauris editors kept the project going. I am greatly indebted to Joanna Godfrey, editorial director at I.B. Tauris for her continuous follow-up on my book development and for her comments on my early chapters. Several I.B. Tauris readers made critical comments and valuable suggestions on early drafts to which I am greatly indebted. I am also indebted to Sophie Campbell, production manager for following up the final editing and production of the book. Bayan Itani, my graduate assistant, went through boxes of clippings and files organizing them by subject and date. She also was instrumental in providing me with supporting electronic documents. I owe her a debt of gratitude for help beyond the call of duty.

Preface

Recent attempts at investigating the media and its role in society tend to focus on the present media situation, particularly on the new and social media. The process of communication is an important component in the maintenance and development of social life, and it is rooted in the past. An appropriate investigation of the role the media in society therefore requires centering the attention on both the biography and the history of the present communication structures in the country.

The past is a prologue. Understanding the past is a necessary preface for the understanding of the present and for planning the future. The purpose of this study is to examine the media situation in Lebanon by investigating the different historical changes in the structure and the forces at work on these media. A historical investigation of the Lebanese media (that is unfortunately, underscored by new Lebanese media studies) is essential for a proper examination of the Lebanese media situation. Such an approach is crucial to provide a critical assessment of the prevailing forces that contribute to the fragmentation and conflict in this small state, which represents an amplified model of the situation in the Arab East region. Because the study is historical in nature, it delves into as much media management details as needed in this historical context. This is why this study goes to great lengths in discussing Lebanese print media, which is the first Lebanese mass medium.

The study and investigation of the role of the Lebanese media in the Lebanese society has been the core of my research for the past half century. My interest in this subject was stimulated by my early interactions with media channels in Lebanon in the 1950s and 1960s as the business manager of a student college paper, as news editor of a local Lebanese paper and as director of information at a university in Lebanon. I developed firsthand knowledge of the business dealings with Lebanese publications, the editing "ethos" in Lebanon, as well as the role of public relations and personal contacts in the Lebanese media context. Over the years, I have acquired a large volume of notes and documents that were the basis for my book on the Lebanese media: *Disoriented Media in a Fragmented Society*, which appeared at the end of the Lebanese Civil War, in 1993, and did not receive adequate exposure and dissemination.

In preparing this manuscript, I have updated and restructured the relevant material in the 1993 book and incorporated parts of some of my recent articles to demonstrate the vast changes that these media have undertaken. I was careful to free my presentation from any ideological interpretation of the media situation. I am here as a scholar and not as a politician.

While this manuscript integrates parts of my past work, it does not represent a new edition of this work. Rather, my new input provides a different orientation that focuses on the history and biography of the Lebanese media. It presents a synthesis of my Lebanese and Arab media observations. I have, thus stayed away from discussing at length the social media in Lebanon, as this form of media has only a short history, which is still in the making. However, I related these to the folk media inasmuch as one may view the social media as a mediated form of face-to-face communication.

In particular, I have included a distinct and critical discussion of the social media in Chapter 5 on "From Folk to Social Media," in which I suggest the importance of involving the social media with the cultural background of society. I present a case for the need to focus on social media's social responsibility and to imbed it into its culture. This may be achieved by relating the role of social media to that of the traditional Lebanese folk media.

Dealing with the present realities of the Lebanese media requires being sensitive to domestic realities of the subject matter. This has meant that certain firsthand information, which reflects little credit on several institutions and individuals, had either to be suppressed or presented in such a way that those concerned would remain anonymous. While some readers may regret that, the exigencies of the current situation in Lebanon make this necessary, however, I do not think that it seriously undermines my account. I am mainly interested in offering examples of the kind of behavior that unfortunately taints the handling of the media in Lebanon. Additionally, much of this information was offered to me in good faith, and I have no wish to break the confidentiality of my informants. Readers must bear with me, therefore, if in certain places they find an irritating vagueness in relation to actual people and events, and I must ask them to take on trust the veracity of what I have written. Suffice to say, that in my earlier career as a media practitioner and as a friend and advisor to various media practitioners and officials, I have had many opportunities to learn about many aspects of the Lebanese media—good and bad. My purpose here is to provide readers with an appraisal of the Lebanese mass media and a critical assessment of the role media plays in Lebanese society.

Lebanon is a distinctive country with many contradictions, a country of precarious pluralism and deep divisions, a fragmented society that is going through a controversial state. Its institutions are torn between a situation of change and that of persistence. The peculiarities of the Lebanese situation have a bearing on its media being schizophrenic and disoriented. The fragmentation of the society contributes to disorientation of its media, and the disorientation of these media feeds into the fragmentation of the society. It is a situation locked into a vicious circle of mutual reinforcement.

The examination of the role of the media institutions in the context of Lebanese society, which this study attempts, suggests that the structure and content of the media is unique to the society and region within which it operates. The existing societal forces determine the structure and content of media institutions. These forces develop, through their interaction and styles of life, which are intervening levels between the messages of the media and individual consciousness and behavior.

What this study aims to show is that in a precarious country like Lebanon the basic challenge facing the media is to create cohesion and consensus, both of which are essential for the mitigation and eventual resolution of conflicts among its various segments. Additionally, the study argues that by operating within an information flow that is not tied to societal policies and plans, and by providing their audiences with content that is alien to the real-life concerns of the average citizen, the Lebanese media have furthered the alienation of the average individual. These media have contributed to maintaining and increasing the divisions that exist within the society.

Indeed, the Lebanese media, inasmuch as they generally appeal to individual sects and groups within the country, are helping to sustain the state of sectarian division. Similarly, by tackling their topics and themes within different orientations to different social classes, the media may actually be introducing new divisions into the society, based on class differentiation.

1

Background

The Sociopolitical Picture

Following four centuries of Ottoman control of the Arab region, from 1516 until the end of World War I, in 1918, the League of Nations granted France and England a mandate over a portion of the Ottoman Empire that encompasses what was known as the province of Syria. France demarcated the region of Lebanon in 1920, and Lebanon gained its independence as a sovereign state in 1943.

The Republic of Lebanon (Arabic *Lubnan*) covers 10,452 sq km on the eastern coast of the Mediterranean Sea. Lebanon's coastal location and moderate climate have made it a contact point between the East and the West and attracted foreign powers. Its high mountains that are relatively difficult to access helped make it a refuge place for ethnic and religious minorities in the region. This ethnic and religious pluralism has allowed foreign powers that ruled Lebanon to maintain their dominance.

The nature of its ethnic and religious composition and its small size granted Lebanon a special status within the Ottoman Empire. It also played an important role in Lebanon's future sociopolitical development. The mercantile basis of its economic prosperity, the heterogeneous character of its society, as well as the specific political structures that it developed, have allowed it to maintain its links with both the Eastern and the Western worlds, as well as enabling it to enjoy an atmosphere of relative political freedom and cultural dynamism.

The last census conducted in Lebanon was in 1932,[1] thus sample surveys provide the only possibility for estimating the population size. The latest population estimate by the Lebanese Central Administration of Statistics is 3,759,100.[2] The Lebanese population estimate in the "Mundi Index" of the

CIA World Facebook is 6,229,794.[3] The World Bank's estimate of the Lebanese population is 6,806,668.[4] The Lebanese figure, however, does not include the Palestinian and Syrian population in refugee camps or foreign workers, which may explain the discrepancy between it and the other two figures.

For three decades after its independence, the country prospered under a free-market economy. However, growing hostility among its confessional groups erupted into a long and costly Civil War (1975–1989). Disagreement over the reconstruction plans after the Civil War resulted in furthering the fragmentation of the Lebanese society and the endless political and social conflicts, as will be discussed in this chapter. Today, Lebanon is a fragmented society that is going through constant political and economic conflicts.

The independence of Lebanon in 1943 limited its long-established interaction with the Syrian towns of the interior and deprived it of its natural hinterland. The geopolitical changes in the Arab region in the late 1940s and early 1950s contributed to developing Lebanon into a regional Arab center.

The establishment of the State of Israel in 1948 resulted in the termination of trade and economic relations between Palestine and the Arab countries. Consequently, Lebanon took over the role of Palestine as the main center for transit goods to Jordan and the Gulf States. The series of military coups that took place in Egypt, Syria and Iraq in the wake of the creation of the State of Israeli prepared Lebanon to be the principal politically and economically stable Arab state in the region and subsequently it became the chief Arab center for business and diplomatic missions.

The Sectarian/Economic Delineation

Lebanon was a fitting area for the European powers to penetrate the Ottoman Empire. This was achieved by continuously exploiting the heterogeneous composition of the population, playing off the religious groups, one against another. Each power claimed itself to be the "protector" of the rights and interests one of the sects, initially among the Christians. France thus, supported the Maronite Christians; the Greek Orthodox Christians looked to Russia; and Great Britain gave support to the Druze. After independence, several relatively powerful countries in the region (Egypt, Iraq, Saudi Arabia,

Syria and most recently Israel) also began to exploit this situation by appealing to various sects.

Lebanon has long had a "confessional" system of political appointments, which is based on the belief that each religious community is a separate entity whose interests are distinct from those of other sects. Under this system, the Maronite Christians have held the highest offices in the country since the 1932 census showed that this group made up the largest minority group at that time.

The first constitution of the modern state of Lebanon was drawn up in 1926 and was modeled after the French Third Republic. This constitution continued to be applicable until 1990 but was amended several times. In addition to the written constitution, representatives of the major religious factions agreed to respect an unwritten "National Pact," which was drafted in 1943 by a Muslim Sunni leader, Riad el-Solh and a Maronite Christian leader, Bichara el-Khuri. This pact stipulated the distribution of key government positions among the major religious sects according to the 1932 census population figures. While the old constitution did not explicitly specify the distribution of key political positions, the "National Pact" pact was firmly respected. Thus, the presidency was earmarked for a Maronite Christian, the position of prime minister for a Sunni Muslim, and that of the speaker of the house for a Shi'ite Muslim.[5]

Article 95 of the pre-1990 Lebanese constitution stated that "for reasons of amity and justice government posts should be equitably distributed among the various communities." As demographic changes indicate that Muslim sects at present clearly outnumber Christian sects, the 1990 constitution modified this by limiting the equitable distribution to top government positions only. It spelled out that the distribution of senior government positions should be "equally divided between Christians and Muslims without restricting any position to a particular sect." However, to alleviate the fear of Christians of losing their prominent role, the 1990 constitution definitely specified that the presidency is to be restricted to a Maronite, the speaker of the house, to a Shi'ite Muslim, and the prime minister to a Sunni Muslim.

Besides religious diversity, Lebanon also has ethnic diversity. The present-day ethnic composition of Lebanon has been affected by numerous local, regional and international conflicts. Most important among these were the migration of Armenians from Turkey after World War I, the Palestinians during the Arab–Israeli War in 1948, the Egyptians, Syrians and Iraqis after the *coups d'état* in Egypt, Syria and Iraq in the 1950s, and the flux of Syrian refugees escaping the ongoing fighting in Syria since 2011.

The emergence of the Palestinians and Syrians as a political force after 1967, the 1990 Syrian army presence in Lebanon and the mass movement of Syrian refugees after the 2011 Syrian armed conflict has caused several crises in Lebanon inasmuch as it has tipped the delicate balance of political relationships. The alliances of several groups and sects with the Palestinians and Syrians have brought about frequent political crises and civil disturbances during the past five decades.

The present Lebanese political system, as spelled out in the 1990 constitution, put power in the hands of the Maronite president, who is elected by the parliament for a period of six years. Next in actual executive power is the prime minister. A Sunni Muslim leader is named by the president, "after the Speaker of the House of Parliament conveys to him the results of binding parliamentary consultations." The prime minister stays in power as long as he has the confidence of the parliament and participates with the president in the selection of a cabinet, which has traditionally been "a coalition of local sectarian and even tribal interests."[6] Despite the existence of political parties in Lebanon, these play a minor role in the political life of the country. The major role is played by the notables (*zu'ma*) and religious leaders who formed the core of Lebanon's ruling elite since its independence. The following observations, made in 1966 by a Lebanese scholar, Labib Zuwiyya Yamak, are still applicable:

> Legislatures since independence have generally been dominated by notables, mostly landowners, of the various sects. The major families have always been represented … Since the most common electoral procedure has been that of the long electoral list, notables have come to enjoy a tremendous power that is sometimes not commensurate with their own personal electoral strength. This procedure … makes it difficult, if not impossible, for parties to have any appreciable influence on the outcome of elections in districts firmly controlled by the traditional notables. All this has resulted in legislatures that have no definite national policy or program and which are generally willing to do the bidding of the Chief Executive … Lebanon has not yet had a government that is accountable to a Parliamentary majority nor is there yet a genuine party system in Lebanon.[7]

The Lebanese ruling elite did not genuinely seek to transform its sectarian and family base to a truly national one. Rather, the ruling elite practice policies that strengthen this state of affairs without regard to the constitution and with no legal pursuit.[8] This violation of the constitution is covered by a tacit agreement among Lebanese politicians and religious leaders.[9] The daily concerns of the average Lebanese are generally addressed not by the government, which is composed of a coalition of traditional notables (*zu'ma*), but by the traditional notable, or *zaim*,[10] of each particular group.[11] The 1989 Taif Agreement did not succeed in ending the control of traditional notables. Rather, it resulted in adding new partners to them—the militia bosses whose leadership is also based on family and sect.

Confessional contradictions are the easiest to observe within the Lebanese structure. In terms of geographic distribution, the population clusters along confessional lines with predominantly Christian zones and predominantly Muslim ones. In Beirut, for instance, Ain el-Remmaneh and Achrafieh are Christian quarters, while Basta and Shi'ah are inhabited predominantly by Muslims. In areas where there was some mixture, such as in the Shouf, the Civil War of 1975–1989 brought it to an end, creating in its place confessional "purity."

Not only do confessional divisions affect the geographical distribution of population, they also affect education and the schooling system. A Christian student is most likely to attend one of the Catholic schools, most of which were established by nineteenth-century European missionaries. A Muslim, on the other hand, will probably study in one of the schools of the Muslim associations such as Al-Makassed. In these schools, children are socialized into different political appeals, and their cultural identities asserted along different genealogies, "histories" and loyalties.

The confessional identity of the Lebanese is further strengthened in various domains of social interaction such as youth associations (there are two Lebanese boy scout federations, one for the Christians and one for Muslims), sport clubs (facing the Muslim *Nejmeh* is the Christian *Racing* football club), and even humanitarian organizations (a "Lebanese Red Cross" and a "Lebanese Red Crescent").

Political divisions between the "Right" and the "Left" are largely a reflection of confessional attachments. Political parties have generally appealed to specific confessional audiences. Those that attempted to cut across confessional lines and to articulate nonsectarian ideologies have remained marginal because they required the giving up of religious allegiances from their constituencies. These parties were born largely as a result of the penetration of Western political ideals in the Arab world. Their ideologies—built around the modern European concept of nation-state democracy or social welfare—mean little to a society in which family, clan, tribe and sect are the instruments of collective action, and the symbolic universes of meaning.

Behind the more obvious confessional divisions of the Lebanese society lie more complex socioeconomic contradictions that have developed from the gradual penetration of capitalism in the Arab world. As in most Developing countries, this penetration has been accompanied by the slow destruction of a young, unprotected industry—the silk industry in the case of Lebanon—and the expansion of the service sector, highly sensitive to the fluctuations of the world market. The birth of a capitalist mode of production has thus created a contradiction between a mercantile bourgeoisie interested in a laissez-faire economic policy and a so-called industrial bourgeoisie, which has called for the imposition of heavy custom duties on imported goods that compete with local industry.

Since its independence, Lebanon has officially had an open economy dominated by the private sector with a flexible exchange rate and no restrictions on capital transfers. Domestic fiscal policy aims at restraining credit expansion in the public sector. As a result, Lebanon experienced relative financial stability until the beginning of the Civil War in 1975.

Lebanon's open economy, its political stability after World War II and its geographic location have attracted foreign capital and stimulated domestic investment. Beirut became a major banking and commercial center in the Middle East and until the beginning of the Civil War, there was a consistent surplus in the Lebanese balance of payments.[12]

However, whereas the policy of an open economy led to the development of the industrial and service sectors prior to 1975, the lack of social planning hampered the development of the agricultural sector, which is a primary source of income and employment in rural areas.[13] In 2009, agricultural employment in rural areas reached 25 percent of the labor force and represented 80 percent of Lebanon's gross domestic product (GDP). This sector "while not among the largest contributors to the national production and wealth ... accounts for 4 percent of Lebanon's Gross Domestic Product."[14] In 2013, the total agricultural exports accounted for 19 percent of total exports and the total agricultural imports represented 16 percent of total imports.[15]

A Heterogeneous State within a Volatile Region

The Lebanese economic structure reflects Lebanon's societal relationships where, in certain regions, tribal arrangements are still operative; in other places, feudalism has resisted or accommodated modernizing influences and ideologies. The coexistence of these contradictory socioeconomic systems is accompanied by a wide disparity of income and resources. The disparity is partly geographical: Beirut is in the center of Lebanon; consequently, it provides a wide range of services and monopolizes the majority of the national income. The south, north and east of Lebanon do not share in the prosperity of the country to the same degree. And it is partly social—within Beirut, a misery belt of slums and deprivation contrasts with the luxurious quarters of the business elite. The Lebanese economy can thus be described as highly fragmented.

On the other hand, because of its nature as a small state with a heterogeneous population mix in a politically volatile region, Lebanon has always been affected by regional and international political changes. And because of its governance system, which is based on unpredictable coalitions between the chieftains of the different religious sects, regional and international powers have been able to squabble on its territory. The 1968 Arab–Israeli War was a major event that had an earthquake effect on the region. Lebanon's delicate sectarian and ethnic fine balance was thus seriously disturbed and the country witnessed serious economic and political problems.

The Muslim population, encouraged by the presence of a large number of Palestinian refugees living in a depressing state and the demographic population changes in their favor, initiated demands for a greater role in Lebanon's governance. Consequently, regional sociopolitical developments provoked the eruption of a Civil War in 1975. It lasted until 1989 when members of the Lebanese parliament signed a regionally and internationally patronized accord in the Saudi city of Taif. This accord was guaranteed by powerful regional and international powers and was expected to end the Civil War. It constrained the previous extensive role of the Maronite Christian president[16] and stipulated a more balanced governance system as well as a regulated presence of Syrian forces during the initial stages of the implementation of its clauses. The emerging new ruling elite was formed mainly from leaders of the warring militias who were allied to the different regional powers. Nevertheless, it continued to represent the different factions of the Lebanese ethnic and sectarian mosaic.

Fragmentation of the Lebanese factions and serious disagreements over reconstruction plans lead to continuous economic and political conflicts, which intensified the fragmentation of the Lebanese society and forced (or encouraged) the deferral of implementing vital articles in the Taif Accord. Among the deferred articles was taking formal steps to gradually end the sectarian system of governance as well as the establishment of a national senate that would represent the different sectarian mix of the state. The Syrian forces in Lebanon played the role of a mediator among the conflicting factions at the beginning but ended up interfering in all aspects of governance.

The Civil War destroyed most of Lebanon's physical infrastructure and resulted in administrative and political chaos, the spread of corruption and the mass departure of many of the capable talents needed to rebuild the country. This situation lessened Lebanon's regional and Arab importance. Its currency dropped by more than 500 percent. To address the economic problems of the country, priority was given to borrowing funds in order to rebuild the physical infrastructure of the country, hoping to draw foreign investments and to revive the economy. This was not coupled with administrative reform or with tackling the state of corruption that was heightened by the Civil War militia leaders ascending to power.

Additionally, the economic policy adopted by the government did not give due attention to the middle class and the professional groups, who formed the core of the population needed in the reconstruction phase. No deliberate efforts were exerted to motivate these groups to participate and be involved in the rebuilding process. The government's economic policy focused on enticing the wealthy population by reducing their taxes as well as appeasing the lower classes by giving them substantial compensation for their losses in the Civil

War. To secure the needed funds for the success of this policy heavy indirect taxation was imposed, the burden of which fell mainly on members of the middle class. As a result, many members of these groups fled the country seeking better living conditions.

The early post–Civil War period was characterized by economic and political instability. The fierce opposition of the ruling elite to any attempt to investigate possible corruption among supporters of the "old guard" of politicians obstructed efforts for reform. The inability of the government to generate concrete change in the living conditions increased the people's frustration. The economic crisis and political instability also infected the Lebanese media and allowed wealthy politicians to own or control most of the major media outlets in the country. Media voices exposing the failure of the ruling elite to attend to serious daily needs such as the restoration of electrical power, or who were critical of economic and reconstruction plans that were designed to suit the interests of wealthy politicians and business people, were suppressed or ignored.

The first phase of the post–Civil War lasted until 2005 with the assassination of a popular political figure, Rafik Hariri. Hariri had steered Lebanon's economic and political affairs for some 15 years as a philanthropist, prime minister and leader of a political trend supportive of Saudi Arabia. During this phase, Lebanon undertook sweeping reconstruction plans that placed it in heavy debt, yet it did not succeed in attending to the basic daily needs of the people. It also witnessed the growing power of Lebanese and Islamic resistance forces to the continued Israeli occupation of Lebanese land that resulted from the 1982 Israeli assault on the Palestinian resistance forces in Lebanon. This resistance forced the withdrawal of Israel from most of the occupied Lebanese areas in 2000 but at a heavy destruction cost that added to Lebanon's economic plight.

The assassination of Hariri was a turning point in the modern history of Lebanon and ushered what some call the "Cedar Revolution," or the "Second Independence Revolution." Supporters of Hariri accused Syria of being behind this assassination. The country was now split into two opposing factions, one calling for the withdrawal of Syrian forces from Lebanon and the other was supportive of Syria. The faction supporting Syria held a massive demonstration on March 8 that assembled in downtown Beirut—it was claimed to include some 1 million demonstrators. This was followed by another massive demonstration and assembly of people on March 14 calling for the withdrawal of the Syrian forces in Lebanon—it was also claimed to include some 1 million demonstrators. The two factions were thus named after these two dates.

Stern regional and international reactions to the assassination of Hariri[17] forced Syria to withdraw its forces from Lebanon. The Lebanese government headed by a Syrian supporter resigned to be replaced by a new Lebanese government headed by a former Hariri assistant and dominated by March 14 politicians who took hold of the country's affairs. New parliamentary elections held in May 2005, resulted in a victory for the March 14 group. Lebanon henceforth entered into some 12 years of strife. The two groups, having relatively equal popular support, struggled for influence and subsequently paralyzed the country's institutions.

In May 2007, the struggle reached armed level in the streets of the capital, Beirut which prompted the ruler of Qatar to mediate and help both groups arrive at a new accord, the "Doha Agreement." A new electoral law was agreed upon in September 2008 with the understanding that it was to be implemented only once. The outcome of the 2009 elections showed similar results to those of 2005. Demands for an electoral law based on proportional representation were now voiced. Failure to produce such a law by the time new elections were due in 2013, and fear of the same outcome by both groups forced an agreement to extend the mandate of the parliament until 2017. When by 2017 an agreement on a new law could not be reached, another extension for a one-year final term was granted, with a binding clause that no further extension was possible. Both groups had no choice but to agree at the last minute on a new electoral law based on proportional representation. While both factions admit that the new law has many defects, an election date was set for May 2018.

Institutional and political confusion did not only interrupt the Lebanese legislative branch but also the functioning of the executive branch. In 2013, a politician, Tammam Salam, designated as prime minister by the parliament, needed 14 months to form a government. And when the term of President Michel Suleiman expired in 2014, the parliament went through 14 fruitless attempts and needed two years and five months before a new president was elected, in October 2016. In the meantime, the affairs of the country were managed by a caretaker government that had limited legal power.

This disorderly state of affairs added to country's living conditions and the alienation of the population. Corruption news was spreading, employment opportunities declining and basic daily needs such as an uninterrupted power supply and regular water were now exposed.

The December 2010 wave of demonstrations and protests (dubbed as the "Arab Spring") that erupted in Tunisia and Egypt triggered similar protests by Lebanese civil society groups. Incited by the success of the Tunisian and Egyptian demonstrations, in February 2011, waves of massive protests erupted by Lebanese youth and civil society groups demanding a secular civilian order and calling for political, economic and social reforms.[18] Public school teachers subsequently demonstrated demanding raises to their minimum wage.[19]

The forced resignation of the government at that time, however, diverted public attention to this new political crisis. It was not until August 2015, when the government was unable to collect the waste that was piling in the streets of Beirut and other areas, that public protests erupted and caught impetus. Small spontaneous demonstrations in some streets of Beirut grew and were intensified. The demonstrations soon became a daily event in downtown Beirut in the afternoons. The protesting masses adopted the Egyptian catchphrase "The People want the downfall of the regime" (*'sh Sh'b urid iskat an-nitham*).

Politicians were alarmed, some tried to infiltrate the protesters and others sought confrontation. A civil movement, "Til'at Rihitkum" (Your Odor Is Exposed) emerged to coordinate and lead the protests. Soon other civil society groups such as "Bidna Nhakim" (We want to Prosecute) appeared. The initial slogan calling for "changing the regime" shifted to "reforming the regime" and eventually specific demands became the focus of separate groups. Consequently, disagreements among the protesting groups contributed to its losing momentum. The social and traditional media played an important role in both the rise and deterioration of this movement, as will be discussed in Chapter 5. The heterogeneous demographic structure of the Lebanese society also played a role in the course of impact and effect of the media, particularly the social media on the route and disposition of the public sphere.

The Media Scene

The Lebanese press reflects, and in turn reinforces, the characteristics and contradictions of Lebanon's political and confessional society. The Lebanese press originally emerged in the 1860s and 1870s to play the role of "social pamphleteers" and to advocate social reform and national unity, however, the autocratic rule of the Ottoman Sultan Abdul Hamid II in the late 1880s and the 1890s triggered the shift in the orientation of this press from being socially oriented to an "Arab nationalist" and a politically oriented one. The press then shifted from viewing itself as operating within an Ottoman order, which is a continuation of the Caliphate system, to being Arab under an alien Ottoman (Turkish) rule.

During the French mandate, the political orientation of the Lebanese media was augmented by a repressive policy of the French authorities, whose mandate over Lebanon lasted throughout World War II. The French authorities actually prosecuted newspapers calling for independence and backed those supporting the French mandate. This policy transformed Lebanese newspapers into instruments of political mobilization, making them the channels through which opinions were exposed and support sought for policies, personalities and parties.

The Lebanese press under the French mandate, thus expressed and in turn strengthened ideological divisions within the society, at a time when the society was beginning to experience serious attempts of building its national institutions and establishing the ground works for national unity.

After independence and as a result of geopolitical and economic changes in the area, which will be discussed in Chapter 2, the Lebanese press was broadened in outlook to the larger "Arab" region. It began to play the role of a forum for the Arab world, accessible to all the conflicts and ideological battles being waged in the Arab world at the time.

The dangers of this state of affairs were criticized by a former president of Lebanon, Charles Helu (1964–1970). Receiving the then newly elected council members of the Lebanese press union in 1969, President Helu in his address to the council inquired with mild irony: "Now that I have met you in your official capacity, may I learn what foreign countries your papers unofficially represent? Welcome to your second country Lebanon."

Later, in a magazine interview, Helu explained: "We don't have a 'Lebanese press'; rather we have a 'press in Lebanon.'"[20] A somewhat similar statement had come from another Arab leader a few years earlier when the late President of Egypt, Jamal 'Abdul Nasser, told a group of Lebanese journalists visiting his country: "You have freedom of the press but lack a free press."

The "pan-Arab" role of the Lebanese press contributed to its miraculous growth in the 1950s. Ironically, this same role was one of the contributing factors for its deterioration in the late 1970s and 1980s. The discordant picture of the Lebanese press became clearly evident during the 1975–1989 Civil War period which witnessed an increasing polarization of opinions within the press. It also witnessed the appearance of illegal media channels clearly addressing themselves to very specific audiences, manipulating a language of conflict and subversion, and widening the gap between the various groups of society.

The Civil War period saw the migration of Lebanese media institutions to London and Paris, and media professionals to the Arab Gulf region, where they were instrumental in the development of the Gulf press. The Lebanese press could not regain its prominent professional role after the Civil War and it continues to face serious economic and organizational difficulties.

The reasons why both Presidents Helu and Nasser felt justified in criticizing the Lebanese press can perhaps be explained within the confines of Lebanese history. Throughout this history, the strategic location of the Arab world has made it a crossing-place and meeting point of the East and the West and encouraged foreign powers to interfere in its local affairs. Lebanon has been vulnerable to this interference as early as the beginnings of Ottoman rule and remained so after independence. Among the reasons for this is Lebanon's religious and ethnic composition as well as the contemporary events of the Arab region and Lebanon itself.

It was quite possible that foreign interferences in the affairs of Lebanon were encouraged, if not brought about, by the heterogeneous composition of its population. The country contains 18 officially recognized religious sects, the most prominent of these being the Sunni and Shi'a Muslims, and Maronite (Catholic) and Greek Orthodox Christians. None of these sects comprises a majority.

The growing spread, in the past two decades, of satellite radio and television as well as the Internet and social media have had a great impact on the Lebanese public. This needs serious attention from officials and examination by scholars.

Satellite broadcasting and social media networking have created a new space for dialogue and discussion. In addition to activating the public sphere, which the German sociologist Jürgen Habermas[21] describes as "the sphere that allows civil society to discuss and criticize ongoing issues," these interactive technologies also contribute in activating what Michael Hardt and Antonio Negri call a civil domain that generates a new political and social nature.[22] It can be said that interactive communication technology if well designed can help to contribute, via the Internet, in the emergence of a new consciousness that establishes new social development. Misuse of such technologies can lead to the alienation and loss.

The 2015 civil movement in Lebanon, it can be argued, was significantly influenced by broadcast and social media. The media's coverage of the so-called Arab Spring was effective in activating an alienated Lebanese civil society. On the other hand, the media played a central role in the expansion and retreat in public involvement.

The overall picture of the Lebanese media scene suggests that multiple contradictions within the Lebanese society expose this media to the influences of opposed ideologies, countries and coalitions. Consequently, these influences will unavoidably have diverse forms of impact on the public sphere that needs to be examined. Lebanon is a society through which many regional and international battles can be fought. The Lebanese media in all its forms have been obviously affected by this state of affairs. There is no doubt that the media have contributed to the eruption of conflicts and hostilities. This role as actor and reactor deserves careful investigation. The ultimate purpose should be to augment its role as an actor, but in a positive and constructive sense, as many of the post-war people in Lebanon hope for.

The Print Media: Unceasing Challenges

Historical Background

Arabic Printing Preceded Gutenberg Printing Press

It is often mistakenly assumed that the Arab world was rather late to employ printing because Islam prohibited printing. Actually, there is evidence that the Arabs knew the art of printing on paper and silk by engravings made on wood (block printing) from the early days of Islam, long before the Gutenberg printing press.[1]

Restriction of the use of Arabic script in printing was implemented in the latter part of the fifteenth century, during the decline of the Ottoman Empire. Muslim religious authorities (*uluma*) were reluctant to support the use of movable type to print Arabic either for fear that some may distort religious texts or may challenge their interpretation of religious texts.[2] The Ottoman rulers at the time also feared that Arabic printing would enlighten the people and thus may endanger their uncontested authority.[3] Accordingly, printing was proclaimed by the *uluma* as "an abomination of Satan's work."[4]

The Ottoman Sultan Bayazid II banned printing using Arabic script in 1485. Nevertheless, European powers, who contended defending minority groups in the vulnerable Ottoman Empire, pressured the Ottoman authorities to grant permission to the Jews in 1494 to establish presses using Hebrew script. Those same privileges were later extended to the Armenians (in 1567) and then to the Greeks (in 1627). The permission for these minorities to print was conditional on them not using Arabic script.[5] This situation lasted until 1727, when the change in the social and political mood provoked a *fatwa* (religious declaration) by Sheikh el-Islam allowing printing. This prompted the Ottoman Sultan Ahmad to issue a decree (*Khat Hamayuni*) permitting the use of Arabic script in printing.[6]

The Roman Catholic Church (later the Orthodox Church; then the Protestants) were not concerned with this obstruction by the Ottomans and employed Arabic printing in their missionary work in the areas of Ottoman Empire with Christian inhabitants, mainly the area known then as "Bilad ash-Sham" or Syria.[7]

Printing using movable type in the Mount Lebanon area of the Syrian Ottoman province may be traced back to 1610, when a group of Maronite priests brought a printing press from Rome to the St. Isaiah (Mar Kazhia) monastery in North Lebanon. This printing press used Syriac letters, which were understood and read only by a small group of clergymen. Historians agree that this printing press did not have much impact on the country because of the low literacy rate at the time and because of its use of Syriac letters.[8] It is reported that: "this printing press went into oblivion soon after it completed its first and only job: printing the 'Psalms of David.'"[9]

The use of printing presses did not gain ground in Mount Lebanon until the Christian missionaries began competing with one another in an effort to attract adherents from among the Lebanese populace. In 1733, a Catholic deacon, Abdallah Zakher el-Shammas, established the first printing press, using Arabic letters, in the St. John (Mar Yuhanna) Catholic Monastery near Shweir in Mount Lebanon. Zakher developed his printing skills in Aleppo, Syria, when he helped the Greek Orthodox Patriarch establish the first Arabic printing press in the Arab region in 1706.

The Greek Orthodox priests reacted to the Zakher press by establishing the first Arabic printing press in the city of Beirut, in 1751. The Maronites followed by establishing an Arabic printing press at the St. Isaiah monastery in 1808. In 1834, the American Protestant missionaries moved their Arabic printing press from Malta to Beirut. The Catholic Jesuit missionaries also entered the rivalry by setting up the third Arabic printing press in Beirut in 1848.

The competition among the different Christian missionaries helped spread literacy and education but also contributed to planting the seeds of sectarianism in the country.[10] Each printing press produced religious publications advocating the doctrines of the particular mission that maintained it.

Popular printing not connected to religious orders appeared in 1857 with the establishment of the "Syrian Press," the fourth Arabic printing press in Beirut, by Khalil el-Khuri a former director of publications in the Ottoman administration. El-Khuri published the first popular Arabic newspaper in Lebanon and, indeed, the Arab world, *Hadikat al-Akhbar* (*The Garden of News*).[11] It began to appear in both Arabic and French in 1870.

Shortly after the publication of *Hadikat al-Akhbar*, a series of popular Arabic newspapers began to appear in the Syrian province of the Ottoman Empire. Lebanese intellectuals and men of letters mostly published these papers. Butrus al-Bustani, a renowned man of letters, for example, followed Khalil el-Khuri by publishing *Nafeer Souria* (*Call of Syria*). Bustani's paper appeared in 1860, during the great fight between the Maronites and Druze in Mount Lebanon. In his paper, Bustani called for the restoration of brotherly relations among the different religious groups.

At the same time, another famous man of letters, Ahmad Faris esh-Shidiak, published in Istanbul *Al-Jawa'ib* (*The Unusual News or Events*), which appeared regularly for 33 years and became the most prominent Arabic paper of its time. A fourth paper, *Barid Baris* (*Paris Mail*) was also founded during the same year. It appeared in Arabic, in Paris, published by Rashid Dahdah. All these papers were published weekly. The first daily Lebanese paper, *Al-Ahwal* (*The Situations*) did not appear until 1894.[12] Early papers addressed social and literary matters but not politics. It can thus be argued that early Lebanese journalists were social pamphleteers and were not concerned with political reporting.

Early Ottoman Period: Social Pamphleteering

Lebanon's early newspapers were started during times of crisis by a group of men of letters and intellectuals who sought to educate and guide members of their community.[13] During their early stages, the Lebanese papers developed in an atmosphere of strict political control by the Ottoman authorities. However, there was no specialized body to enforce the January 6, 1857 Ottoman "legislative list" (*La'iha*) of Sultan Abdul Majid,[14] that regulated printing and printed matter under the jurisdiction of the Ministry of Education in Istanbul; it delegated the supervision of the print media outside Turkey to the "Librarians" (*maktubjis*) of the districts.[15] The most serious restrictions imposed on the media by this "list" were those imposing prior restraint (censorship prior to printing), forbidding "any criticism of government actions" and banning discussions that might negatively affect relations with other states.[16]

Lebanese papers, however, prospered under the press law issued by the relatively liberal Ottoman Sultan Abdel Aziz, in January 1865. This law granted a restricted degree of freedom to the newspapers published by Ottoman subjects (including Arabs), but was strict in dealing with the press owned by foreigners (particularly the missionaries). The law subjected all papers published in the Ottoman Empire to Ottoman law and not to foreign consuls, as was the practice before 1865.[17] The most serious danger to the national press in this law lays in its Article 13, which legalized the "administrative suspension" of papers should they publish material that threatens societal values or endangers the security of the state, causing "excitation, or agitation."

The 1865 law, together with a "protocol" that was forced on the Ottomans by England, Prussia, Russia, France and Austria in 1861, guaranteed a special status to a predominantly Christian province of present-day Lebanon (Mount Lebanon). It also provided relative freedom to Lebanese journalists.[18] This freedom, coupled with the development of the Lebanese educational system (due largely to the influence of Christian missionaries), provided an atmosphere that made it possible for Lebanon to be ahead of the other Arab countries in terms of the number of newspapers according to density of population and area.

Lebanon could be regarded as the true cradle of Arab journalism, because popular newspapers other than official gazettes were published in Lebanon almost continuously after 1858. Popular publications appeared a little later in Egypt, but much later in Syria, Iraq and Palestine.[19] However, the record of Lebanese papers suggests that only a few of the early Lebanese newspapers managed to continue publication for long periods, and that many did not appear regularly.[20] Indeed, several Lebanese newspapers, which appeared during this period, were edited and published by famous men of letters and intellect. Not surprisingly, they disappeared with the death of their publishers.

The prime purpose of early Lebanese papers was to call for unity of the people during a period of heightened ethnic or religious strife. News coverage was subjective and newspapers focused mainly on editorials advising or educating the people. The primary aim of publishers during this early period was to educate rather than entertain or inform.

Second Ottoman Period: Political/Nationalist Press

The access to power of Sultan Abdul Hamid II (1876–1908) changed the attitude of the Lebanese press. At the beginning of his rule, Abdul Hamid promulgated a constitution that guaranteed relative freedom for individuals as well as journalists (Articles 10 and 12 respectively). The Sultan intended to dilute the public unrest that preceded his takeover of power, particularly after the death of Sultan Abdel Aziz and the exile of Sultan Murad V. During his early period of reign, journalists were relatively free to express themselves and were allowed to report about delicate events such as the assassination of a number of Ottoman ministers and the overthrow of Sultan Abdul Aziz—even the victory of the Russians over the Ottomans in 1877.[21]

When Abdul Hamid succeeded in gaining control over the power in the empire, he began imposing restrictions on his subjects as well as on the print media. He took advantage of the Russo-Turkish War (1877–1878) to declare martial law and to abolish some of the prevailing liberal press regulations as well as to impose censorship on the press.[22] The 1878 restrictions, however, did not provide the Sultan with sufficient controls. In 1884, he issued a stricter law that empowered the granting of newspaper licenses to the police department. This law also allowed for regular police inspection of printing plants and paper warehouses. To facilitate police control of printing plants, Articles 14 and 15 of this law required that doors of printing plants should not be locked, and that these plants should not have many doors or windows that may be used as exits in the event of a police raid.

As an example of Ottoman control of the print media during the rule of Sultan Abdul Hamid II, Uthman Nuri listed ten directives, which were issued to journalists by the Ottoman governor. The following is a translation of some of these directives:

> Newspapers must first enlighten the public about the esteemed health of the Sultan, and then they may discuss agricultural crops, and the advancement of industry in the Empire.

> Papers are forbidden to publish any item without prior approval by the Ministry of Education. Non-controversial social items are exempted.

Lengthy articles dealing with ethical or social issues are forbidden. Expressions such as "to be followed," or "continued" or any other expression indicating that the subject is incomplete are forbidden.

The use of blank space or repeated dots in place of censored items is forbidden. This may cause confusion and allows for unnecessary interpretation by the public.

The press are forbidden to report individual or public complaints about government officials or even to mention that such complaints have reached HRH the Sultan.

Important official personalities should not be criticized. Should a ruler be accused of theft, nothing should be reported. Should he be accused of bribery, no reference to it may be published. Should a ruler or high official be murdered, all reference that may imply that he died in an unnatural way should be omitted and the press should merely report that he passed away.

It is forbidden to publish the names, or make reference to, the enemies of HRH the Sultan.

It is forbidden to report about revolts in the Kingdom or about any historical revolt against any king.[23]

A sample of the subjects which newspapers were not allowed to discuss appeared in *Al-Manar* newspaper in 1912. These included such topics as:

reform, awakening of the Arabs revenge, attention, nation, history of the Abbasid Caliphate, history of France, alerting the unaware, execution, criticism, extinction, disorder, confusion, mentally unbalanced, crazy, madness, bribe, bribery, meeting, gathering, republic, depose, poison, etc.[24]

The pressure applied by the regime of Sultan Abdul Hamid on Lebanese journalists, however, served as a unifying factor. It helped to establish a link between journalism and politics as well as create a nationalistic outlook among Arab journalists. The pressure by Abdul Hamid and his Ottoman regime on Arab journalists prompted Lebanese journalists to shift their orientation from advocating social reform to calling for independence and political freedom for Arabs under the Ottomans. Thus, it has been said,

this historical link between journalism and politics does much to explain the extreme political character of the contemporary Arab press ... Today it is a tradition, which is just as "right" in the minds of Arab editors as is the not-very-old American tradition of objective reporting.[25]

When the Ottomans increased their pressure on journalists, many fled to Egypt where they enjoyed relatively more freedom to express themselves, as Egypt had autonomy after 1831. These journalists became very influential to an extent that they almost monopolized the publication of newspapers in Egypt. Lebanese journalists continued to be prominent in Egyptian publications until the middle of the twentieth century.[26] Some of the papers that were started at this time by Lebanese are still being published in Egypt. Among these is the leading Egyptian daily paper *Al-Ahram* and the leading weekly *Al-Musawwar*.

Pressure by the Ottomans, however, did not stop a number of magazines and papers from emerging in Lebanon during the reign of Abdul Hamid. The strict Ottoman pressure on journalists lasted until 1908, when a new elite, the Young Turks, came to power. The new regime was more liberal than the previous one and showed interest in reviving and modernizing the Ottoman Empire. In 1909, a new press law was introduced. The law abolished prior restraint and provided easier working conditions for the print media in the form of a reduction of postal rates for publications and facilitating the granting of newspaper licenses. The 1909 law clearly defined the profession. It dealt with: 1. Publication rules (37 articles); 2. Printing rules (13 articles); 3. Authorship rules (42 articles); and 4. Press crime rules (eight articles). This law was amended several times: in 1912 and 1914.

The change of Ottoman regimes emboldened many Arab journalists. New papers emerged seeking to guide and liberate the Arab people. Over the period of just a few weeks, the number of Arabic papers in Lebanon rose from 7 to 29.[27] However, this liberal period was short-lived. The new ruling group, which came to power with Sultan Mohammed V in 1909 began a period of suppression of non-Turkish subjects of the Ottoman Empire, now clearly a "Turkish Empire." While Turkish journalists were granted a greater degree of freedom, efforts were made to control non-Turkish newspapers.

The new restrictions did not inhibit Lebanese journalists from playing an important role in bringing about national awakening, particularly since the new ruling Turkish *elite* was quite open in discriminating against Arabs and other non-Turks. Tempted by the degree of freedom promised by the 1909 press legislation, several Lebanese journalists, who had been practicing their profession outside Lebanon, returned home and were instrumental in reviving the Lebanese print media.

The first attempt at gathering journalists together in a union took place during this period, when Khalil Sarkis and Sheikh Ahmad Tabbarah established a "press committee" (*Lujnah sahafiya*) in Beirut in 1911.[28] The committee declared that its aim was to protect the rights of journalists, promote the profession and improve its standards, as well as serving the "state and nation." A price, however, had to be paid for the boldness of the journalists. On May 6, 1916, 31 Arab leaders, including 16 journalists, were hanged in the public squares of Damascus and Beirut for stirring public opinion and calling for independence.

Ottoman attempts to check the growth of the Lebanese print media were always frustrated by the resoluteness of journalists, but World War I succeeded in achieving this goal. The poverty-stricken state of Lebanon and the scarcity of paper and resources permitted only a few papers to survive the war.

The occupation of Lebanon by the Allies, at the end of World War I, brought hope for a press reform, particularly after Marshall Allenby, the British Commander of the Allied Forces, issued a directive abolishing censorship of the press in September 1919. The journalists quickly resumed their efforts to organize themselves and, in 1919, established the first Lebanese press union of both journalists and publishers. The new union was headed by Ramiz Sarkis. It lasted until 1938.

French Mandate Period: Spread of Corruption

When Lebanon was placed under the French mandate by the League of Nations, the mandatory government not only upheld the Ottoman restrictions on journalists but also increased press restrictions through a special "bureau" in charge of the press. This bureau was in complete control of the affairs of the print media in Lebanon and Syria; not even local government officials could take action concerning journalists without securing permission from this office. The bureau was in charge of "suggesting" to the local government the suspension of papers, should they violate its censorship code. In the event that local government officials failed to suspend the paper, the French authorities would implement the suspension nonetheless.

In 1924, a law of 66 articles governing the press was enforced. This law failed to include any reference to the organization of the profession of journalism and declared the practice of this profession open to anybody (the 1909 Ottoman law had restricted this practice to those with at least seven years of education as well as to those who had spent a period of apprenticeship).

The Lebanese journalists opposed the 1924 law and waged a strong drive against it. To silence the opposition, the mandate added, in 1925, a 67th article to the law, allowing the government to suspend any newspaper prior to a court decision. In 1926, the French High Commissioner imposed prior restraint on the print media of Lebanon and Syria. In 1940, the French authorities decreed that Lebanese papers may not appear in more than one sheet (two pages) in order to cut down on the consumption of paper, which was becoming scarce during World War II. Magazines were also forced to make drastic reductions in size.

These measures were aimed at weakening the opposition but could not silence Lebanese journalists. In 1941, the Lebanese editors formed a distinct union, and the publishers followed by setting up their own union in 1942.

More new Lebanese papers continued to appear. Many of these papers championed the call for independence and the editors were compelled to pay the price for this stand. In most cases, the price was imprisonment. This position by the Lebanese journalists boosted their public image. It also had a negative effect: journalists developed a tendency to concentrate on "*views*" in their reporting and not on "*news*," an orientation that was carried on and is still apparent today.

On the other hand, several papers supported the French authorities in return for rewards. It was during this period that the practice of "bribing" journalists became common, as testified to in the memoirs of leading journalists of that period, Aref el-Ghrayyeb and Iskandar Rayashi. Both of these prominent journalists "bragged" about the fact that they received financial as well as other favors in return for journalistic services they rendered to officials.[29]

Toward the end of the French mandate, the picture one gets of the Lebanese print media is that of a clear division between papers championing independence and others supportive of the French regime. By the end of the mandate, there were about 246 political publications that had been discontinued as a result of financial difficulties or the political pressures exercised by the authorities.

Early Independence Period: Professional Confusion

During the early stages of independence, the 1924 French press law continued to be implemented. The authorities were even stricter in enforcing its penalty clauses. The paucity of measures relating to the organization of the profession and the "financial favors" officials provided to "loyal" journalists led to the emergence of several papers that were managed as business enterprises and were hardly governed by professional ethics. The public image of the profession therefore suffered. Journalism became the refuge for high school failures and those with political ambitions. Nevertheless, a good number of journalists of that period continued to carry the torch of professionalism and to call for reform.

When several journalists exposed the corruption of the first government under independence, of President Bichara el-Khuri, as well as the rigged elections of May 1947, the government reacted by enacting a new press law in 1948. The law, in general, granted journalists more freedom than before, yet it gave the government several outlets to increase its restrictions on papers opposing the regime. This law, of 70 articles, regulated the affairs of the print media and organized all journalists into one union.

The campaign of the journalists against these restrictions was faced with a strong and determined government that suspended seven publications in one day (*An-Nahar, Al-Bayrak, As-Sayyad, Ad-Diyar* and *Al-Ahrar*).[30] This government action prompted the Lebanese press union to call for a general strike. When the parliament and the government held firm, the union decided to boycott all news about the deputies loyal to the government, government leaders, as well as official government statements. The stand of the union was supported by Lebanese opposition parties as well as by the press unions of Cairo, Baghdad and Damascus.

The Golden Era: Rise of a Pan-Arab Lebanese Press

The continuous campaigns by journalists against President el-Khuri played an important role in bringing about public discontent with his regime. In September 1952, popular resistance to the regime led to the resignation of the president and to the peaceful fall of the government.

The new regime of President Camille Chamoun was grateful to the journalists. In October 1952, a liberal legislative decree lifting most of the restrictions of the 1948 law became effective. It legislated that press offenses be addressed by a special court. It organized journalists into two unions: a union for publishers and another for editors. However, the decree opened the door for granting licenses to new papers, a right that had been temporarily suspended by the 1948 law. This resulted in another increase in the number of daily political newspapers.[31] Beirut alone had more than 50 daily papers sponsored by different leaders or groups. Thus, in April 1953, the government, upon the request of the union of publishers, issued another legislative decree (Number 74) legislating that no new license for the publication of political newspapers would be issued as long as Lebanon has more than 25 political dailies and 20 political weeklies and periodicals. This decree, however, permitted publishers owning more than one license to change the name of a publication, provided that the new license would cancel two old ones.

The "rush" to publish newspapers in the early 1950s was a result of the great economic and geopolitical changes that Lebanon and the area were facing, changes that made Lebanon prosper as a leading center of finance, business and diplomacy in the Arab region. The significance of the Arab region grew after the end of the World War II as this region was an important potential outlet for Western products and an important source of oil. Lebanon's position as a major commercial and trade center in the Arab world was strengthened when the port of Haifa and its oil refinery, as well as the pre-1948 Palestinian transit routes fell into Israeli hands, thus becoming unavailable for those interested in trading with Arab countries. Lebanese transportation routes became the new transit routes for the Arab East and consequently the oil pipelines from the Arab Gulf that used to reach refineries in the Palestinian port city of Haifa were diverted to Lebanon, where two refineries were constructed in Sidon and Tripoli.

With *coup d'états* in Syria and Egypt that ensued the establishment of the State of Israel in 1948 and the resulting political and economic instability in Egypt and the region, Lebanon became the most important center for foreign diplomatic missions from where both secret and public foreign agents could operate. The Egyptian print media, which until the early 1950s were the leaders of the Arab press, began to lose their accessibility to several of the Arab countries, thus losing their pan-Arab role. The Lebanese press took over the role of the Egyptian press and acquired a pan-Arab status.

The magnitude of influence of foreign interest in the Lebanese print media increased sharply after the 1948 Palestinian war. By the late 1950s, Lebanese papers were being distributed widely all over the Arab world. Some Lebanese papers had, during its golden period, wider circulation outside Lebanon than within. To avoid confiscation and to ensure regular distribution in Arab countries, the Lebanese print media made continuous compromises, since circulation of these media in the Arab world was not always guaranteed, due to the frequently changing censorship policies and the changing political regimes in the area.

It was a common practice for Lebanese papers and magazines to have different editions. Items, or even pictures, that may be sensitive in an Arab country were replaced by "neutral" ones in the edition that would reach this country. Thus, *Ash-Shabaka* magazine, for example, had on its cover of the March 19, 1973 issue a picture of a girl in a bikini bathing suit. The edition reaching Saudi Arabia and Libya had only the face of this girl. Indeed, all the semi-nude pictures, which were common in this magazine, were removed from the other editions.

The growth of the modern Lebanese print media in the 1950s began with technological developments made possible through foreign money, which began pouring into press institutions by those interested in the affairs of Lebanon and the region. Foreign embassies and business firms were by this time buying the support of the Lebanese print media by helping to build modern newspaper plants and by purchasing new printing presses and equipment. None of the pre-1950 Lebanese papers had office space larger than a few rooms; most had their editorial space in a corner or in the vacant area at the printing press where the paper was printed. By the late 1960s, the editorial and business staff of almost every major Lebanese paper occupied huge buildings. Most of these papers possessed advanced technology that was not always utilized but was nonetheless welcome since it was, in many cases, made available free in return for services.

During the work of the author as a journalist in a leading Beirut paper, he recalls that the editorial staff of the paper once requested new equipment, which the publisher could not provide because of lack of funds. One evening the staff observed with surprise the visit to the publisher of the CEO of an organization that was the subject of a corruption campaign launched by the paper. Directly after meeting, the staff received instructions to end the corruption campaign. Within few days, the equipment the staff had requested was installed in the editorial offices.

The power of the Lebanese press became so apparent in the 1950s that no government could possibly afford to ignore it. It is perhaps fair to claim that the direction of growth of the present-day Lebanese print media was set in the 1950s. Three journalists may rightly be called progenitors of this direction: Kamel Mroueh, publisher/editor of *Al-Hayat* (*The Life*), George Naccach, publisher/editor of the French language daily *L'Orient*, and Ghassan Tweini, publisher/editor of *An-Nahar* (*The Day*). Mroueh pioneered the technical aspects of developing Arabic fonts and types suitable for the modern printing, production and distribution of Lebanese newspapers: he introduced new Arabic typefaces for printing his paper, as well as adopting modern methods of printing. Naccach pioneered by paying considerable attention to the development of the human element in the profession. He pioneered the employment of experienced and reputable university graduates on his staff and was also the first to pay them professional salaries. Tweini combined the contributions of both Mroueh and Naccach and went further than both in building the image of Lebanese journalism as a modern and respectable profession.

The organization and proper establishment of the profession of journalism, however, did not materialize until the regime of President Fuad Chehab, who made a serious effort to reform the Lebanese administration. In September 1962, a new liberal and enlightened press law was introduced in which the profession and the practice of journalism were clearly defined. Journalism was defined in Article 9 of the law as "the profession of publishing news publications." The freedom, of this profession could not be limited, except by the general laws of the Republic.[32] A journalist was defined as anyone whose profession and main source of income was journalism. He/she should: 1. Be Lebanese of at least 21 years of age; 2. Hold at least the Lebanese baccalaureate (second part) or its equivalent, and have practiced the profession for at least four years after applying for apprenticeship, or hold a *license* degree (BA) in journalism from an institute of the Lebanese University or any equivalent degree in journalism acceptable by the University; 3. Have an orderly judicial record; and 4. Have journalism as his/her only profession.[33] This law, however, exempted from its second requirement all those who were practicing journalism at the time, on condition that they do not leave the profession for a continuous period exceeding two years.[34]

The 1962 law also organized the Lebanese journalists into two separate syndicates (orders): the Lebanese Union of Publishers (*Nakabat as-Sahafa*), including owners of political press licenses; and the Lebanese Union of Reporters (*Nakabat-al-Muharireen*) including all active journalists. A Lebanese Press Union (*Itihad as-Sahafa al-Lubnaniah*) was formed from the executive officers of the two unions to represent the Lebanese profession and to attend to professional matters of journalists.

Furthermore, the law created a "Higher Press Council" composed of the executive officers of the first two unions, two elected members (one from each of the unions), and the head of the press and legal affairs department at the Lebanese ministry of information. This council was entrusted with the power of dealing with "all problems of common interest to journalism and journalists in general, with the exception of those problems that are primarily the concern of each of the two syndicates." The Higher Press Council was also responsible for "drafting the bylaws of the Lebanese Press Union."

Another specialized committee established by the 1962 law was entrusted with defining the privileges of journalists, as well as developing a retirement plan. Foreign journalists operating in Lebanon as well as Lebanese journalists serving as correspondents to foreign papers were also organized by the 1962 law within a special union: "The Union of Foreign Correspondents."

The 1962 law provided the press with minimal formal state censorship and established the limits within which the freedom of the press might be exercised. These limits were determined by the special nature of the Lebanese system. Thus, "news which endangers national security or the unity or borders of the state: or which degrades any religion or arouses sectarian or racial grudges," were pronounced punishable by the law.[35] The law also declared the publication of false news with intent as well as the use of the profession for direct or indirect blackmail punishable by the law.[36]

In practice, the limits set by the 1962 law did not affect the freedom of the Lebanese press. The main threat to this freedom came from unofficial and external sources, which will be discussed later in this chapter. To limit the possibility of state intervention during periods of national crises, a national voluntary association was set up by the Press Council to apply a self-styled form of censorship upon the journalists. This voluntary body proved quite effective during times of crisis.

The Onset of Press Setbacks

The 1962 law continues to be enforced to date, with modifications introduced since then by the various governments. These modifications were introduced to meet the challenges that emerged during the Civil War and the different political crisis in the country. Many of the changes, however, represent setbacks for the modern Lebanese press. The golden days of this press began in the early 1950s with the regime of President Camille Chamoun and ended after some ten years with the regime of President Fuad Chehab. While it is true that the regimes of both Presidents Chamoun and Chehab witnessed attempts at restricting the freedom of the press, these attempts were mainly carried out by zealous officials. They did not represent the orientations of the regimes, which were clearly liberal. The Lebanese press reached the peak of its professional development and acquired maximum freedom during these two regimes. From then onwards, the Lebanese press started to lose what it has acquired.

At the 1965 Arab League summit meeting, several Arab leaders officially criticized the role of the Lebanese press, which included attacks directed at them or at their regimes. To appease these critics, the government of President Charles Helu introduced a special decree amending Article 62 of the 1962 law. The decree, now commonly known among journalists as "the law of kings and heads of state," forbids the print media from criticizing foreign heads of state.

Other restraining measures followed. When President Suleiman Franjieh sought, in the early 1970s, to punish a magazine, *Al-Hawadith*, which accused a member of his family of illegal financial deals, he introduced then a decree prohibiting foreigners from owning shares in Lebanese papers. This decree was directed at the magazine, which was believed to be largely financed by non-Lebanese Arabs.[37]

The most serious modifications to the 1962 press law, however, were introduced by President Elias Sarkis in 1977. President Sarkis represented the same liberal and reform-oriented trend of President Fuad Chehab, and yet he blamed the Lebanese media for contributing to the intensity of the Civil

War. The first legislative decree Sarkis issued, thus, was to introduce temporary prior restraint (decree Number 1, of January, 1977). He followed this by issuing another decree, amending the 1962 law, particularly the section on penalties for libel and irresponsible action (decree Number 104, of June 30, 1977).[38]

The penalties for libel under the 1962 law were unreasonably low, and the amendments by President Sarkis reversed the picture by introducing harsh punishments. These amendments, among other unusually harsh clauses, did not accept privileged information as a defense against libel. The amendments also allowed the Council of Ministers to impose prior restraint. Most importantly, these amendments obliged publishers to submit detailed financial statements every six months.

The former Prime Minister Salim el-Hoss told this author in a private interview that the 1977 amendments were forced on his government by certain Arab governments. These governments, he said, requested imposing official pressure on the Lebanese press in return for the continuation of the presence in Lebanon of the Arab Deterrent Forces as well as the activation of the mission of the "Committee of Four" (foreign ministers of Lebanon, Kuwait, Saudi Arabia and Syria) that assisted the Lebanese government in retaining order in the country.

Later, in January 1, 1984, *An-Nahar* newspaper quoted el-Hoss as saying that "legislative decree number one was issued after several newspapers in Beirut were raided amidst certain Arab circumstances subsequent to the Cairo Summit meeting. It was no secret that this legislation was inspired by these circumstances." In another newspaper interview, el-Hoss was reported to have said:

> The first legislative decree of 1977 which enforced press censorship was introduced in an Arab atmosphere which was polarized against the role of the Lebanese media and the freedom it enjoyed. In December 1976 several major newspaper offices were raided [by the Arab Deterrent Forces]. When the proposed legislative decree was presented to the Council of Ministers I asked President Sarkis the reason for issuing this decree as the first of our legislative decrees. He whispered to me that this action is an Arab request and we have to disregard any objections to it at a time when we are in bad need for Arab support.[39]

The amendments were strongly resisted by journalists as well as by numerous politicians. Like most decisions made by President Sarkis that were faced with strong opposition, they were not implemented during his term of office.

Although the amendments were approved by the Council of Ministers, signed by the president and published in the official gazette, the president agreed to freeze them. Later, President Sarkis reintroduced prior restraint, as a temporary measure in an effort to contain the Civil War, through restricting the propagation of sensational news and the exploitation of sensitive information by political groupings. Censorship was limited here to local news.

The government of President Sarkis could not properly apply prior restraint for two basic reasons. First, not all papers agreed to this prior censorship, and most of those who ignored it had backing by militant political bosses thus evaded government punishment. Second, the officials entrusted with implementing prior censorship were either unqualified or biased, and thus treated the law-abiding papers preferentially and, most of the time, arbitrarily.

The author is in possession of a collection of items censored during this period. These include such items as a news story reporting the death of the mother of the Maronite Patriarch. The item was censored because it mentioned that a Lebanese Communist Party leader sent a cable of condolence to the Patriarch. Another censored item was one reporting that a leftist group distributed aid to war victims. The official censor requested that the item be changed to suggest that only the Lebanese Red Cross was actually responsible for this distribution.

With the election of President Amin Gemayel, in 1982, his first government was given legislative powers by parliament, thus press officials began a dialogue with government representatives to reconsider the amendments made during the regime of President Sarkis. The increased political hostility and antagonism to the regime of President Gemayel, however, prompted his government to maintain the Sarkis amendments. In December 1983, a leading opposition newspaper, *As-Safir*, was suspended and its senior editors brought to trial for publishing material that was not cleared by the censors. The government also introduced a new decree (Number 12/83: September 16, 1983) requesting that any intended buyer of a political newspaper license should present the ministry of information with a statement about the source of his capital (both for the purchase of the license and the operational expenses of the paper for a period of one year). The decree gave the government a priority to purchase any newspaper license that was for sale or whose owner

Figure 2.1 Sample of copy planned for publication in *As-Safir* newspaper with rejection "censoring" marks by the official censor. Among these is an item reporting that the secretary general of the Communist Party sent his condolences to the Christian Patriarch for the loss of his mother.

had passed away. The decree also froze issuing nonpolitical press licenses for a period of three years.

The deterioration of the security situation in Lebanon early in 1984 and the government's consequent loss of control over a large part of the country allowed the press to ignore restrictions and to operate at liberty. The success of the opposition, in May 1984, to force President Gemayel to form a new government brought hope for lessening the restrictions on the press. However, the affairs of the press had a very low priority on the new government's agenda as it was facing serious political, social and economic problems that paralyzed it.

The serious deterioration of the security situation in the country and the escalating collapse of the Lebanese economy during the regime of President Gemayel threatened the very existence of the Lebanese press. With the actual division of the country into areas controlled by warring militias, the circulation of the Lebanese papers dropped sharply because no paper could distribute in all areas. The militias practiced censorship, confiscation of issues or simply banning the entry of certain papers to the areas under their control. The revenue from advertising also dropped and the price of printing material and other basic print supplies soared as a result of the sharp devaluation of the Lebanese currency.[40] The challenges facing the Lebanese press during this period were not simply censorship—survival was now the main challenge.

In three years, the Lebanese press had to raise the price of the newspaper from half a Lebanese Lira (LL) to LL1,000 and LL2,000, which was a price the average Lebanese could not easily afford.[41] Unable to raise the price of the papers further, for fear that the circulation may drop sharply, the Lebanese press decided, beginning with 1988, to cut down the number of their pages to ten only (from 12 and 16). Earlier, they stopped issuing the free supplements, which were distributed with the Sunday issue. The papers also cut down on their number of foreign correspondents.

Lebanese Press after the Civil War

Loss of Pan-Arab Character

A review of the evolution of the Lebanese print media suggests that the sectarian alignment of this press as well as its entanglement with Arab affairs have constantly subjected it to political and economic pressures. The critical problems of this press were actually not related to its lack of freedom from government. This press has constantly managed to "outsmart" the government by going around regulations and maintaining a qualified freedom to operate. The main problem of the press lies in its failure to free itself from the powerful sectarian and business chiefs who control its organization, management and financing, and consequently its inability to serve the genuine interests of the Lebanese society.

Indeed, the early tendency of Lebanese journalists to speak for specific groups and to promote their interests led newspapers in Lebanon to concentrate more on the dissemination of views and opinions than on news and facts. This gave outside powers and interests the opportunity to play active roles in the affairs of Lebanon through the Lebanese media. Each paper came to support a certain group and was looked upon as a representative and spokesperson for that group. In this, foreign interests have not actually changed the structure of the press system. Rather, they exploited it and, in doing so, they accentuated the differences among people. This characteristic became so apparent during the Civil War that any claim to objectivity made by the press is viewed with skepticism.

In a pertinent public lecture on the state of affairs of the Lebanese print media in 1967, the veteran journalist Ibrahim Salameh made this sarcastic description, which is still relevant:

> The print media that are published in Lebanon represent all the countries and states of the world ... but not Lebanon ... These media are not at all free; rather they are mortgaged and in debt to those ... who possess money and manage to "rent" them. Naturally, it is impossible for the rented media to violate the rent contract ... The print media in Lebanon are rented to capital in all its mobile forms, nationalities, and levels, and it is, in the final analysis, bound, not free... The condition of the print media here very much resembles that of the driver of a private car owned by a "Bey," Sheikh, or prince ... The driver may appear as the master of the car, riding and driving it with his hands and feet ... But he is practically and contractually not free, because all his movements are responses to gentle whispers or dry commands from the master reclining on the back seat. And so, our journalists look at the world through the context of bonds and contracts and not through radio stations, wire services and facts. The Lebanese print media write for their subsidizers and not for their readers.[42]

The perpetuation of this situation is due to the makeup of the Lebanese press system that is crowded with a large number of licensed political publications, and which is not reasonable for a country with a small population and advertising budgets. Lebanese papers in the 1950s and early 1960s operated with tolerable production costs and their purpose then was to appeal to certain local social, political and religious groups. Sponsorship of these papers then was affordable by local business and sectarian endeavors. However, as a number of professionally gifted journalists succeeded in injecting a pan-Arab appeal into their papers, the Lebanese press grew into one that was feared and appreciated. Regional and foreign business and political enterprises were then prepared to subsidize it in return for its support. Sponsorship, thus, became a common feature of the Lebanese press. The flood of political and business subsidies to the press triggered the rush to establish political papers whose publishers were not necessarily journalists but were mainly after financial or political profit.

The escalation of the Civil War in the 1970s lead to the migration of talented Lebanese journalists to the Arab Gulf states and consequently Gulf newspapers took over the role of a pan-Arab press in the 1980s and 1990s. The Lebanese papers not only dropped drastically in their distribution but also in influence. No longer were regional business and political enterprises interested in sponsoring Lebanese papers. The rising costs of production of newsprint and the depletion of advertising budgets drastically affected the print media. All were forced to increase their prices and appear in fewer pages.[43]

By the end of the 1990s, the vast majority of Lebanese papers were facing financial difficulties due to the plunge in their circulation and advertising revenues. This situation predisposed even the most prominent papers to boldly seek financial assistance from outside sources at the price of mortgaging their professional independence, as will be exposed later in this chapter.

According to 2016 figures by the Lebanese Union of Publishers, Lebanon has 110 licensed political publications (including 58 dailies, 48 weekly magazines, and four monthlies—seven in French, two in English and three in Armenian. The nonpolitical publications are over 300 in number. The greatest majority of these publications appear in Beirut and only a handful appear in the cities of Tripoli, Sidon and Zahle. While the small papers could manage to continue with irregular and humble operation through modest sponsorships, the leading papers were now unable to maintain a large-scale operation and a large staff. A leading newspaper, *As-Safir* made public its financial plight and ceased publication at the end of 2016. Other leading newspapers are expected to follow.[44] Presently, none of these papers can actually sell more than 10,000 copies.[45]

Free from Government not from Sectarian/Business Bosses

The nature of the print media system in Lebanon makes publishers open to overtures of financial assistance from foreign groups in exchange for editorial support.[46] It also makes foreign interest groups turn to the Lebanese print media as an intermediary through which to present their interests and exert influence on internal and regional affairs. Each foreign interest group tries to secure at least one media outlet to promote its point of view. This has prompted journalists to compete for securing a license for a political paper as a freeze was imposed on issuing new licenses.[47] None of the present publishers is willing to surrender his/ her license in the hope that he/she will be able to receive subsidies in times of crisis or to rent the license to an aspiring individual or political group.

This state of the print media reflects the fact that Lebanon is essentially a country of services. Lebanon's economic role was and continues to be that of a middle-person, who transports consumer goods from the West to Arab markets and participates in overseeing these markets. The prosperity of Lebanon after independence was neither the result nor the cause of genuine national development. Lebanon's role, no matter how one explains it, was and still is reflected in the country's mass media, which tend to take the color of the money poured into them.

A consequence of this characteristic of the Lebanese press is that it does not hesitate to express interests other than its own, and sacrifice credibility and professional standards for material profit. The absence of a national consensus in Lebanon is, to a large extent, exacerbated by this state of affairs. During the pan-Arab period of the Lebanese press, financial assistance and other forms of support flowed to the Lebanese press. It was common for foreign embassies, business firms and local political groups, including the Lebanese government, to patronize Lebanese papers.[48] In return, the recipient newspaper was expected to propagate and support the policies of its subsidizer.

The country faced serious economic problems after the Civil War. The war destroyed most of its physical infrastructure and resulted in an administrative chaos as a result of the intensification of corruption and the mass departure of many of the talents capable and necessary to rebuild the country. This situation lessened Lebanon's regional and Arab importance. Its currency dropped by more than 500 percent.

To address the economic problems of the country, an affluent businessman, Rafik Hariri, was asked to form the government in 1992. He gave priority to borrowing funds in order to rebuild the physical infrastructure of the country, hoping to draw foreign investments and to revive the economy. Hariri, however, failed to attend to administrative reform. He also failed to give serious attention to the conditions of the middle class and the professionals in the country, in order to persuade them against migrating in search for better opportunities abroad.[49]

The assassination of Hariri in 2005, and the so-called Cedar Revolution in 2005 ushered a new period in the modern Lebanese press, and indeed in Lebanon's political unfolding. This incident resulted in an acute ideological and political polarization. While allegiance of Lebanese papers prior to this period had been scattered along religious and ethnic loyalties, a paper's loyalty could now be classified along two poles: a pro-March 8 group (supporting the so-called Confrontation Front); and a pro-March 14 group (supporting so-called moderate pro-Western Arab states). Sectarian and ideological commitments were now more obvious. Political subsidies from regional and world resources flowed at the beginning but started drying up with the support shifting to active and militant groups, particularly after 2011 with the eruption of Arab popular demonstrations and the fighting in Syria.

The political and economic confusion in Lebanon became wide-open in 2012–13 when, following the end of term of President Michel Suleiman, it took the politicians almost a year to agree on forming a government, and the parliament failed, for over two years, to attain the necessary quorum to elect a new president. As a result, the Finance Ministry reported that Lebanon's net and gross public debt by the end of August 2017 had reached L£101,228 and the country's net public debt by the end of 2016, as a percentage of GDP had reached 129 percent.[50]

The instability of the Lebanese society for over three decades contributed to the professional deterioration of the Lebanese media and consequently to the drastic drop in its audiences as well as its income from advertising—and thus, to its inability to be financially self-sufficient. Most major media outlets in the country are subsidized or controlled by political and sectarian bosses and their content is manifestly promoting political agendas.

Lack of Order and Professional Ethics

Bribes to newspapers and journalists are commonly accepted as normal. A leading Lebanese publisher announced in a seminar held in Beirut that "the present situation of Lebanese print media is such that the publisher who does not take bribes is an ass."[51] At the same seminar, a prominent lawyer stated that during a court case that he handled, when it came to the knowledge of the judge that the paper under trial had received a payment from a foreign embassy, his only reaction was to give the publisher a sarcastic look.[52]

At another seminar deliberating the need for a media code of ethics in Lebanon, a prominent journalist, Faysal Salman of *Al-Mustaqbal* newspaper, declared:

> let's not go too far in dreaming up what's unattainable. We all know one another.... . Why do you want me to fight the dragon? I won't be able to defeat it ... Where's the logic of having a journalist's pay set at $200 and you asking him to be an angel from heaven? This isn't in defense of deviation, but a call for rationality, of objectivity.[53]

Responding to Salman, the then President of the Lebanese Order of Journalists Melhem Karam, said: "What my colleague, Faysal Salman, said was forthright. He said what every journalist must say." Perhaps the following statement (confession) by a leading journalist, Charles Ayyoub, which appeared on the front page of his popular daily paper, *Ad-Diyar* is most revealing about the ethical stands of some Lebanese journalists:

> Gen. Wissam Hasan [Head of the Security Branch in the Lebanese Public Security] called me to enquire if my newspaper "Ad-Diyar" was willing to adopt a middle-road line between [two opposing political groups]. I replied

in the affirmative ... Hasan said: "I will pay [you] $150,000 a month to highlight the news of the Future Party in 'Ad-Diyar'."

Of course, people talk about payments [to journalists] but they do not bear in mind that *this payment is actually a form of an exchange that allows the publisher to pay salaries and cover the cost of paper and printing.* General Hasan ... afterward informed me that ... the amount will be ... $100,000 in return for straight and good news about March 14 Front, to occupy a space of six pages in the newspaper.

Later General Hasan ... informed me that he met in Paris with [Prime Minister] Hariri and that they had decided to stop the assistance. I was given no explanation [for this decision] except that Saad Hariri's financial circumstances were tight. But [I told him that] "Ad-Diyar" had honored its commitment ... and as a consequence its circulation dropped by two thousand copies. *Ad-Diyar* had respected to the word, its deal to publish news of March 14th, and it followed, General Hasan's request to be a Christian middle road paper and not against March 14.

I stated [General Hasan] that we ... made no mistake. He said "It's not a matter of your having done wrong. On the contrary, you were right. The point is that Saad Hariri is in a difficult financial position." I told him I was not convinced, and that [he] and Prime Minister Saad Hariri, as well as the third party who created conflict between us, were responsible for ending the subsidy. [I told him] *You will see now what it feels to have "Ad-Diyar" opposing you.* [This is how] I started my press campaign against the Future movement, Saad Hariri, and General Hasan, *to make them comply with our agreement.*[54] [Emphasis mine]

Media institutions in Lebanon have no qualms in expressing interests other than their own, and sacrifice credibility for material profit. The absence of a national consensus in Lebanon is, to a large extent, exacerbated by this state of affairs. Financial assistance, or other forms of subsidies, pour into Lebanese media from foreign embassies, companies and business firms, as well as from local groups, including the Lebanese government. In return, the recipient medium is expected to propagate and support the policies of its "subsidizer."

The services rendered by Lebanese papers to their patrons can be classified in three general types: 1. Complete editorial commitment and news slanted in favor of the country or group; 2. Planting articles of "news" items, either supporting and defending, or attacking and denigrating a group, country, policy or an official; and 3. Promotion of policies. Lebanese media institutions often make contracts with more than one patron to promote more than one policy.

Subsidies to Lebanese papers come in a variety of forms. One is when the patron government or group rents out the entire publication for a certain yearly or monthly fee. Under this condition, the patron pays for all the costs of production as well as for the staff during the period of the contract.

Another form of subsidy is through payments to promote certain programs or causes. The amount of such payments depends on the patron but can be quite handsome, as was revealed in 1967 during a press conference held by the former President of the Lebanese Union of Publishers, Zuhayr 'Usayran. 'Usayran held a press conference to announce his resignation from the presidency of the Order because of a disagreement with his cabinet members over a L£1 million payment (at that time worth $200,000), he had received from the late King Saud of Saudi Arabia. He said the payment was made to him personally in return for promoting the image of the deposed king in the Arab world and he, therefore, would not share it with other members of the Order. 'Usayran also revealed at this conference that he had earlier distributed to Lebanese publishers another payment—which he claimed he could document—of $100,000 from the former king.[55] Commenting on this incident at the time, the English daily paper, *The Daily Star*, remarked: "What was shocking about the million-pound-deal is that none has questioned the principle; the outcry centered on why the amount hasn't been shared among the various newspapers."[56]

A somewhat similar public announcement was made when a publisher of a leading magazine reported that he had turned down, in 1962, a "first payment" of $200,000 from Egypt to publish a new daily newspaper, with an offer of an exclusive interview, to appear in the first issue of the paper, with President Nasser of Egypt. He wrote that the "first payment" was delivered to him through the Egyptian Ambassador in Beirut, but that he returned it "because daily journalism was not his specialty." He wrote that he suggested to President Nasser to give the amount to another Lebanese publisher. "I am your soldier," he reported telling the president, "but I prefer the profession of weekly journalism."[57]

Subsidies to journalists are also provided indirectly through gifts of equipment or paper. Sometimes they are in the form of salary payments to one or more employee. On some occasions, payments are made to employees directly and without the knowledge of the media institution, particularly when that institution is supposed to be neutral, as in the case of the government-run radio station and the government-supervised television station. Such types of payments were exposed by the former President of the Union of Publishers, the late Riad Taha at a press conference. Taha reported that "there are contracts and secret deals which link certain television announcers and non-Lebanese parties to promote the news of other countries, thus giving the impression that the Lebanese state is biased in its Arab and foreign policies."[58] He said he had presented evidence about this to the Lebanese government and to the television authorities. No official statement was made in reply to Taha, nor was any action been taken by the authorities.

Another form of subsidy is provided through concentrating the advertising budgets of some businesses in papers of favorable and supporting political, sectarian or ethnic background. Most Lebanese newspapers face sizeable financial expenditures, which can only be met through relatively large advertisement contracts or through high circulation figures. At a public meeting, a Lebanese minister of information suggested that by concentrating the advertisements of its supporters in a particular paper, a political group or personality can request the support of that paper in return.[59] Many companies advertise in newspapers on the basis of the paper's editorial policy and the political identity of the editor.[60]

Complementary to this, political and religious factions as well as interest groups pay newspapers to keep silent about certain issues or events, which are unfavorable to their image. Support of one group may place another at a disadvantage. The media institution is paid, then, not to support that group.

The policy of the Lebanese Union of Publishers itself has accentuated the commercial nature of the Lebanese media. Indeed, prior to the 1962 press legislation, a commonly circulated statement about the state of affairs of Lebanese journalism was: "Lebanon is full of journalists but does not have journalism." The statement described accurately the situation then. Journalism at that time was a means of gaining political power or financial success. The practice was saturated with people for whom journalism was a means to an end, not a profession. Such people drifted into this profession and corrupted it.

An Associated Press (AP) official told this author that, shortly after AP opened an office in Beirut, a well-known publisher approached him saying, "I've been following your wire service and I like it. How much would AP pay my paper for using its copy?"[61]

Most of the present holders of licenses for political newspapers could not objectively be classified as professional journalists, yet they form the body that elects the managing board of the Union of Publishers. Thus, when the 1962 press law gave newspaper publishers the power to manage the affairs of the Union of Publishers, they introduced restrictions on the functioning of successful papers. The Order made it hard for the better papers to develop into large national papers as well as to develop an audience cutting across confessional, political and socioeconomic boundaries.

The Union of Publishers, for example, did not permit newspapers to increase the number of pages in their papers without increasing their price, thus setting limits to the size of the papers. The Union also controlled the freedom of publishers to distribute free Sunday supplements. Papers, furthermore, were not allowed to appear more than six times a week.[62] These and other similar measures hampered the growth of successful professional papers and gave smaller papers unnecessary protection. The measures also increased the fragmentation and disorientation of Lebanese public opinion.

Control of the Lebanese press through violence is almost as frequent as non-violent forms of control. This form of control is not unique to the Civil War—it existed before the war. Numerous examples can be cited of violence used as a means to intimidate the Lebanese print media and to silence its editors. Different methods are used, one of which is the assassination of journalists. Another is the bombing of their printing plants or editorial offices. These crimes serve both as a punishment to editors as well as a warning to others.

In 1966, a prominent press magnate, Kamel Mroueh, was concluding his editorial when an armed man walked into his office and shot him. Court trials revealed that an Arab regime was linked to this assassination. The death of Mroueh, the publisher of three Lebanese papers, achieved its intended goal: his major paper, *Al-Hayat*, dropped from the position of the highest circulation Lebanese paper in the Arab world to one with slim circulation figures, and eventually an Arab Gulf prince purchased its license and moved its headquarters to London.

Another assassination was that of a leading Palestinian journalist, Ghassan Kanafani, who was killed by Israeli terrorists in front of his home, while starting his car. Salim Laouzi, a leading publisher of the Lebanese magazine, *Al-Hawadith*, was the victim of another assassination. In 1980, he was kidnapped while on his way to the airport. His body was found in a deserted area. A year later, the president of the Union of Publishers, Riad Taha was shot dead while on the way to his office. The editor and publisher of *As-Safir*, Talal Salman, was also the target of an assassination attempt. He survived, however, but was forced to flee the country for a while. The former editor in chief of the leading paper *An-Nahar*, Michel Abu Jawdeh, was stabbed in the face in the early 1960s. He was later kidnaped twice by a group whose identity Abu Jawdeh refused to publicly reveal. His release came after the intervention of "high level" sources. Other journalists have been targets of assassination plots but survived, with major or minor injuries.

Bombing or throwing explosives at newspaper plants or offices has also been a common practice of intimidating the press, even before the outbreak of the 1975–1989 Civil War. In December 1972, three explosions took place at the offices of a leftist paper, *Ar-Ra'i*, causing the death of one employee and injuring three others, as well as causing the complete destruction of the paper's printing plant. The attack was said to have been prompted by a conflict between two factions of a political party.[63]

In April 1973, explosives were thrown from a speeding car near the offices of *Al-Muharrir*, which at that time was a leading "progressive" paper that consequently discontinued publication. This was thought to be in retaliation for *Al-Muharrir*'s publication of an article and a caricature critical of an Arab king.[64] A weekly news magazine, *Al-Hawadith*, was also the victim of an explosion that caused heavy material damage. The magazine's editor accused an Arab government of this incident, in retaliation for his magazine's strong campaign against it.[65] Other newspapers have also been targets of similar attacks, including two leading Beirut newspapers, *An-Nahar* and *As-Safir*. Bombing of newspaper offices became a common phenomenon during the Lebanese war.

Lawless activities of intimidating the journalists continue. The government, most of the time, is able to uncover the organizers and executors of such activities; and when it can, however, it is usually unable to take action against the organizers or even to expose them. This situation persists because of the fragility of Lebanon's political structure, and the sensitivity of its mercantile economy to reactions of retaliation from neighboring countries in response to negative Lebanese press coverage. It is claimed that many of the lawless activities against journalists in Lebanon are organized and executed by officials or agents of foreign countries. Should Lebanon expose them, it would face retaliation by the country exposed, as has been the case in the few instances when Lebanon took action.[66]

The historical circumstances that accompanied the development of the Lebanese print media together with the structure of the media themselves have resulted in encouraging the press to focus on services and opinions. The 1948 and 1952 press legislation helped limit this unhealthy state of affairs but did not solve the problem of congestion in the profession. By then, Beirut alone had some 52 licensed daily political publications. Most of the holders of these licenses could not factually be classified as professional journalists.[67] The meddling of the Union of Publishers in the production affairs of the press made it difficult for the healthier papers to develop into large national papers as well as attract an audience that would cut across confessional politics and socioeconomic boundaries.

The Civil War intensified the country's fragmentation and sharpened the manipulation of news for political or sectarian mobilization. A large number of illegal unlicensed political publications appeared during the Civil War. The library of the American University of Beirut has copies of 80 such unlicensed publications. Almost all of these appeared in tabloid formats. Most important among them was *Al-Watan*, published by the political council of the "Nationalist Movement," *Amal*, published by the Amal Shi'ite movement, and *At-Tahrir al-Lubnani*, published by the "Lebanese Supporting Front."

These papers were, often, directly financed by political groups or religious communities, and thus they addressed themselves to restricted audiences. Most of them were distributed free of charge, but contributions toward their publication were usually forcibly sought (sometimes under the threat of a gun). In terms of content, they were close to underground pamphlets, making heavy use of a vocabulary of mockery and irony, of caricatures and cartoons, of imaginary trials, poetry, and open letters to abolish the "enemy," all of which were designed to build up cohesion and a sense of identity among members of the group they represented.[68] Often, they backed their highly biased reports or analyses with exaggerated figures, and did not hesitate to manipulate specific historical incidents to justify and legitimate the actual position of the group in the conflict. The appearance of these papers was inversely related to the power of the government to cope with the problems facing the country. The more the government spread its control over the fighting "zones" and warring groups, the fewer illegal papers were published.

An Overview of Lebanese Newspapers

General Structure of Newspapers

Most Lebanese daily political publications that were published before 2000 appear in a broadsheet format of 58 x 42.5 cm with a 5-cm column width. Papers that have appeared more recently, such as *Al-Akhbar*, *Al-Balad* and *Al-Jumhouriya* appear in tabloid format. The weaker papers are published in four to six pages, while the successful ones appear in 12, 14 or 16 pages—depending on advertising space. While the Union of Publishers prohibits daily papers from appearing more than six times a week, several leading papers manage to appear every day. The seventh-day edition used to carry an additional logo of another licensed political paper, which was usually rented out from publishers of weak papers that do not appear regularly.

Lebanon has numerous local news agencies. The most important among these are the two state-owned agencies: "The National News Agency" (NNA) and "The Central News Agency." Prior to the Civil War, foreign language Lebanese publications had relatively large audiences and were fairly influential but the demographic change in Lebanon and the drastic decrease in the circulation of Lebanese papers has reduced their status. Most important of foreign language papers are the French papers, which are distributed widely due to the fact that French was a dominant language in Lebanon. The Armenian and English papers are less influential. The Armenian papers circulate only among the relatively large Armenian community in the country, the Armenian language being spoken exclusively by this community. The English language papers circulate mainly among the foreign community since these papers, unlike the French language papers, are directed at the foreign reader. While

Figure 2.2 Above: Front page of Hadikat *Al Akhbar*, the first Lebanese newspaper. Below: When the Order of Publishers increased its pressure on successful papers not to appear on Sundays, these papers appeared on that day by using "rented" licenses of negligible papers that do not appear regularly. The picture shows three samples: *Al-Hayat* newspaper appearing as *Az-Zaman*; *An-Nahar* appearing as *Al-Itihad al-Lubnani*; and *Al-Anwar* appearing as *At-Tayyar*.

Figure 2.2 Front page of Al-Anwar carrying the logo of At-Tayyar newspaper. *Continued*

Figure 2.2 Front page of Al-Hayat newspaper carrying the logo of Az-Zaman newspaper. *Continued*

Figure 2.2 Front page of An-Nahar newspaper carrying the logo of Al-Itihad al-Lubnani newspaper. *Continued*

the French language papers do not differ in their content from the Arabic language papers, the English language papers usually includes more US and foreign news as well as more entertainment.

With the increased integration of the Armenian community in the Lebanese society, the Armenian language papers are losing circulation and importance. Only those papers that are backed by Armenian political groups have survived. The leading French daily paper is *L'Orient-Le Jour*. *The Daily Star* is the English daily paper. It was discontinued when the number of the foreign community in Lebanon was depleted in the mid-1980s and resumed publication with the normalization of the situation in the country. The three Armenian daily papers *Zartunq*, *Aztaq* and *Ararat* are each directed at one of the three main Armenian political factions: Tashnag, Hunchak and Ramgavar.

Opinion in the Lebanese press is usually incorporated within the news story; either in the form of a subjective presentation and selection of facts or in an outright expression of opinion within the context of the story. Lebanese papers do not have specialized editorial pages. The important editorials usually appear on the front page. Most leading papers have specialized sports, cultural and economic pages but other specialized pages are few and mediocre. The main focus in the Lebanese press is on Lebanon and the Arab world. The capital and urban areas receive almost exclusive attention in the local news coverage.

While the Lebanese media are strong in their local and Arab background features, they are weak in investigative reporting. Lebanese papers stayed away in the past from investigative journalism mainly because of the pressure of political and economic power groups who obstruct the exposure of negative factual information about them, also because of lack of trained investigative journalists and, most importantly because such an undertaking is expensive.

The founding of a number of nongovernment organizations (NGOs) with Western support have recently succeeded in promoting interest in this area. Among the important NGOs promoting investigative journalism is Arab Reporters for Investigative Journalism (ARIJ), which was founded through European support.

Subservient not Watchdog Press

The Lebanese press generally tends to oppose government authority. This does not mean that this press acts as a "watchdog" to safeguard the Lebanese public interest. Its opposition to the government is actually because it supports another political or economic power group, or possibly several groups, that are active on the Lebanese scene. This power group need not necessarily be Lebanese. Lebanon has numerous active political and economic forces that share with the "government authority" the political power in the country. Therefore, the claim by the Lebanese press that it is relatively free from "government authority," while true, does not necessarily mean that it is free from the authority of other forces in the country.

The Lebanese papers' political allegiances are amply evident in most of their news coverage, editorials and features. It is possible to determine the orientation of Lebanese papers merely by a careful reading of their headlines. It is also possible to do so by examining their selection of news events covered. Additionally, the fact that a paper supports a particular authority does not mean that it will continue to do so. Lebanese papers regularly shift their political orientation.

Content analysis studies of Lebanese daily newspapers by this author show that the press provides more news coverage to political events at the expense of other news.[69] Minor news of politicians and power groups receive extensive coverage, while news concerning the livelihood of the average citizen is generally given little or no attention. The relatively small space devoted to editorials and commentary in the Lebanese press may be misleading: they give the impression that there is not much in the way of opinion. On the contrary, opinion is included within the news report itself.

Labor and business news get comparatively better coverage than news about rural areas because such news is linked to two groups active on the Lebanese political scene: labor unions and business, industrial and financial communities. Interestingly, right-wing papers attend more to news of the business, industrial and financial communities, while left-wing papers focus on the news of leftist labor unions.

The Lebanese system of governance, which became more disorderly after the so-called Cedar Revolution and the split of the country into two major camps, "March 8" and "March 14," "tolerates" employing approachable political influence by the press to evade legal restrictions.[70] The high polarization of public opinion and the open scuffle between members of the government of opposing political orientations in 2005 boldened the press to violate the enacted media laws. The divergence became wider with the involvements of both factions in the fighting in Syria. As a consequence, attacks on regional powers and officials became common features of the Lebanese press. The attacks covered a fairly broad range of political opinions and ideologies without concern for possible penalty.

Prominent Lebanese Papers

The radical social and political changes within the Lebanese society during the past 20 years have affected its media in many ways. One of the effects of these sociopolitical changes has been the sudden rise and fall of political newspapers. Relatively obscure papers have risen to prominence and several leading papers such as *Al-Muharrir, Lisan-ul-Hal, Al-Jarida*, and most recently, *As-Safir* have folded and disappeared. Few of the licensed daily Lebanese papers appear regularly today. Of those that do appear regularly only a handful are prominent and have a respectable circulation.

The nine leading Lebanese daily papers that have played an important role in Lebanese affairs during the past decade, in terms of their influence, strong editorial position and professional competence, are perhaps *An-Nahar, As-Safir*,[71] *Ad-Diyar, Al-Akhbar, Al-Anwar, Al-Mustakbal, Al-Jumhouriya, Al-Liwaa* and *L'Orient-Le Jour*.

Al-Akhbar (literally, *The News*) is a daily Arabic-language tabloid newspaper that was founded in 1938 as a communist paper. It ceased publication in the 1950s but was reinstated in 2006 by a group of distinguished leftist journalist intellectuals spearheaded by Joseph Samaha, a former editor of *As-Safir* newspaper. *Al-Akhbar* is dynamic and daring in its reporting but is often criticized for "mixing facts, rumors and opinion." The paper focuses more on interpretations of news, on features and investigative reporting. It usually prints articles by leading leftist intellectuals. *Al-Akhbar* ran a popular online English version until March 2015 that was discontinued because of lack of funds.

Al-Liwaa (meaning *The Flag*) is a right-of-center broadsheet newspaper. The paper has an Arab nationalistic outlook and generally addresses the Sunni Muslim community in Lebanon. Its editor in chief, Salah Salam, is a respected journalist who ran unsuccessfully for the position of president of the Union of Publishers.

Al-Jumhouriya (literally The Republic) is a tabloid daily right-of-center newspaper that was founded in 1924 and bought in 2011 by a powerful Greek Orthodox Christian politician, Elias Murr. It began as a forum representing Murr's right-wing Lebanese nationalist position but has recently acquired importance by employing established journalists representing different political and ideological orientations.

An-Nahar (*The Morning* or *The Day*) is a broadsheet daily paper that was established in 1933 by a Greek Orthodox Christian politician, Gibran Tweini. His son, Ghassan, as its editor in chief developed it to occupy, in the 1950s, 1960s and 1970s, a leading influential position among Lebanese and Arab papers. The paper's influence, however, began declining after Ghassan's retirement and is presently experiencing financial and professional difficulties. *An-Nahar* is a relatively moderate right-of-center paper. It has a consistent record of public service and strong editorial positions. It achieved prominence in the past mainly because of its strong, but sober, opposition to all governments. Its appeals mainly to the middle to upper classes, as well as to the Greek Orthodox Christian groups.

Al-Mustaqbal (*The Future*) is a broadsheet right-of-center daily newspaper. *Al-Mustaqbal* was launched in 1999 by Rafik Hariri, the former prime minister—the assassinated leader of the Movement of the Future. The newspaper expresses the views of the Movement of the Future and supports the Lebanese March 14 Alliance. In addition, this daily is one of the foremost anti-Syrian publications in the Lebanon.

As-Safir (*The Ambassador*) is a left-of-center broadsheet paper that gained prominence at the beginning of the Lebanese Civil War but was forced to cease publication in January 2017 due to financial difficulties. The publisher of the paper, however, still comes out with regular online editorial comments on Arab and local events. In the past decade, *As-Safir* had, possibly, the highest circulation in Lebanon. Established in 1951 by a Maronite Christian, *As-Safir* was bought by a Shi'ite Muslim in 1974 to champion Arab nationalist causes. It achieved success because of its aggressive policy of opposition to the government and because of its solid news coverage and excellent background articles written by noted intellectuals. It used to appeal to Arab nationalist and Muslim masses. Its highest circulation was within the Muslim areas, in south and north Lebanon as well as in the Bekaa.

Al-Itihad (*The Unity*) appeared in October 2017, when the former journalists of *As-Safir*, headed by veteran journalist Mustafa Naser, revived an obsolete political paper, *Al-Itihad al-Lubnani* (*The Lebanese Unity*) by purchasing its license. The publisher of this broadsheet paper described his move as being motivated by his belief that: "the print media is not dead, rather it is old journalistic reporting that has become obsolete." Like *Al-Akhbar*, this paper focused on interpretation of news, features and investigative reporting. The paper was not able to secure advertising support at the beginning and the sudden death of Naser forced its disappearance.

Ad-Diyar (*The Homeland*) has recently risen to the rank of leading daily papers when a former Lebanese army official, Charles Ayyoub, bought its license and published it in 1987. The success of *Ad-Diyar* is perhaps due to the bold stands it took in defying powerful political and militia bosses in the country. While Ayyoub is a declared member of the Syrian Social Nationalist Party (PPS), his staff represent most of the ideological groups in Lebanon. Journalistically, the paper is managed in an amateurish nonprofessional way. Its success may be attributed to the fact that it addresses popular issues in blunt ways which professional papers shy away from. This seems to satisfy the average Lebanese reader, who is anxious to find a paper that addresses his/her everyday problems. *Ad-Diyar* is a middle of the road broadsheet daily, which appears seven times a week, in defiance to the decision of the Union of Publishers. The paper's layout is primitive and unprofessional.

Al-Anwar (*The Lights*) was founded in 1950, by the publisher of the leading weekly magazine *As-Sayyad* (*The Hunter*), to champion the cause of "Nasserism" in Lebanon and the Arab world. During its first 20 years, *Al-Anwar* was among the prominent Lebanese papers and, perhaps, had the highest circulation of all Arab papers in the Arab Gulf states and Syria. It's simple and attractive layout as well as its emphasis on light feature stories appealed to the average Arab reader. However, with the beginning of the Lebanese Civil War, *Al-Anwar* had to dilute its Arab nationalist slant because its offices and printing presses were located in the Christian-dominated section of Beirut. Consequently, the paper lost many of its readers in Lebanon and the Arab world. *Al-Anwar* is a middle of the road broadsheet paper that appears six days a week. Its sister magazine, *As-Sayyad* suffered the same fate and, in an effort, to improve its circulation moved its offices to London where it is now published. In October 2018, the publishers of *Al-Anwar* and *As-Sayyad* announced that they can no longer sustain losses and that both publications will cease publication immediately.

L'Orient-Le Jour is, perhaps, the most widespread daily broadsheet newspaper among the French educated Lebanese people. *L'Orient-Le Jour* (The Orient—The Day) is a result of the merger, in 1970, of *L'Orient* and *Le Jour*, the two French language papers that played a major role in early Lebanese politics. *Le Jour* was founded in 1934 and supported the Constitutional Bloc that dominated Lebanese politics during the early period of independence. *L'Orient*, on the other hand, was founded in 1944 to support the opposing National Bloc. At present *L'Orient-Le Jour* is published by the same institution that issues *An-Nahar*. Although it appears in French, *L'Orient-Le Jour* is directed at the Lebanese reader and not at foreigners. Prior to the Civil War, the paper was considered to be the most serious Lebanese paper because of its sober news coverage and strong editorials. This right-of-center paper used to circulate widely among Lebanese middle- to upper-class Muslims and Christians. With the death of its publisher and editor in chief, George Naccach, the paper lost its prominent position among Lebanese readers and the objectivity of its news coverage is questioned.

Summing Up

In a 1963 survey of the print media, radio and television, the role of the Lebanese print media was shown to be slowly shifting from educating and guiding to informing and entertaining.[72] This finding suggested the possibility of the emergence of a paper appealing to different groups across the whole of society. Such a paper would be able to boast a national circulation and an income from advertising that permits it to be less dependent on further sources of income to support its operations. The protection given to weak papers by the Union of Publishers, however, did not allow the materialization of such a possibility.

The continued failure to solve this problem was mainly due to an error of orientation to the problems of the print media in Lebanon by all: government, Union of Publishers and media professionals. Journalists campaigned for more freedom and became so involved in this campaign that the essential requisites for shaping and unifying the profession were underscored.

When the print media were able to acquire the freedom of operation they demanded in 1952 and 1962 (from Presidents Chamoun and Chehab), journalists focused their attention on improving the physical facilities of their papers, believing that all other professional problems would be automatically solved. Improvements in the physical structure, however, only sharpened the need for new media structures within which to grow.

At the outbreak of the Civil War, in 1975, a number of solutions for this problem were debated. The first solution called for free competition among the papers so that only the healthy ones would survive. This would require allowing free competition among papers by opening the door for issuing new licenses. The second and third solutions called for government interference. One such solution suggested that the government implement the procedure adopted in Syria early in the 1950s on the licensed papers by requiring the merger of every two or three papers. The second solution was for the government to buy the licenses of struggling papers. This last alternative seemed to appeal to the majority of members of the Union of Publishers. The difficulty of implementing it, however, rested in the lack of government funds and the lack of interest of previous governments to finance such a venture.

This uncertain situation persisted at the beginning of the 1970s with, on the one hand, a multitude of small papers circulating among members of the same sectarian faction, political orientation or socioeconomic community. Several of these papers now appear sporadically and manage to be supported by local sponsors. On the other hand, a limited number of papers, with a relatively wider audience made attempts to shift from straight political ventures to channels representing a national trend of apparent secularization that was beginning to have an appeal among intellectual circles as well as among business elites. This dialectical process was abruptly changed by the outbreak of the Civil War and the ensuing national disorder and deterioration in the economy.

Indeed, the Civil War altered the picture in the direction of intensifying the fragmentation and conflicts in the country and of sharpening the earlier tendency to manipulate news for purposes of political or sectarian mobilization. This period witnessed the appearance of a large number of illegal unlicensed political publications, some of which managed to keep publishing regularly for a long time, while others vanished as silently as they had appeared.

The mushrooming of illegal publications conveyed a need for information on the part of anxious audiences. "Information" of a biased nature conveyed in a personalized style, however, can only make sense to a narrow group of people, even narrower than the groups mobilized by the pre-war papers. Illegal publications, thus, were a means by which these smaller elements of the Lebanese society formulated and reasserted their identity in the midst of a violent storm that threatened their cohesiveness and their capacity to survive.

On the other hand, the readership and content of the licensed papers were often modified by the new environmental circumstances created by the war. These licensed papers had to reflect the opinion of the faction that controlled the area in which their offices and printing presses were located, for fear of being blown up or prevented from distributing their issues. Consequently, the readership itself was affected, generally along the lines of an increasing polarization of opinions that corresponded to the geographical division of the country. Few papers managed to maintain a moderate and balanced outlook.

By the late 1980s, most of the illegal papers disappeared, except for an occasional publication in times of increased tension. The phenomenon of illegal papers, however, was serious proof of the dangerous role the print media can play in the promotion of divisions within the Lebanese society. The signing of the Taif Accord did not usher an improved or positive situation for the press that was now exhausted and ridden with depleted physical resources, poor circulation and advertising resources. Reconstruction attempts failed to bring about economic revival or to aid the press in regaining its pan-Arab role. Attention was now more focused on the concerns of satellite television.

Faced with poor circulation and poor advertising revenues, coupled with a government absorbed in internal national conflicts, the press was incapable of coping with the competition by the now professionally mature and affluent media in the Arab Gulf. To regain its previous readership and advertising budgets, several papers chose partial and sensational reporting as a path to attract readers and sponsors. Biased reporting and sensationalism reached their peak in 2005 with the split of public opinion into two opposing factions.

This period witnessed the increased public dependence on the broadcast and social media as sources of fast news. At the same time, interest by regional and business organizations in subsidizing the Lebanese press was declining. As a consequence, most of the leading papers are in serious financial difficulties. A leading daily paper, *As-Safir* folded in January 2017 and several other leading papers, including *An-Nahar* are unable to pay the salaries of their staff and are sacking many of their employees.

Some forecast that the demise of newspapers in Lebanon is forthcoming and that "the print media is dead." Historical evidence, however, proposes that no communication medium was entirely replaced by a new one. Rather, the old media generally adapts to the environment fashioned by the new media. It is not the print media that is dead but rather the old style of journalistic reporting that is becoming obsolete. Thus, the path for the survival of the Lebanese print media ought to be one that allows it to provide its audience with content that the other media cannot provide as well. To meet the challenge of the new media, the press needs to concentrate on providing its readers with a content that the social media are not suitable to provide effectively: such a content includes critical interpretation of events, investigations of vital affairs and thought-provoking features. Two journalists ventured onto this route, Ibrahim el-Amin of *Al-Akhbar* and Mustafa Naser of *Al-Itihad*. *Al-Akhbar* is in the elementary stages of this experiment and its growing circulation and popular impact is promising. The death of Naser and the folding of *Al-Itihad* ended its experiment.

Only time will tell if this is the right path for reviving the print media in Lebanon.

Radio Broadcasting

Overview

If the Lebanese print media were born essentially as an answer to a need, felt by a few intellectuals, to educate and guide the people and mobilize them around social and communal accord, radio broadcasting was introduced in 1938 by the French Mandate to propagate its own political agendas. Indeed, radio broadcasting in Lebanon was developed "to bring closer together the French and Arab cultures in both Syria and Lebanon"[1] and to combat Nazi and Fascist propaganda beamed at the Arab world from Radio Berlin in Germany and Radio Bari in Italy. It began and was to remain until the beginning of the Civil War in 1975, under strict control by the national ruling elite.

Radio broadcasting in Lebanon was designated as a government monopoly and Radio Lebanon was, until 1994, the only agency legally authorized to transmit radio signals from within Lebanon. It was used chiefly to propagate the plans of the government and those of the ruling political personalities.

Political control of radio broadcasting in Lebanon has been applied and tolerated by all Lebanese regimes since the inception of this medium. The former Prime Minister Saeb Salam explained in a 1973 interview that because the government has no newspaper to defend itself, Radio Lebanon is its "paper." Since then, a number of senior government officials have regularly echoed this statement.

Radio Lebanon is the official broadcasting organ of the Lebanese government and operates within the Lebanese Ministry of Information. It is headed by a director who is the overall coordinator of activities and the link between the authorities and radio services. In principle, this organization is independent in its day-to-day operations of broadcasting, except for the news bulletin, which is controlled by the official National News Agency. In practice, however, broadcasting is controlled by the director-general of the ministry of information, who is in turn subject to the authority of a number of ministers or political *zu'ma* (bosses). The broadcasting of any local program, except music, requires prior approval. Politicians and personalities not approved of by the government and the ruling *zu'ma* are usually banned from the radio studio altogether. Radio Lebanon has a separate budget within the ministry. Its expenditure on programs and on personalities is often influenced by political pressure.

Customarily, Radio Lebanon attempts to balance the function of the Lebanese press, which is typically critical of the government and does not usually give it fair coverage. In actual practice, however, Radio Lebanon reflects the government and the political elite only, in an unskilled and ineffective fashion, often losing its audience and failing in its mission.

Throughout its long history, this official radio broadcasting system has failed to develop into a genuine popular channel of information and entertainment accessible to the diverse Lebanese communities as well as to the different socioeconomic groupings. It has also failed to play the role of a forum for the various political, intellectual, artistic and cultural circles of the country.

The official Lebanese radio was a medium that one used to turn to out of suspicious curiosity, something alien to the people that stood above them. Aside from music programs and certain live broadcasts, this medium does not signify very much for the people. Indeed, the history of radio in Lebanon suggests that the investment in, and development of, this medium was a function of the interest of politicians in exploiting radio broadcasting for their political ends more than a function of the interest in serving the people. The political interests of the ruling elite, not the interest and needs of the general public, determined the direction and nature of growth of radio broadcasting in Lebanon.

The historical circumstances that accompanied the development of radio broadcasting enhanced the alien character of this medium in the eyes of the Lebanese. Instituted by the French mandatory authorities, the Lebanese broadcasting operations were kept under strict control by the French High Commissioner during the mandate period. When a protocol was signed between the French government and the newly independent Lebanese government to hand the radio station over to the Lebanese authorities in 1946, more than two-fifths of its programs continued to be prepared by three foreign embassies: the French, the British and the American. The reorganization of the radio in 1961 discontinued the British and American programs but maintained the protocol with France, according to which French-prepared programs would continue to go on the air. No political dialogue was allowed through the radio, thus restricting access to broadcasting to the government and the ruling political elites.

In subsequent years, no government official made any effort to reorganize radio broadcasting or to draw new frames and directions along which radio should develop. For them, it was sufficient that news programs covered governmental policies and protocol activities. In their zeal to maintain an uncompromising status quo, mildly referred to as "national stability," they discouraged innovation and change. The only aspect of radio broadcasting that witnessed some modernization and improvement was the technical. Programs continued to be managed on a day-to-day basis, with little or no long-range planning.

With the failure of the authorities to involve its official radio station in covering the civil hostilities or to provide essential information about events of the hostilities during two civil war periods (1958 and 1975–1989), illegal politically oriented radio stations went on the air. These illegal stations propagated the conflicting positions of the different warring groups.

With the signing of the Taif Accord that ushered the end of the Civil War in 1989 and with the central government gradually taking control over the affairs of the state, an audio-visual law that organized broadcasting in Lebanon was adopted by the Lebanese parliament in 1994. The new law ended the state monopoly over broadcasting and authorized the granting of radio and television licenses to private stations. Under the new law, the official Lebanese radio continued to operate as an organ of the government.

Although the medium of the radio is popular in Lebanon, Radio Lebanon services ranked low in prestige and influence among the broadcasting outlets in the country. Research findings by this author[2] early during the Civil War suggest that the Lebanese public prefers to seek information, even entertainment, from other radio services. The official government radio station is unable to gain genuine national appeal and it maintains its original character as propagator of policies of the political ruling elites. The Lebanese public does not perceive it as serving its interests, or even fulfilling its information needs.

Historical Background

The first radio broadcasting station in Lebanon was established in Beirut in September 1938. At the request of the French authorities, a French company, Radio Orient, built and managed this station as the official station for both Syria and Lebanon, under the name: Radio Levant (Arabic: Radio ash-Shark). It had a power of half a kilowatt and transmitted on medium wave.[3] Short wave signals were added in December 1940. Transmission was limited to four hours: two hours at noon and two in the evening. The power of the transmitters, situated in Khaldeh on the outskirts of Beirut, was clearly insufficient. Transmitters that are more powerful were ordered from France but the war did not permit their delivery.

Radio Levant began operation with one room, which housed four employees (the manager, an engineer, an announcer and a secretary in charge of music); a small studio; and a five-man orchestra. The personnel were under the strict control of the information department of the High Commissioner.[4]

In 1941, the French Vichy government destroyed the station's transmitters when the Allied Forces entered Lebanon. Using parts of a transmitter salvaged from a ship that sank near the port of Haifa in Palestine, the Allies rebuilt the transmitters. The station resumed broadcasting with a one-kilowatt medium wave transmitter and a 200-watt short wave transmitter.

In 1946, three years after Lebanon gained its independence, the station was formally handed over to the national government. A protocol allowing France the daily use of the station for 145 minutes was signed between the governments of France and Lebanon. England and the United States requested similar privileges and were granted 60 and 30 minutes respectively to air daily programs. The station was renamed the Lebanese Broadcasting Station and was subordinate to the Directorate of Propaganda and Publishing, a branch of the Ministry of the Interior.

Daily broadcasts then lasted 570 minutes, of which only 60 percent, or 335 minutes, were Arabic programs. The remaining 235 minutes were allocated to French, British and American programs prepared by the embassies of those countries. This practice continued until April 1960, when the British service aired a pro-Zionist program. Faced by a media and public uproar, the Lebanese government was forced to withdraw permission from the British and American embassies to use the station. A separate English language unit was set up within the radio structure. Because of the protocol signed with France, the French program was continued. However, it was placed under government supervision. French programs were now prepared by the French broadcasting organization ORTF, not by the French embassy. After 1974, French programs on Lebanese radio were entrusted to one of the companies created in the wake of the restructuring of that organization, the "Institut National de l'Audiovision" (INA).[5]

The demand for a regular and organized information network provoked the need for a separate information ministry. As a result, the Ministry of Guidance and News was formed in 1949. The radio station was attached to it. During the period 1946–1952, several attempts were made to strengthen the broadcasting station. In 1948, the government expressed its intention in setting up a more powerful radio station. This decision was prompted by its embarrassment when Lebanon had to use Turkey's broadcasting facilities to relay the proceedings of the third UNESCO conference that was held in Beirut.

A group of Lebanese emigrants volunteered to raise funds to establish an international Lebanese radio service to link Lebanon with Lebanese emigrants worldwide. The government approved the proposed plan and the emigrants contributed to the project. A Marconi technician was commissioned to make a feasibility study. However, nothing came of this plan due to disagreements among the donors. The US government proposed that a relay station be established in Lebanon for the Voice of America in return for its contribution to the construction of a 1,000 kilowatt Lebanese radio station. This offer, along with others from foreign and local business groups interested in setting up commercial radio stations, was rejected.

Clearly, developing radio and other mass media did not rank high among the priorities of the Lebanese political authorities at the time. The political and economic changes in Lebanon and the region, however, as well as the election in 1952, of a new president who was more aware and persuaded of the power of the mass media, changed the order of priorities. In 1953, a legislative decree was issued to organize the print media and another (legislative decree 39) to regulate radio broadcasting. Under this decree, radio broadcasting continued to be a branch of the Ministry of Guidance and News. It was now to have two departments: one for administration and the other for production. The latter included a section for programs, another for music, and a third for technical services.

That same year, the sum of L£0.5 million (then equivalent to US$170,000) was allocated in the budget for the new radio station. Two United Nations experts were commissioned to prepare a plan for a more powerful station. This sum was later raised to L£8.5 million (US$3 million).

The new plan, which was approved, required two 100-kilowatt transmitters on the short and medium waves, as well as a modern building to house the new studios and offices of the station. The short Civil War of 1958, together with other administrative and contractual issues, delayed the completion of the project until 1961.

To confront the "rebel" stations that had established themselves by the force of their supporters, the government urgently sought to improve the power of transmission of its radio station. A ten-kilowatt transmitter on medium wave was introduced in 1958. By 1959, another four-kilowatt transmitter on medium wave length commenced to broadcast foreign programs.

In 1959, the Ministry of Guidance and News was reorganized and the radio department was upgraded. Broadcasting became part of the ministry's general directorate. Meanwhile, a French expert on tourism was commissioned to prepare a new organizational plan for the radio station. As his expertise was in tourism, he was sent to a number of European capitals to study their broadcasting systems before presenting his plan.[6] His recommendations were adopted in 1961, when the Ministry of Guidance and News was again reorganized and renamed the Ministry of Guidance, Information and Tourism.[7]

The new structure of the ministry promoted the Lebanese radio station to an agency with a separate budget within the ministry. The Lebanese radio, thus, became financially independent from the ministry, though it stayed administratively under the ministry's jurisdiction. Article 8 of this August 1961 organization (legislative decree 7276) gave the government radio agency a monopoly over radio transmission and the freedom to produce "directly or through others" its programs and, "in cooperation with the Ministry of Post, Telegraph, and Telephone, to consider all technical matters related to the utilization of radio channels."[8]

Under the new arrangement, however, news programs became the responsibility of the National News Agency, a newly formed branch of the ministry. The 1961 organization did not permit radio to broadcast any political dialogue. Access to radio was now possible only for the ruling politicians, who had the sole right of access to this medium.

The new station was inaugurated on June 4, 1962. Radio transmission now covered Africa, North and South America, Europe and the Middle East. Broadcasting time doubled and programs in five languages—Arabic, Armenian, English, French and Spanish—were now broadcast regularly.

Radio broadcasting on FM was introduced in October 1965, when the government received a displaced FM transmitter as a gift from the Arabian American Oil Company (ARAMCO). Transmission on FM was mainly limited to broadcasting musical programs. Stereophonic transmission was introduced in 1973.

Within a decade, the Lebanese radio had become an increasingly important voice for the government in the service of its political purposes. This, coupled with the fact that powerful radio stations were introduced in neighboring countries and were affecting the reception proper of the signals of the Lebanese radio, prompted the government in April 1972 to adopt a new plan, the "Great Radio Lebanon Project," for the further development of radio broadcasting in Lebanon.

The name of the Lebanese broadcasting station was also changed by the plan to Radio Lebanon. Its first phase of development was completed in March 1975. The project was scheduled for completion in the spring of 1976, but the Civil War and the state of political unrest in the country forced the government to freeze putting the project into operation.

The government's plan for the "Great Radio Lebanon Project" aimed at increasing the total transmission intensity and providing complete FM coverage to all Lebanese regions by placing transmitters in different locations. It also aimed at providing adequate and powerful coverage on the medium wavelength to the whole of Lebanon and its neighboring countries, as well as improving the programs directed to Lebanese emigrants all over the world.

The plan included installing: a 1,000-kilowatt transmitter whose power could be strengthened to 2,000 kilowatts for the central station; a number of transmitters, with power ranging from 25–500 kilowatts, in locations that ensured covering all of Lebanon with both FM and medium wave AM transmission; and a 250-kilowatt short wave transmitter.

With the election of President Elias Sarkis and the belief then that he would be able to end the Civil War and bring about normalcy, unfortunately, the political realities did not allow his government to go ahead with the project. The delay then was forced by a dilemma facing the government officials. One of the influential rightist warring groups had seized the area of the site (Hamat) chosen to be the center of the network of transmitters of the radio project and had assigned had it as a location for a surrogate airport. All through the Civil War period, the government did not have the resolve to remove these forces from this area. Should it attempt to evacuate them now, it would be understood as an act of hostility toward this group. On the other hand, not evacuating them would be understood by the opposing leftist group as taking side with their opponents. The officials thus chose to delay the implementation of the project.

Later in 1979, the Hamat site was captured by the Arab Deterrent Forces, who came to Lebanon upon the request of the government of Sarkis, and the airport site was destroyed. Fearful of upsetting the rightist forces, the Sarkis government decided to move the site to South Lebanon, near the town of Tyre. Rightest groups opposed the decision because the South was populated by leftist groups and was threatened with Israeli occupation, thus, the government would be venturing into a risky investment. The government complied and suggested Amshit as an alternative site. This new site was appraised to be not suitable. The government, thus, came up with a plan to carry the construction on a 180-meter float in the sea. Deputies from South Lebanon opposed the plans this time and the government postponed final action.

Resumption of fighting and the escalation of the Civil War forced the government to shelve the project. With the ending of hostilities in 1989, the government was preoccupied with serious economic and political problems; thus, little attention was given to radio. In 1994, the adoption of a new broadcasting policy legalizing private radio channels kept the government from paying serious attention to this medium.

Structure of Lebanese Radio

Radio Lebanon has a separate budget within the ministry of information. The government provides this budget in full. There is no outside source of income.[9] No annual license fees are paid for radio (or television) sets, nor is commercial, nonpublic advertising allowed on radio. The budget of Radio Lebanon, though independent, is part of the total budget of the ministry of information. It has increased steadily, from L£24,000 (US$8,000) in 1946 to L£5,221,600 (US$1.7 million) in 1975, to L£784,820,000 (US$261 million) in 1991 and L£7 billion (US$2.3 billion) in 2015.[10] However, this growth in the budget of Radio Lebanon constitutes less than 0.5 percent of the budget of the state and this reflects a lack of proper attention by officials to this medium.

Foreign programs on Radio Lebanon are limited to those received from some 27 Arab and foreign radio stations with which Lebanon has exchange agreements. Such programs, however, are few and require prior clearance from the ministry. Direct relays from abroad are rare. These are transmitted only when important officials are on visits abroad and they are arranged with the cooperation of the Ministry of Post, Telegraph and Telecommunications (PTT).

There are no specialized agencies to direct Radio Lebanon, nor is there a clear plan for the future management and upgrading of quality of the human element in charge of radio broadcasting. It is governed on a day-to-day basis, which is often confusing, not only to the public, but to the officials and other employees as well. Programs that are introduced one day may be stopped the next, if an important official or politician so decides. Scheduled programs have often been interrupted to broadcast a report, or a favorite song, for an important official.

In this state of affairs, programs are introduced or disappear according to the importance and the power of the agency promoting or opposing them. For example, the Center for Educational Research and Development (CERD), established upon the advice of people close to the former President Suleiman Franjieh and headed by a director close to this president, was able to introduce regular educational radio programs early in 1974. When the president left office, the director of CERD took a long leave of absence and the power of the Center diminished. Consequently, the educational programs were discontinued.

Radio Lebanon is expected to operate as the mouthpiece and champion of the government. This role is perhaps its biggest handicap because the government has taken radio broadcasting for granted. It does not give it the attention or the funds needed for its development, although it is the country's most readily available medium of communication.

The management of Radio Lebanon is usually unprofessional. The inadequate organization and staffing of the various departments result in poor quality productions. The authorities have been both unwilling and unable to change this state of affairs, mainly because change requires a management with initiative and expertise, that is to say, a qualitative change of the human element is involved. Such drastic change is not possible under the present system, which is based on the appointment of officials according to sectarian considerations rather than qualifications.

In the first decades of Lebanese radio broadcasting, the humble quality of radio and its inability to meet the needs of the audience were blamed on inferior facilities, poor technical equipment and poor organization. A series of technical improvements were introduced then, but it soon became clear that the improvement needed was in the area of the human element, not the technical resources. The government did not value the need for improving the human element in its radio structure, nor did it make use of offers for such improvements by qualified agencies. This lack of proper official and government attention to its own broadcasting medium resulted in Radio Lebanon losing its audience and influence to emerging radio stations that were able to operate, illegally prior to 1994 and under license since then. These stations addressed public needs for information and concerns about overall security during the Civil War. Many of the illegal stations were consequently able to legalize their status and adjust their operations to the changing public mood as well as to recent emerging challenges of new media technologies, as will be discussed in this chapter.

Civil War and Radio Broadcasting

Emergence of Illegal Radio Stations

During periods of great conflict and insecurity, the public demands more information from the existing media than what they usually provide. When these media fail to meet the demands of the audience, new outlets are sought. The Civil Wars of 1958 and 1975–1989 modified the environmental conditions within which radio broadcasting was operating and introduced new challenges to the existing structures.

The Civil War demonstrated that Lebanese radio audiences were not content with the placid news bulletins of Radio Lebanon, which were designed to give a mild version of a savage war and to maintain, in spite of this chaotic state of affairs, an image of order and institutional vitality. Radio Lebanon's local bulletins were filled with reports about activities of government officials and with meetings among the various political leaders. On the other hand, heavy weight was given to international news, sometimes as much as four-fifths of the airtime, thus avoiding the embarrassment of having to report about worsening local events.

During the relatively short 1958 civil strife, three rebel radio stations began airing the rebels' perspective of the events going on in the country. Each station propagated the ideas and news of its own faction. These were the Voice of Arabism (controlled by the "Najjadah," Muslim coalition); the Voice of Lebanon (representing the "Kata'ib," Christian Maronite Phalangist); and the Voice of People's Resistance (broadcasting from Tripoli and representing a Muslim leader, Rashid Karami). These stations operated for nine months before closing down, with the stabilization of the political situation. Because of their short-lived existence, the programs of the stations were essentially unprofessional. Managed on a day-to-day basis, these programs were limited to propaganda songs and news that was manifestly slanted.

During the early period of the 1975–1976 Civil War, the existing official radio and television operations were paralyzed by the general state of confusion that prevailed at all levels of the state institutions. The minister of information, who was also the prime minister, represented one warring faction while the president of the republic as well as the director-general of the ministry of information belonged to another. Agreement on a common information policy was impossible, so the official radio and television services simply ignored the fact that the country was going through a civil war. This situation prompted the emergence of illegal radio channels, which added to the troubles and confusion of the government.

The illegal radio stations were few and without significant appeal to the Lebanese masses during the first period of the Civil War (until March 1976). However, the policy of the officials to ignore the turbulences in the different parts of the country ultimately contributed to nurturing an appeal for the illegal stations. For instance, when a devoted civil-minded anchor on Radio Lebanon altered his usual daily "live" traffic program to report about areas in Beirut where hostilities were going on and about location of sniper areas, he was reprimanded and consequently fired. The intention of this anchor was to warn drivers about the shifting hostility areas. Nevertheless, although program became very popular and developed to occupy most of the morning broadcasting time, the change in the program was carried out without the authorization of radio officials and was regarded as a cause for public agitation. The dismissed anchor of the program, Sharif al-Akhawi, a shy schoolteacher, became a public celebrity.

The Division of Radio Lebanon

On the evening of March 11, 1976, a new phase in official broadcasting began. On that evening, an army officer, the army commander of Beirut, forced himself with the aid of a few soldiers into the studios of the Lebanese Television Company (CLT) as the news program was being aired. He read a statement declaring himself the military ruler of the country and asked the president to step down. From the CLT studios, he moved to the nearby official radio station and occupied it to broadcast the same statement.

Immediately after the broadcast, the supporters of the president occupied the other television station, Tele Orient, and the radio transmission sites in Amshit and Mount Ayto. Thus, began an open division of the official broadcasting stations in Lebanon—a division that lasted throughout most of the regimes of two presidents, Elias Sarkis and Amin Gemayel. Both radio and television transmitters were divided among the battling groups. Radio transmitters in Amshit and Mount Ayto were in the hands of one faction; those in Beirut and Ma'aser esh-Shouf were in the hands of another.

The appointment of the first government under President Elias Sarkis, in September 1976, was expected to usher the end of the Civil War, with the support of a deployed "Arab League Deterrent Force." Immediately after the government took office, the two stations were reunited. The news department, however, remained divided for several months. It was agreed that the two opposing groups separately prepare news programs and that they be broadcast in alternate news placings.

When a new director-general for the ministry of information was appointed, he reunited the two opposing factions in one department. Radio Lebanon was once again integrated. With this task accomplished, several efforts were made to improve the quality of programs to make them competitive with the illegal pirate stations, but these efforts failed for three main reasons: the first was that the appointment of those expected to manage the radio stations was based on loyalties not qualifications; the second was that government officials took Radio Lebanon for granted and thus provided it with little attention and funds; and the third reason was the continued abrupt changes in the leadership of the ministry of information. Consequently, no stable plans for radio could be adopted.

When President Amin Gemayel came to power in 1982, after the Israeli invasion of Lebanon, and the intervention of the French, Italian and US forces to aid the new government, he was expected to move swiftly and address himself to reunite the country. His first government was given legislative powers by the parliament. However, it did not produce any legislation in the area of broadcasting. Radio broadcasting was low on the priority list of the authorities and received little support and funds. At one time, Radio Lebanon went off the air for a whole day because there were no funds to repair some of its essential equipment.

Illegal Stations Taking Root

The number of illegal stations and their negative input to the state of division in the country increased during the 1975–1989 period.[11] The length of the war and the profusion of funds available to the warring groups allowed the rebel stations to improve their services and produce programs that were more professional.

The Voice of Lebanon was the first of the rebel stations to go on the air. It began its operations in June 1975, continued for a few months, closed down during a brief ceasefire period, and then resumed broadcasting. This station represented the rightest Phalangist party and was transmitting 24 hours a day. It developed the widest audience during the regime of Phalangist President Amin Gemayel (1982–1988), because of its close connection to the Minister of Information during the regime of President Suleiman Franjieh.

The Voice of Lebanon was able to obtain a disputed "permit" to function. A heated debate over the legality of this permit was resolved during the regime of President Elias Sarkis by a decision not to recognize the "permit" because it contradicted an article in the Lebanese constitution (Article 89). This article maintains that: "no license or commitment to utilize any natural resource, or utility or monopoly of public nature may be granted except by a law and only for a limited period of time." The "permit" also contradicts Article 8 of the legislative decree 7276 of 1961, which gave Radio Lebanon a monopoly over radio broadcasting.[12]

Consequently, early during the regime of President Sarkis, on August 1, 1978, Prime Minister Salim el-Hoss replied to a parliamentary question concerning the illegal radio stations by stating:

> The existence of private radio stations is an illegal phenomenon triggered by the events of the last two years. This phenomenon constitutes a threat to the authority of the state and a source of confusion and agitation which conflicts with efforts being exerted for peace on the land of this nation. There is no final solution to the problem of security in Lebanon in the presence of these stations. The government will work to close all these stations down.[13]

Unofficial and illegal stations continued to emerge ignoring official opposition. These stations crowded the FM Lebanese radio airwaves during the Civil War. Illegal stations were not restricted to politically oriented ones—many stations aired exclusively music and talk programs.

The rival and counterpart of the Voice of Lebanon was the Voice of Arab Lebanon that was founded in 1978 by al-Murabitun leftist Arab nationalist movement. This station was stormed by armed supporters of a rival group and ceased broadcasting, then resumed after several years. Among the powerful stations that were still broadcasting at the end of the Civil War were: the Voice of the Homeland, an organ of the Makassed Sunni Muslim institution; the Voice of the Mountain, an organ of the Socialist Progressive Party representing mainly the Druze population; the Voice of the People, an organ of the Communist Party; and the Voice of Free Lebanon, the official station of the Maronite Christian "Lebanese Forces."

The outburst of violence in 1983 and 1984 forced Gemayel's first government to resign and seriously weakened the authority of the president, who had no control over a large part of the country. Accordingly, more illegal stations went on the air. In May 1984, a new coalition government was formed including leaders of the "opposition" and "loyal" warring groups. Instead of addressing itself to uniting the country, this government was further divided with its members unable to agree on almost all issues, with each minister acting on his own.

The continued clashes among members of the second Gemayel government lead to the resignation of the prime minister and the inability of the president to form a new government. Thus, the government continued as a caretaker government until the end of the term of office of Gemayel. During this period, the ministers declined to hold joint sessions and no serious legislation or policies could be considered. The prolonged inability of the different government officials during the Civil War to take action and address themselves to address the confused broadcasting situation provided the illegal stations a kind of de facto recognition, which was slowly being routinized. In a magazine interview on November 1982, the then Minister of Information, Roger Chikhani, said that these radio stations present a "delicate problem." He held that they

> did a good job during the war, providing the citizens with valuable services, especially where security was concerned. One cannot deny this fact. But what may one do about them now? Frankly, I do not know. One thing for certain: the law must be applied ... But there is a possibility that the law will be altered.[14]

By the end of the Civil War, the reorganization of radio broadcasting became an urgent yet complicated problem that plagued government officials. On one hand, some of the illegal stations grew in influence to an extent that it was difficult for any government to eliminate them, even if it decided to do so. On the other, it was "irrational to permit religious or sectarian radio stations ... to continuously threaten the unity of society and become institutions of agitation."[15]

In the absence of an effective army and security forces, the government was actually powerless and could not prevent the operation of pirate stations. By the end of the war, when the government regained relative control over the country, these stations sought official recognition and declared themselves private and commercial channels. The long period of operation of these radio stations and the power of the groups behind them forced the authorities to search for a new position that was suitable for the existing stations.

During the regime of President Gemayel, Radio Lebanon operated similar the illegal radio stations. It converted to become a spokesperson for one of the warring groups and its public image and its credibility declined further. With the end of the Civil War, the newly elected President Elias Hrawi was required by the agreement that brought him to power to reach a solution for the confused state of affairs of broadcasting. The Taif Agreement, which addressed the demands of the warring groups and ushered the end of hostilities, mandated that: "all broadcasting channels should be reorganized within the law."[16]

While publicly declaring pirate stations illegal, the post-Taif government could not take action against any of them. In the early post-Taif period, the ministry of information officials were of the opinion that the illegal stations could not possibly continue without continued subsidies from the faction supporting them. Time, they believed, was against these stations.

The Taif Agreement included special reference to the broadcasting media requesting the emerging national partnership government to address the problem of reorganizing these media "within the framework of responsible freedom in a way that serves the aspirations for national accord and ending the state of war."[17] In line with this, the Minister of Information organized a special seminar in 1991 to discuss this reorganization. A wide range of media practitioners, officials and scholars participated in this seminar that was broadcast live on one of the unlicensed television channels.

In his opening remarks of the seminar, the Minister of Information, Albert Mansour urged that

> we have to get out of the circumstances of war and change the methods of war which included the [use of] the media. These media cannot continue to be instruments of war ... we have accepted to abolish the militias and gave this decision priority of implementation in an effort to move from the state

of war to a state of peace. We thus have to agree that media channels are not militia instruments, which fire words instead of bullets.[18]

After some three years of deliberations between the different national sectors concerned with broadcasting, the Lebanese parliament approved in 1994 an audio-visual media law, which was perhaps the first law organizing broadcasting in an Arab region. The law distinguished two general radio broadcasting categories: the first permitted the broadcast of news and political programs; and the second allowed broadcasting general programs only, without the right to air news. The audio-visual law established a "National Council for Audio-Visual Media" (NCOAVM), which is to serve as an advisory board that oversees broadcasting and recommends to the government granting broadcasting licenses.

The implementing the 1994 audio-visual law demonstrated a lack of official concern for the broadcasting medium. On September 17, 1996, the government granted broadcasting licenses (on the FM band) to 11 radio stations. Few of the stations were permitted to broadcast news and political programs, which meant excluding the majority of stations from "airing any program concerning the government's foreign or domestic policies."[19]

The general director of the ministry of information at the time, Mohammed Obeid, conceded in an interview with the *Washington Post* that the selection of the stations to be licensed was, in part, "a political decision."[20] The number of radio stations licensed by the government reached 32 by December 2015. However, several unlicensed stations continue on the air illegally. Two of these unlicensed stations belonged to eminent religious authorities thus were given a debated "special" approval.[21]

Radio stations that are licensed to broadcast political topics and news include Voice of Lebanon (Sawt Lubnan), the rightist organ of the Phalangist party, founded in 1975;[22] Voice of the People (Sawt ash-Sha'b), founded in 1987 leftist radio affiliated with the Communist Party; Voice of Tomorrow (Sawt al-Ghad), founded in 1997 and affiliated with the Free Patriotic Party of President Michel Aoun; Voice of Free Lebanon (Sawt Lubnan al-Hurr), launched in 1985 rightist organ of the Lebanese Forces Party; Radio Orient (Itha'at ash-Shark), founded in 1995 and affiliated with the Future Movement, and Voice of the Horizon (Sawt al-Mada), established in 2009 and affiliated with the Free Patriotic Party.[23]

Radio stations in the nonpolitical category are of two types: one that exclusively airs religious programs advocating a culture of peace and promoting human and religious values and interfaith dialogue. Stations in this type usually stand for the different religious denominations and most operate without authorized licensing.[24] Prominent among the religious radio stations are: the Virgin Mary (Radio Pax) that airs light religious songs dedicated to Christ; the Qur'an Kareem Radio that airs exclusively religious programs and recitations of the Qur'an.

The other radio type airs a variety of entertainment and music genres in both Arabic and foreign languages. Among the major stations of this type are: Radio One, an online music station that airs international music; Mix FM, an Internet-based online radio broadcasting varieties of music genres; Arabic Music Radio an Arabic language station broadcasting Arabic Music; Radio One, operates from the town of Beit Meri and plays English and international music.

Entertainment radio stations usually include a "listeners' choice" music programs as well as "call ins" when a presenter indulges the callers with simplistic exchanges. Some of the "call in" programs shift attention late at night to provide advice on personal and family problems usually by incompetent presenters who play the role of "therapists."

The advisory role of NCOAVM has been continuously criticized and calls are growing for granting it more powers to restrain political influence by the government in broadcasting regulation. The status of NCOAVM is presently under review by the information and communication committee of the Lebanese parliament. A draft law integrating regulations for the print, audio-visual and electronic media is now before the different parliamentary committees for consideration. If approved the draft law will give NCOAVM licensing power among other managerial responsibilities.

Future of Lebanese Radio

What is the future of radio broadcasting in Lebanon? What policies may the government adopt to adjust the muddle in this area and to improve the performance of this medium?

The radio medium has always received little attention by all Lebanese governments. Lebanese officials were indeed not interested in this medium or in its advancement. They failed to provide it with the professional and technical capability or know-how to succeed. It was an inheritance from the French that they were not anxious to acquire. They did not know what role this medium can play in their governance system, nor were they concerned in learning about this role. Thus, it took them two years after gaining independence to officially receive the radio station facilities from the French authorities. And then they readily approved requests to grant three foreign governments (France, England and the United States) the right to broadcast their programs on this national medium.

During the Civil War, the ruling powers were in no mood nor were they in a position to consider national broadcasting plans and policies that may allow this medium to play a positive role in the state's affairs. Moreover, ruling politicians and active power groups presented conflicting views on this subject. The prolonged inability of the different governments during the Civil War to take action and address themselves to the confused media situation, particularly the radio medium, gave the illegal stations a sort of a de facto recognition that was slowly being routinized.

By the end of the Civil War, the reorganization of radio broadcasting became an urgent but complicated problem that plagued government officials. On one hand, some illegal stations grew to a level that it was difficult for any government to suppress them, even if it chose to do so. On the other, it was "illogical to permit religious or sectarian radio stations … to continuously threaten the unity of society and become institutions of agitation."[25]

Faced with diverse proposed remedies the government opted to end the state monopoly over broadcasting and to adopt the French broadcasting regulation model by creating an audio-visual board to oversee broadcasting matters. However, unlike the French model, this audio-visual body was given only advisory role; final decisions on aspects of regulation and licensing were reserved to the minister of information and the government. Additionally, the board membership has to maintain a sectarian balance in its composition; thus, the main criterion for membership on this board was sectarian representation and not professional qualification: members of the board need to represent the major religious sects in the country. Professional qualification was secondary to sectarian representation on this board of ten: five appointed by the government and the remaining five elected by the parliament.

Another predicament facing radio broadcasting was the fact that attention focused more on developing broadcasting technology than on upgrading and developing the human element in this area. The tendency therefore was to acquire new technologies and train "technicians" to operate this medium. Thus, government, media professionals and universities were concentrating on producing media "technicians" who can manage and repair the technologies, rather than on creating media "engineers" who can attend to the "big radio picture" and can draft media policies and plans that are based on Lebanon's societal and cultural needs.

The advancement of radio in Lebanon cannot be achieved by a mere focus on the technology sector of this medium. The cultural component of the medium is essential for its development. Unless broadcasting institutions are able to inject the cultural, particularly the folkloric element into this medium it cannot play an effective and significant role in addressing popular and national problems. The impact of the social media on attitude and opinion change can be realized in a more positive manner when these media are fused with the folk media, as will be discussed in Chapter 5. Lebanese radio today, both the official and private, is contributing to introducing low culture and "kitsch" that may appeal to public impulses but not to their needs.

Additionally, the political partisanship of present private Lebanese radio stations inhibits them from reaching national coverage. The FM radio stations are either commercially profit-oriented channels or religious channels. The commercial channels concentrate on music, games and talk shows that are usually presented by amateurs. The religious channels are mainly fundamentalist and focus on preaching. Neither type pays attention to "tuning" their programs to Lebanese cultural and national needs. And the government does not seem to be concerned with developing plans and drafting policies in this direction. Thus, a state of entropy prevails in radio broadcasting. Political and commercial profit are the chief factors that "guide" the operation of this medium.

In conclusion, Lebanese radio broadcasting lacks government interest as well as the involvement of competent professionals. It lacks concerned official as well as media executives who are trained not only in the technical aspects of this medium but also, and most importantly are knowledgeable in its role in the Lebanese society. The partnership of both can produce essential policies and plans that can advance this medium so as it may contribute to Lebanese national development.

Television

Historical Background

The history of television in Lebanon is one of supervisory and structural changes as well as of a "tug-of-war" between government and private enterprise. The beginnings of Lebanese television correspond to the setting in motion of an era of economic prosperity in Lebanon, the late 1950s. Private enterprise was instrumental in introducing the television medium in Lebanon. Thus, while the print media developed as a reaction to social need, and radio developed as a reaction to specific external political circumstances television was prompted by economic prosperity and the growth of business and finance. This perhaps explains why the print and radio media in Lebanon are more oriented to education and persuasion (propagation) while television concentrates more on entertainment.

The initiative to establish Lebanese television belongs to businesspersons who had little experience in the exigencies of television broadcasting. They conceived of their project in essentially commercial terms. In this lies Lebanese television's main weakness, for the logic of a commercial enterprise in developing countries often runs counter to that of public service and societal welfare.

A review of past performance of television in Lebanon suggests that measures taken by the government to regulate television broadcasting were not designed to stimulate awareness of television officials in the needs of the public. Nor were they to encourage original productions, or to promote local talent, or develop responsible organizational structures. Rather, enforced broadcasting regulations aimed at allowing the government and the reigning political bosses to exploit this medium for their own political goals. Political bosses legitimated their monopoly over television news bulletins and the censorship of material that might threaten their political goals or the status quo.

The first attempt to start television broadcasting in Lebanon goes back to October 1954 when two Lebanese businesspersons, Wissam Izzedine and Alex Arida, submitted an application for a license to establish a television broadcasting company. After two years of negotiations, on August 1956, the government approved an agreement granting a license to "La Compagnie Libanaise de Television, SAL" (CLT). The license was not a monopoly as the applicants had requested. It was simply a license to broadcast television signals on two channels: one (Channel 7) devoted to programs in Arabic or with Arabic subtitles; and the other (Channel 9) for foreign, mainly French, programs. CLT thus was the first commercial television station in the Arab world.[1]

The civil troubles of 1958 interrupted the construction work on the station. On the evening of May 28, 1959, the station inaugurated its service and began transmission with a power of half a kilowatt. The first three months were devoted to the transmission of experimental programs; less than ten sets received the first transmission.

The agreement between CLT and the government left the door open for other companies to apply for television broadcasting licenses. The most important term of the 21-article agreement stipulated that the government would not grant monopoly rights to the company and that television broadcasting was to operate under government scrutiny. It further agreed that the new company was not to broadcast programs that would threaten public security, incite religious hostilities, threaten public morals or enhance the image of any political personality or party.

Television programs, under the terms of this agreement were restricted to education or entertainment. Advertising was not allowed to exceed 25 percent of the broadcast time. The agreement also required that there should be at least 20 hours/week of broadcasting and that the company should undertake to broadcast, free of charge, news programs and official bulletins submitted by the Ministry of Guidance and News.

The first phase of the project, according to this agreement was the construction of a main 400-watt transmitter, to be increased to 4 kW, and the installation of relay stations covering the whole of Lebanon. The agreement gave the government the right to take over the station directly and operate it should the television company stop broadcasting for 30 days on two occasions during a one-year period without a compelling. The government had the right to cancel the license without any indemnification.

In addition, television was subjected to Lebanese laws regulating the operation of press and authors, as well as to national or international laws regulating wireless communications and broadcasting institutions. Television was also required to exchange sound programs with the official Lebanese radio.

The agreement was to remain in force for 15 years, after which the government had the right to buy all the company's related facilities. To be able to concentrate on production and programming, CLT established a separate company, Advision, which assumed the administration of the company and the responsibility for selling advertising time. Time-Life Broadcasting Corporation was a partner of Advision during the early period of the company. This partnership, however, lasted for a short time. In 1967, Sofirad, a French government-financed institution that controls and coordinates several private French broadcasting stations including Radio Monte Carlo, bought Advision in association with Intra Investment Company and several small Lebanese shareholders.

In April 1959, another group of Lebanese businesspersons, financed by an American corporation, *ABC,* approached the government with a request to set up a second television station, the "Compagnie de Television du Liban et du Proch-Orient" (Tele Orient). The group sought to draw up an agreement similar to that with CLT, but with certain adjustments including a change in length of contract. It requested a 25-year contract (instead of 15). The group also proposed that should the government decide to cancel the agreement it must allow for a period of ten years (instead of four as with CLT) to terminate the operations of the company. The government refused the propositioned modifications. In July 1959, an agreement identical to that of CLT was signed with Tele Orient. Transmission of one program on Channels 5 and 11 began on May 6, 1962. In 1965, the London-based Thomson Organization, together with the Rizk Brothers of Beirut, formed the Thompson-Rizk Group and bought the ABC shares in Tele Orient.

From their inception, both television companies faced financial difficulties. Both were incurring financial losses during the early period of their operation.

The two companies endeavored to sell locally produced programs to television institutions in the Arab countries. At first, Sofirad subsidized CLT and the Thompson Group backed Tele Orient. After a number of unprofitable years that witnessed tough competition and lack of adequate management, especially in selling airtime, an agreement was signed in 1968 between CLT and Tele-Orient. This agreement marked the beginnings of policy and programming coordination. Advision, which was in charge of advertising and the management of CLT, became responsible for advertising on Tele Orient programs. The arrangement was an improvement on past experience but did not end the financial losses of both companies.

A second step in the cooperation between the two companies was reached in October 1972 with the establishment of Tele-Management SAL, a private independent company equally financed by CLT and Tele Orient. This company was to handle advertising and to coordinate the scheduling of the programs of the two companies. Advision continued to be in charge of the administration of CLT. Immediately after its establishment, Tele-Management successfully adopted sophisticated sales methods and coordinated the scheduling and marketing of programs, which increased the advertising revenues of both companies.

Revenue from advertising on television was increasing before the setback during the Civil War. Total television advertising income in 1974 was L£13 million (then about US$4.5 million). This represented a 19.5 percent increase over 1973 and constituted 35.3 percent of the total 1974 advertising expenditure in Lebanon.

Tele Orient had an additional income from its sales of locally produced programs to the Arab countries, which represented 12 percent of its total income in 1974: the rest came from advertising. CLT sold fewer programs, perhaps because its local programs were directed more to the Lebanese audience.[2] The income from the sale of CLT programs in 1974 covered only 5 percent of its total income.

On December 31, 1974, after negotiations between the Ministry of Information and Representatives of the French Ministries of Foreign Affairs and Information, the Lebanese government renewed the exploitation license of CLT, which from that date absorbed Advision. Under the new arrangement, the government was to purchase the installations of CLT and then lease them to it. The renewal was for a period of nine years. Thus, between December

1974 and December 1977 there were two sets of regulations for television broadcasting, one set applying to Tele Orient under the provisions of its 1962 license, and the other applying to CLT under its 1974 arrangement.

The 1974 settlement with CLT had essentially one purpose: to institutionalize and formalize the government's role in the political control of CLT. The new arrangement specified that two government "censors" be placed at the station to regularly observe its operations. It also requested CLT to broadcast a daily one-hour evening program prepared by the government. The new arrangement stipulated that the government collect 6.5 per cent of the company's net advertising revenue, and that a maximum of nine minutes of advertising per hour of programs would be permitted, with a maximum of three minutes during the news.

Furthermore, the agreement made vague recommendations demanding that programs be "of the highest possible standards." It required that CLT transmitters be redistributed to extend its national coverage and requested it to upgrade the professional proficiency of "production and technical" employees. The government, however, had no role in the implementation of these recommendations.

Color programs using the Secam system were introduced by CLT in October 1969. Tele Orient began producing color programs in 1975. Rather than using the same system employed by CLT it used the PAL system and converted it to Secam for local transmission. This arrangement allowed Tele Orient to sell its color programs in Arab markets that use the PAL system.

During the first two years of the Civil War (1975–1976), the two companies faced difficult challenges. The war seriously reduced their advertising revenues, and both companies incurred heavy losses. While both stations managed to maintain their technical equipment and keep their transmitters operational, they could not keep their production studios functioning. New programs could not be produced and television officials were eagerly seeking programs to fill their broadcasting schedules. One UN agency information executive told this author that a television official borrowed, and used, all the films in the agency's library. He said that the television official did not bother to find out what the content of the films were. His concern was the time span of each film.

This situation lasted until March 1976 when an unsuccessful *coup d'état* resulted in the occupation of both stations by militias representing the two warring factions. Consequently, the news program in the west Beirut station (in Telet el-Khayat) was managed by the "nationalist forces" (mainly Muslim) and that in the east Beirut station (in Hazmieh) by the "Lebanese forces" (mainly Christian). Coordination between the two stations in presenting a common news program was severed,[3] but they maintained coordinating scheduling their entertainment programs. The period of the split witnessed a serious escalation in the war. Broadcasting installations became targets for the warring groups. Television installations were bombed and badly damaged as each station had installations in the areas occupied by opposing factions. Transmission was also badly affected by power failures, which now became acute. Power supply became irregular and rationed.

The use of rotary antennas during the Civil War led to an increase in viewing foreign terrestrial television stations. Several foreign terrestrial television transmissions were then received in Lebanon. Syrian television as well as Egyptian and Israeli television signals could be received by sets with proper antennae. Cypriot signals could sometimes be received as well.

During the first two years of the Civil War, Lebanese television was virtually absent in North Lebanon. Television services in Syria and Cyprus were the only services north Lebanese audiences could receive. Syrian programs attracted more Lebanese viewers because of both language and cultural similarity. Tele Orient signals became unavailable to viewers in the Bekaa region (east Lebanon) as of March 1976. This lasted until 1991 and left the airwaves open to programs from Jordan, Syria and Israel. In South Lebanon, only CLT's Channel 7 was received, as were Egyptian and Israeli telecasts.

Surveys conducted in 1974 for Tele Management by the Associated Business Consultants[4] showed that more urban Lebanese watched television than any other medium. A study conducted by the author during the war (in 1978) revealed that television had its most impact on the lower income classes but hardly affected the elite, who did not give it serious attention, and who restricted their television viewing, if they engage in it at all, to foreign serials. The lower income groups considered their use of television as a means of entertainment. Both lower and upper income groups sought Information about national and world problems from newspapers, which were regarded as being more reliable.[5] The overall level of television set ownership in Lebanon, according to the ABC survey, was close to 75 percent of all homes in 1974.

Another survey estimated that, in 1974, the number of Lebanese households with "television sets in working order" was only 64 percent.

There are no individual television license fees in Lebanon. The fact that all television sets were imported and that these sets were heavily taxed, limited the spread of this medium. However, with the emergence of illegal seaports controlled by different militia groups during the Civil War, television and video sets were smuggled into the country and prices dropped significantly.

The heavy losses incurred by both companies moved them close to bankruptcy. The only prospect for them to continue operation was to secure financial assistance from the government. They officially requested the interference of the government at the end of 1976. At that time, a new president, Elias Sarkis, was elected and the pace of hostilities diminished. People were hopeful that the new regime would end to the Civil War.

The first government of President Sarkis faced a dilemma. If it refused to give support to both companies, Lebanon would be without television. This would add a further blow to the already battered image of the country and would be a bad beginning for the new regime. If it agreed to extend aid, the government would have to find a formula whereby it would aid other institutions affected by the war. To add to the urgency for action by the government, the license of Tele Orient was also due for renewal.

In an effort to resolve this dilemma, the government appointed a special committee to examine the state of affairs of television in Lebanon. The committee, which included representatives of the two companies, had the task of recommending the role television should play in what was believed to be the post-war period and making recommendations to maintain the operation of this medium. The committee recommended founding a new company with an exclusive right for television broadcasting. The new company was proposed to be structured on an equal partnership between the public and private sectors with an option for CLT and Tele Orient to purchase the shares of the public sector. The government, which then had temporary legislative powers by the parliament, approved the report and asked the committee to work out the details of implementing its recommendations.

On December 30, 1977, a legislative decree (number 770) legalized the birth of a new television company, The Lebanese Television Company, Tele Liban. The company was "to manage, organize and exploit the various television transmitting installations, and to undertake all commercial and production tasks relating to Lebanese television as a joint enterprise." Tele Liban had a 25-year license and was given monopoly over television broadcasting in Lebanon. Its capital (30 million Lebanese pounds in 300,000 shares) was distributed equally between the government shares and the two existing companies.[6]

A board of directors of 12 members manages the new company: six representing the government, and the remaining six representing the two companies. The two companies elect the latter. The Board elects its chair upon the recommendation of the ministers of information and finance. The formation of Tele Liban, thus, was not a result of a new government policy to define the role of television in Lebanese society but simply the result of *force majeure*. It was the only possible move that the government could take at the time in order to support television and maintain its operation that was threatened with collapse.

The merger of the two early television companies within the new structure was planned to inject experience into the new company. The declared function of Tele Liban, according to an official of the Ministry of Information, was "to bring together the best of what the public sector has to offer—its primary concern for the needs of the country and the public—and the strength of the private sector in dynamic management and profit making." However, both government and business interests, which jointly managed television under the new plan, continued to broadcast programs that were selected based on their private political or economic interests rather than by the public interest. The efforts of these two groups, therefore, did not contribute to the advancement of television.

Indeed, the creation of Tele Liban did not improve this medium's public service. The private sector in television enjoyed sanctuary and was assured of financial liquidity since the government was now its partner. On the other hand, government officials were content with their control of the overall management of television. Their attention focused on improving the physical aspect of broadcasting which was harmed by the war. No plans or efforts were made to tie the programs of Tele Liban to social policies or national plans needed for a torn society. Thus, instead of both groups joining efforts to improve public service, they adopted a policy of "let the public be damned."

The main contribution of the government to Lebanese television was, therefore, to provide it with financial liquidity. This liquidity made it possible to rebuild and improve the existing transmitters. By October 1979, transmitters that were destroyed during the first two years of the war had been replaced or repaired. In October and November 1981, additional transmitters made it possible for most areas of both North Lebanon and the Bekaa to receive Tele Liban's programs.

The government's material support made it possible to increase transmission time. In 1982, regular afternoon and evening broadcasting became a regular feature of Tele Liban. Typically, however, the government's financial support improved the physical structure of television and little attention was given to develop required quality programs that may address genuine problems of the Lebanese society. Government interference in television broadcasting was far from aiming at initiating a process of improvement of the standards or widening the appeal to programs. Rather, it kept things in a state of stagnation and hampered growth.

During its early period, Tele Liban's programs were mostly imported foreign programs or local programs of inferior quality that hardly addressed societal problems. If they occasionally dealt with such problems, they were careful not to handle problems that may embarrass the political officials and power groups on ground.

Scheduling of programs was intended to yield maximum financial gain and not necessarily satisfy the different audience groups. Thus, one could find a French program for children scheduled late at night for lack of advertisers while an adult comedy scheduled in the afternoon at the time usually assigned to children's programs.

Tele Liban officials endeavored to improve their advertising revenue by contracting a specialized firm to handle its advertising and programming. This required dissolving Tele Management and making administrative changes. Strong opposition from the Syndicate of Tele Liban employees, however, challenged this decision. The syndicate exposed a shady deal in which an outside agency was to be contracted to handle television advertising. Tele Liban management was thus forced to withdraw its decision to dissolve *Tele Management* "pending further study."[7]

An examination of the content of early Tele Liban programs by this author[8] showed that only 41 percent of the afternoon television programs were broadcast in Arabic. One of its programs was aired exclusively in either French or English, with French providing the main share.[9] Noteworthy, however, was that only 17 percent of the programs for youth and 33 percent of those for children were in Arabic. Arabic programs, also, were mostly in classical Arabic not the spoken colloquial Lebanese Arabic.

In addition, 53 percent of the entertainment programs on Tele Liban channels were produced in the United States and 23 percent were produced in France. Half of the "education al and instructional" programs on Lebanese television were American and one-fourth were French. Even television programs of "information" nature had a large share of American (15 percent) and French (23 percent) productions.

Surveys conducted regularly, since 1974, for Tele Management by a Lebanese firm specializing in market research (Associated Business Consultants, ABC), showed that more urban Lebanese watched television than any other medium.[10] The study conducted by the author during the war revealed that television had its maximum impact on the lower income classes but hardly had an influence on the elite, who restricted their little television viewing to foreign serials. The lower income groups considered their use of television as a means of entertainment. Both lower and upper income groups sought Information about national and world problems from newspapers, which were regarded as more reliable.[11]

Tele Liban officials concerted their efforts on imitating Western programs with little concern to address societal needs and public issues. The first Director-General of *Tele Liban*, Dr. Charles Rizk, boasted in a press conference in 1979, that: "the Lebanese viewer can 'now' watch the same programs shown 'now' in New York and Paris." National integration, which is a challenging, task facing a developing nation like Lebanon continued to be ignored. All through the 16 years of civil war, not a single television program addressed itself seriously to the task of bringing the warring sects together. No television serial produced programs featuring Muslims and Christians cooperating and working together for a Lebanese cause.

An examination of the terms of agreements granting television licenses as well as government directives concerning the operation of television reveals that the policy of successive Lebanese governments was to keep television under control by limiting its power. Some television officials occasionally attempted to free themselves from the tight government control. Such attempts took place in November 1991 and January 1992 when personnel of Tele Liban staged a general strike. Their strike, however, was not successful because they had at heart financial profit not public interest.

Former President Gemayel triggered new hopes for improving the role of television in addressing societal needs when, in a 1982 publicized meeting with television officials, he criticized the lack of concern of television for Lebanese problems and the low quality of television programs. It soon became apparent, however, that his concern was for the control of television by his party, both in terms of the orientation of the programs and in terms of the television personnel. Consequently, neither the quality of programs nor technical operation improved in a perceptible way.

With the de facto division of the country and the consequent control of television studios by politically active "militia" groups, Tele Liban officials were "liberated" from the control of central government officers but became subject to a new type of authority. Their concern became focused not on national stability but on portraying the concerns of the militias controlling the area of their studios and justifying the illegal existence of the military activities undertaken by these militias.

The Emergence of De Facto Stations

The further weakening of the central government encouraged some warring factions to establish their own pirate television stations. These pirate stations managed to draw a good share of the advertising budgets, which prompted Tele Liban officials to file a lawsuit against three pirate stations requesting financial compensation for loss of advertising revenue. The lawsuit was based on the government decree granting Tele Liban "monopoly right to broadcast on all channels until December 31, 2012."[12]

Most important among the pirate stations at that time were the Lebanese Broadcasting Company (LBC), which began as the organ of the Maronite Lebanese Forces, and Al-Mashrek Television established by Arab nationalist politicians opposed to the Lebanese forces. Another important pirate station was New Television, NTV (later to dubbed Al-Jadeed TV). The Lebanese Communist Party established this station but aired programs that had no forthright relationship to the ideology of its party.

LBC went on the air in October 1985 with financial and technical support by the Christian Broadcasting Network (CBN) headed by televangelist Pat Robinson of the US fundamentalist "evangelical-moralist" movement. The CBN which then transmitted programs to some 25 countries through a satellite service operated another pirate Lebanese station, the "Middle East Television" that used to transmit from the Israeli occupied southern part of Lebanon.[13] In a short period, LBC captured a wide Lebanese audience and became the leading television station in Lebanon in terms of variety of its programs and size of its audience. During the first two years of its operation, LBC's newscasts were clearly superior to those on Tele Liban.[14]

As was the case with Tele Liban, LBC became subject of a tough struggle between US and French interests to dominate the orientation of its programs. The influence of US televangelists over LBC did not please the French who consequently were able, early in 1988, to have LBC air French programs on a new UHF band (channel 33). Its programs were a selection of emissions on the different French television services. The few English-speaking programs on this channel included French, not Arabic, subtitles. Thus, during its early beginnings LBC had two services, a predominantly US-oriented service with Arabic and English programs and a strictly French service that did not include Arabic programs.

Al-Mashrek Television began its experimental broadcasting in 1989 and started its regular programs in April 1990. Its heavy use of Arabic (mainly using colloquial Egyptian dialect) programs and films and its concerted effort to strengthen its news program attracted large audiences. By the beginning of 1991, Al-Mashrek Television was a serious competitor for both LBC and Tele Liban.

New TV was set up shortly before the end of the Civil War but began its transmission in April 1991. It drew a large audience for airing programs dealing with concerns of the common people, thus, it appealed to a wide range of general Lebanese public. Like Tele Liban's news service, the news services of the pirate stations presented more views than news.

The creation of the pirate television stations faced both the government and the private sector in Tele Liban with a new challenge. The continued disregard of public needs and the deterioration of the professional quality of the human element and technical skills at Tele Liban allowed pirate stations to attract Lebanese viewers to their programs and consequently drew advertisers to them. They were able to attract Lebanese from different factions to their foreign programs that were of a better professional quality and did not fear covering events that were prohibited on Tele Liban. They also attracted the general public to several of their local programs that addressed daily concerns of average Lebanese citizens.

Generally, local programs on LBC and Al-Mashrek dealt mainly with either politics or entertainment. LBC's entertainment programs were mostly replications of US and French quiz shows and variety programs. Its political programs were biased but were more successful in approaching the average Lebanese than those transmitted on the general programs of Tele Liban. Al-Mashrek's programs concentrated on Egyptian films and serials and appealed more to the middle and lower socioeconomic groups. Its management appeared to be less innovative than that of LBC and its personnel less dynamic.

The success of LBC and Al-Mashrek in capturing advertising budgets led to heavy losses by Tele Liban. Faced with this competition Tele Liban officials launched a series of new up-to-date US serials in the fall season of 1988 and arranged for direct relay of many special US television events. Thus, the 1988 debate of the US presidential candidates and several of the television commentaries on the results of the US elections were directly relayed. Even the "Miss America Pageant," hardly known before to the Lebanese public, was relayed from the United States.

Official public broadcasting was given a thrust when a successful businessperson who later became prime minister, Rafik Hariri, bought the private shares of Tele Liban. A new and dynamic executive, Fouad Naim was appointed to chair the station. He was assured official support to introduce administrative and structural reforms.[15] Within few months, Naim was able to build a vigorous professional news team and was moving forth in transforming Tele Liban into a dynamic public service television.

His efforts, however, were letdown when Hariri sold his Tele Liban shares and his government withdrew its exclusive broadcasting rights without compensation. He resigned in frustration. Reflecting on his Tele Liban experience Naim told Zahera Harb in a private 1995 interview: "They [the officials] failed TL because there was no real understanding of what public-service television meant within the Lebanese political milieu ... They were convinced that the state-run television was there to cover their activities."[16]

Consequently, Tele Liban was not able to face the competition from the newly licensed stations who are owned or backed by members of the government. After few years of failed operation, the government decided to close down Tele Liban for three months in order the implement reorganization. The shutdown was extended further for several more months and the new structure continues to strive for survival, facing government interference and tough competition by better-endowed stations.

Television Legislation Becomes an Urgent Need

During a 1989 retreat in the Saudi town of Taif, Lebanese members of the parliament were able to arrive at a regionally and internationally supported agreement that marked the end of the Lebanese Civil War. Among other things, the Taif Agreement, which was later incorporated in the Lebanese constitution, called for the reorganization of the media in Lebanon. The government was thus expected to find a "legal" solution to existing pirate radio and television stations. The deliberations of members of the parliament called for legalizing the existing de facto radio and television stations. Consequently, several politicians and businesspersons hurried to set up television stations to establish their "right" for a broadcasting license. According to an ITU expert 46 television stations were set up in a matter of few months and some ten of the new stations were on the air by the end of 1991, transmitting on UHF channels as all the VHF channels were already in use.

The pirate television stations that "mushroomed" during this period transmitted mainly international films and television programs, which were either received through large dish antennas, or obtained on video cassettes that were easily available in Lebanon. New stations on the air then included: Sigma TV, Laser Vision, Al-Manar (established by the "Hezbollah" resistance movement), Cable Video Network (CVN), Kilykia Television, TV One, Al-Mahabba Television (established by a group of Maronite priests known as the "Children of the Church Group"), Independent Cable Network (ICN), and Murr Television (MTV), owned by an influential Lebanese businessman and brother of the then Minister of Defense, Michel Murr.

The snowballing of television stations resulted in confusion and chaos in the broadcasting industry. The government felt the urgency for introducing new legislation that can put order into this field. This occurred at the beginning of the Elias Hrawi presidency that was faced with the enormous job of reestablishing government authority after the Civil War. Thus, the minister of information at the time, Albert Mansour, submitted in August 1991 recommendations for the reorganization of broadcasting in Lebanon. He recommended granting licenses to television stations whose total resources are Lebanese and were to broadcast on UHF channels. To oversee the industry Minister Mansour recommended setting up an Independent National Communication Agency, which would recommend granting broadcasting licenses and would verify that the different broadcasting channels operate within the officially set technical and professional regulations. The Agency would also serve as a consultative body on all matters relating to broadcasting.[17]

In order not to upset the delicate status quo and until new legislation is enacted, the minister recommended that, exceptionally, Tele Liban lease some of its channels to the de facto pirate stations in return for a fee to be determined by the government. This would ensure the rights of Tele Liban and would provide it with funds to improve its facilities and services. At the same time, the arrangement would allow pirate stations to continue their operation.[18]

The recommendations of Minister Mansour were referred to a special ministerial committee that proposed to the Council of Ministers the adoption of three measures. The first was to purchase all private shares of Tele Liban and reintroduce them to the public on new terms[19]. The second measure proposed was to request Tele Liban to rent some of its channels to applicants for television broadcasting. The third was to subject all pirate television stations presently operating de facto on Lebanese soil to the same controls to which Tele Liban is subjected.[20] In January 1992, the Council of Ministers took the following decision:

Inasmuch as the Lebanese Television Company, half of whose shares are owned by the government, has the exclusive right to broadcast on all available television channels until the year 2012, all television institutions which are presently operating de facto and in contradiction to the existing laws, and anybody who wishes to invest in television, must submit within a period of one month an application for commercial television broadcasting. The application will be referred, through the Ministries of Information, Post, and Telecommunications, to the Council of Ministers for a decision.

The ministerial committee is requested to draw out, for the consideration and approval of the Council of Ministers, the conditions for rental of, and investing in, television channels. The ministerial committee is requested to utilize available television talent and to seek wider and more varied contribution by the private sector in the Lebanese Television Company.[21]

The decision of the Council of Ministers raised a public uproar not because of what it stated but because of what was reportedly discussed in the deliberations of the ministers. According to press reports, the deliberations dealt with the possibility of restricting broadcasting news on television to Tele Liban.[22] Reports about the deliberations suggested that both the President of the Republic and the prime minister called for an end to the chaos and lack of restraint in the activities of media institutions.[23] Criticisms of the deliberations focused on the government's intention to give Tele Liban a monopoly over newscasts. Several members of the Council of Ministers and numerous politicians issued statements criticizing the deliberations. The ambassadors of England, France, the United States and the Vatican also issued statements supporting freedom of the press.[24] One press report quoted an ambassador as having said that suppressing television newscasts was a wish "forced on the government" from outside but that "freedom in Lebanon is a red line which may not be crossed without negatively affecting the country."[25]

The government promptly denied that a decision was taken to restrict news to Tele Liban. The ministerial committee quickly addressed itself to the task of drafting proposals for legalizing the de facto pirate stations. It recommended that, until a new law governing broadcasting in Lebanon is issued, these stations be given annual leases, not licenses, of the available UHF channels. It further recommended the recognition of three types of television stations. The first will have a general type whose transmission would cover the Greater Beirut area, the Mount Lebanon area and at least one other administrative unit. The second would be a specialized station in terms either of its area of transmission, or the specialized programs it broadcasts. The third type would restrict transmission to signals whose reception requires a decoder.[26]

Whatever solution adopted for the de facto pirate stations it was clear that the operation of these stations would be legalized and that they will continue to attract a wide audience. However, these stations, as well as Tele Liban, continued to contribute to cultural pollution by importing foreign programs portraying alien values and norms. Any observer could recognize that many of the costly foreign programs relayed directly were irrelevant to the needs and tastes of the Lebanese public.

Two years of indecision and delays lapsed before the Council of Ministers finally approved a draft law regulating the chaotic use of the broadcasting channels in Lebanon. The new law was adopted with minor modifications by the Lebanese parliament in November 1994.[27] The influence of the active audio-visual lobby was clear in the amendments adopted by the parliament: notably, abolishing the item limiting the time allowable to advertising. No time limit for airing advertisements exists under this law. Under the terms of this law also Tele Liban was to be fully owned by the government and its exclusive television broadcasting right was to be revoked in return for granting it the right to broadcast on all the VHF channels and one UHF channel. No compensation by the de facto stations was granted to Tele Liban.

The law requires that founding broadcasting stations within Lebanese territories or its national waters be subject to prior licensing (Chapter 2, Article 5). The duration of the license is 16 years, renewable (Chapter 5, Article 26). Licenses are to be granted by a government decree upon the recommendation of a new council established by this law, the "National Council of Audio-Visual Media" (National Council). This council has the power to recommend the suspension or closure of stations. It is formed of ten members appointed jointly by the government and parliament (Chapter 5, Article 17). The audio-visual law classifies television stations according to the following four categories:

First Category: Stations that transmit visual programs, including news and political programs, covering all the Lebanese territory.

Second Category: Stations that transmit visual programs, except news and political programs, covering all the Lebanese territory.

Third Category: Stations that transmit coded signals that can only be received by subscribers who possess the necessary technical equipment.

Fourth Category: International stations that transmit via satellite and whose coverage goes beyond the Lebanese territory (Chapter 3, Article 10).

According to the new law, granting a broadcasting license requires, among other things, acquiring approved technical transmission standards; meeting the necessary operational standards in terms of its human and physical resources, and presenting evidence of its ability to sustain expenses for at least its first year of operation. The law, furthermore, requires the station to broadcast a volume of local productions that are fixed by the "terms of conditions" of broadcasting in Lebanon (Chapter 2, Article 7). The law provides for setting-up a technical committee, "The TV and Radio Transmission Organization Committee," to draw the "terms of conditions" for broadcasting and to study all technical broadcasting aspects and to submit recommendations to the Minister of Information (Chapter 2, Article 8).

The law additionally stipulates that granting radio and television licenses be limited to Lebanese citizens or companies. It does not allow "for a person or entity to own directly or indirectly more than ten percent of the total company shares. The husband or wife and all direct relatives are considered to be one person or entity" (Chapter 4, Article 13).

Under the terms of the audio-visual law, broadcasting stations are not allowed to operate at a financial deficit for a lengthy period. Licensed stations are required to submit to the Information Ministry statements of their balance sheets. A number of technical and environmental requirements were proposed but failed to involve the quality and quantity of local programs essential for a country that is flooded with canned programs. The "terms of conditions" sets the required local programs to 16.6 percent of the total aired programs. It requires only half an hour of weekly transmission of local educational programs and another weekly half an hour for rural and agricultural programs.[28]

The new law faced substantial public debate. Again, the influence of the very active audio-visual lobby was clear in press campaigns and statements by politicians warning against "the dangers to freedom in Lebanon." Clearly, owners of the de facto stations and the political opposition were afraid of the way licenses will be granted.

They were right in their fear. In September 1996, the government decided to grant licenses to four television stations, other than Tele Liban. The four belonged to government leaders or their relations, maintaining the sensitive religious sectarian balance, which is of paramount importance in Lebanese politics.

The stations that received licenses were: 1. The Lebanese Broadcasting Company International (LBCI, formerly LBC), which represents Maronite Christian groups and whose shareholders included prominent members of the government; 2. Future Television, representing Sunni Muslim groups and owned by the then prime minister; 3. Murr Television (MTV), representing Greek Orthodox Christian groups and owned by the family of the then Minister of Interior; and 4. The National Broadcasting Network (NBN), representing Shi'ite Muslim groups and owned by the family and supporters of the Speaker of the House of Parliament.[29] Al-Manar, the organ of the Islamic Hezbollah Party, which started broadcasting in June 1991 was given special permission to continue on the air as the "voice" of resistance against the occupation of South Lebanon. It received a comprehensive license in July 1996.[30]

The government decision faced a public uproar because it was based more on political and sectarian than on professional grounds.[31] Stations that were not licensed refused to discontinue broadcasting. The government used both threats and promises to implement its decision. In some instances, it used force to close some stations but in others, it allowed some to appeal the decision.

A Christian religious station "Tele Lumiere" continues to broadcast without a license but with tacit government approval. This encouraged Muslim religious authorities to begin experimental broadcasts for the "Holy Qur'an TV" and a *number* of other religious stations asked for similar treatment but no official action was taken. As religious authorities are very powerful in Lebanon, the Council of Ministers took a decision to enable the different religious communities to air their religious programs through a special channel to be made available by the government owned Tele Liban. Until this channel was available, the authorities kept silent about the de facto (illegal) operation of these stations. In a newspaper interview, the Lebanese Minister of Information declared that the government expects that the programs aired by the religious stations be in agreement with the Lebanese basic positions and with the constitution of the country in a way that will strengthen common citizenship and the service of the nation.[32]

Two years after the implementation of the audio-visual law, the government issued an "Order of Specifications for TV and Radio Channels" (Decree 7997/1996) in which it specified in details broadcasting requirements. The "Specifications Order" makes it clear that broadcasting channels are obliged to visibly differentiate between advertising, partisan policy positions and public information.

Among the public service requirements by the "Specifications Order" is the obligation of terrestrial channels to air a minimum of 730 hours of locally produced programs annually. The type of these local programs is spelled out in Chapter 3 of this "Order." Among these is: 146 hours of programs directed at children and youth; 280 hours of news, and 166 hours of documentaries and development programs.

When a new president was elected, late in 1998, and the opposition came to power, the new government reconsidered the appeals of stations that were denied licenses by the previous government. Consequently, three new television stations were granted licenses. "New Television" (Al-Jadeed TV), owned by a Sunni Muslim opposing the former prime minister, was the first to be licensed, in June 1999. The other two were licensed in October 1999: "The Independent Communication Channel International" (ICNI), owned by a Maronite Christian; and "United Television" (UTV), which is a merger of several of the old de facto stations. Both address different confessional groups. The latter two stations, however, were not able to come into existence.

Lebanese television stations are

> linked to the different political and religious rival factions of the country … The result is a general lack of professional standards in reporting local, regional and international events, while the news agenda is deeply influenced by the different affiliations.[33]

The formats of the stations address different sectarian groups in their news programs, editorial comments, and talk shows. Their orientation is "politically religious" in the sense that their discourse conveys not the religious faith but rather the political and social "positions" of the different confessions they address. Even their entertainment programs tend to stress the political and social beliefs of the confessional groups they address. Thus, the focus of LBCI, for example, is not on Maronite religious programs but on advocating the political and social interests of the "Maronite community." Lebanese television stations present the Lebanese political and social life in different and often contradictory frameworks.

While newspaper readership is not widely spread in Lebanon and the Arab world in general, radio and television are available in almost every household in Lebanese urban areas.[34] Television reception is not only of Lebanese local channels but cable connection is widely spread in the major Lebanese cities.

Development of Satellite Broadcasting

The early 1990s witnessed the accelerating spread of satellite broadcasting in the Arab world. Lebanon was no exception. Satellite reception dishes became among the fastest selling commodities in Lebanon and the Arab Gulf countries. Unlicensed cable television distribution companies began supplying subscription to households. Cable distribution is unregulated and is widely available in Lebanon today as monthly subscriptions cost as little as US$15.[35] By 2005, it was estimated that some "1,300 illegal satellite television distribution companies are operating in the country, servicing up to 780,000 of the country's 800,000 subscribers,"[36] Cable operators usually subscribe to the different satellite systems, such as Orbit, and/or install reception dishes then distribute the signals they get through a cable system. The government fears introducing regulations in this area as it may create popular outrage since such a regulation will necessary increase the cable subscription fee to an unaffordable rate, which the majority cannot pay.

The major cry against the illegal operators comes from local television stations that were losing a major share of their audiences to the cable system. These stations are constantly protesting to the government about this state of affairs but with little success. The satellite stations were not concerned with this practice at the beginning since the Lebanese market was very small and few of the subscribers to illegal operators could afford to pay the high fees for a smaller selection of stations. However, some initiated action to raise the subscription fees paid by the operators and were able to press providers to increase their subscription payments.[37]

Lebanese businesspersons and television officials saw an excellent profit potential in satellite broadcasting. Two stations, LBCI and Future Television, ventured into this field even before being licensed. LBCI established LBCSAT and Future TV launched Future International SAT. The programs of both ranked among the leading satellite programs in the Arab Gulf countries in the 1990s, an important source of advertising income.[38] This tempted wealthy Arab Gulf sheikhs and satellite stations to invest in Lebanese television stations.

Founded in February 1993, Future Television started trial satellite broadcasting, in October 1994; the testing period lasted two months. Future International Television installed 5-meter and 7-meter dishes installed in its Beirut and Sidon sites. An additional 13-meter dish was later installed in the government earth station in Jouret el-Ballout as a redundant uplink facility. Future International TV began covering the Middle East, North Africa and Southern Europe.

Realizing the commercial and professional importance of satellite broadcasting LBCI plunged into this field in April 1996 when it established LBCSAT, a free satellite channel. The channel started broadcasting 22 hours daily on January 1997. Later in 1997, LBC launched three new encrypted channels: LBC Europe, LBC America and LBC Australia.

Faced with the success of both Lebanese satellite stations the government decided that the best way to respond was to have its own station, Tele Liban get into satellite broadcasting. An official government decision was adopted late in 1999 and Tele Liban began its satellite broadcast in March 2000. The TL satellite service began by covering the Arab world and part of Europe. However, it merely airs its terrestrial programming via satellite, not specialized programs to satisfy Arab viewers or the Lebanese Diaspora. A fourth station, Al-Manar requested a license for satellite transmission and its request was approved in April 2000. Its satellite service began on the eve of May 24, 2000, the day of the liberation of South Lebanon. After the Palestinian "intifada" broke out, on September 28, 2000, Al-Manar increased its satellite broadcasting from four to 18-hours/day.

The success of Lebanese satellite stations encouraged two other stations to get into this field. MTV began its satellite service in November 2000, on the eve of its ninth anniversary, and Al-Jadeed TV, which was expected to go on the air in December 2000, announced that it would start its satellite service at the same time.

Early satellite broadcasting in Lebanon faced a number of obstacles during the regime of President Hrawi and Prime Minister Hariri in the 1990s. The first obstacle was to get government clearance for a satellite connection. The second and more serious one was to secure the right to broadcast news. At the beginning, the Hariri government did not permit both *LBCSAT* and Future TV to transmit news on their satellite channels and limited airing news on satellite channels to the official government satellite station, Tele Liban. The argument by the government was that Lebanese satellite news programs might negatively affect Lebanon's relations with some Arab countries inasmuch as these countries may not tolerate the freedom the Lebanese media enjoy.

LBCI challenged the government ban and continued airing its satellite news program. The Hariri government reacted, late in December 1996, by deciding to censor "all news as well as direct and indirect political programs prepared for satellite broadcasting." A special "censorship team" whose members included a number of well-respected journalists was named. Again, LBCI challenged the decision, moved its news studio to Rome, and sought a ruling from the state's judiciary advisory council. The judiciary council supported LBCI; consequently, Lebanese satellite channels won the battle to air political news programs.

Societal Challenges

Television in Lebanon has an unusual status. Although commercially run and in this sense its programs are expected to be determined by the "wants" and/or "needs" of its viewers, its political and economic bonds to the political/sectarian/ financial powers on the ground usually allows these powers to determine the nature and information content of these programs. Accordingly, this medium has rarely been used as one for public service or a promoter of nationwide unity. Lebanese television generally does not take into consideration its responsibility to the people. It lacks civic commitment and is in urgent need for transformation in order to cope with the role it is expected to play in national reconstruction.

Prior to the Civil War, the political "management" of television, coupled with financial pressures generated by commercial interests, led television officials to adopt a "safe" role in Lebanese affairs.[39] This role gave the viewer, by government intent, an image of national stability, rarely broken by visions of internal dissent, disruption, or political problems.[40]

Applied television regulations allow the government the right to exercise censorship over television programs. When the government was strong enough to enforce these regulations, censorship was carried out by two censoring authorities—security officers from the Surete Generale, and representatives of the Ministry of Information. The first censors have control over all recorded programs, local and foreign, in addition to advertisements. The second censoring authority is mainly concerned with checking news and local film commentaries, though the news is prepared by the government's own national news agency and the news films were prepared upon the instruction of government officials.

Even with government overseeing television broadcasting, many complaints were made about foreign attempts to exploit television. Several politicians and civic leaders voiced their complaint that government's concern was directed at censoring political or social matter critical of the government while ignoring exercises by television personnel to "plant" other political or social matter. One such complaint came from a former president of the Order of Publishers, who reported that: "there are contacts and secret deals which link certain television anchors and non-Lebanese parties to promote the news of foreign countries, thus giving the impression that Lebanon is biased in its Arab and foreign policies."[41]

In 1973, the former President Suleiman Franjieh banned two television anchormen from appearing on television for a period close to six months on the grounds that they "acted on their own" in handling certain news items. It is not surprising that one finds films on television that are part of film libraries of cultural or information sections in foreign embassies. Lebanese television was also subject to attacks by the print media, mainly on grounds that it has progressively taken part of the advertising revenues that previously went to the print media.

A large share of Lebanese television programming consists of political news programs, which are the most-viewed genre. Television news usually pays more attention to domestic politics than to socio-economic issues of public service. The coverage of such socioeconomic issues, if aired, is usually presented in the negative. Exposition of such public issues tends to focus on exposing "the other group" (as opposed to the group to which the station is bonded) and not public service.

A blatant example is television blowing up the country's financial difficulties in early 1990s in order to force a government resignation. This resulted in ushering the way for a new prime minister (who was allegedly behind the coverage) at the price of creating a serious financial crisis that lead to an extensive depreciation of the Lebanese currency. Another reprehensible example is television's coverage of the "garbage crisis" in 2015–2016 when its damaging coverage of this crisis contributed to delaying effective solutions and flooding the country with garbage for close to a year.

Because of the high degree of politicization of Lebanese society, current political events are covered in a way that supports the views of each television station with no respect for professional codes and ethics. The UN international commission to investigate the assassination of a former Lebanese prime minister reported that:

> Certain Lebanese media had the unfortunate and constant tendency to spread rumors, nurture speculation, offer information as facts without prior checking and at times use materials obtained under dubious circumstances, from sources that had been briefed by the Commission, thereby creating distress and anxiety among the public at large.[42]

An unpublished 2005 study by the author of the content of television news showed that "political figures" along with "sectarian public figures" were the main actors in a relatively high percentage of the local news items. This reflects a political environment that is torn by sectarian grievances.

The assassination of Hariri in 2005 increased political polarization and was clearly reflected in the news coverage of different television channels. Each channel concentrated on covering its patrons and the slant in new reports were more obvious. Social media that were mainly inundated with social content were now including more political commentary.

The outbreak of so-called Arab Spring demonstrations and the eruption of uprisings in Syria had an awakening effect on Lebanese public opinion.

The rift between the March 8 and March 14 blocks became wider. Slant in news coverage by television and other mass media now took a regional and ideological nature. Classifying television channels in terms of two broader regional political orientations thus became obvious: one orientation supportive of uprisings in Syria and the other viewing these uprisings as a foreign conspiracy.

Failure of the authorities to handle a dispute, which left rubbish uncollected in the streets of Beirut and Mount Lebanon, stirred extensive demonstrations in the summer of 2015 and consequently developed into a popular civil movement. Protesters used the popular catchphrase used during the Tunisian and Egyptian 2011 uprisings: "The people want regime downfall." It may not be an accident that two prominent television channels began extensive live coverage of these civil demonstrations directly after a visit of top executives of these channels to an Arab Gulf state. Reporters of these channels not only provided complete live coverage of the protests but also engaged the protesters in discussions insinuating that the call for "regime downfall" is un-Lebanese.

Continuous thrashing by television programs that the call for regime change is disloyal, the slogan changed to "regime reform." Callers for "regime reform" later split into several groups each backing a special type of reform.[43] Rumors and accusations of foreign involvement in the civil movements became a common subject of discussion on television channels. Differences between the splinter groups became a daily subject of discussion. Consequently, the movement fizzled away.

Conclusion

Broadcasting regulations in Lebanon were not intended to promote themes relevant to the livelihood of the average citizen. Themes that deal with integration between different sectarian and ethnic groups and their working together in national reconstruction and in bringing about unity of the people are almost absent in Lebanese television. Broadcasting legislations were not aimed at promoting original productions, or at providing more opportunities for local talent and developing responsible and professional organizational structures. Rather, state legislation was aimed at allowing government officials and the ruling political bosses to exploit the broadcasting media for their own goals.[44] Television news programs focus mainly on news of politicians, with little reflective coverage of issues that concern the public.[45]

Lebanese television is owned or bonded to diverse tribal/sectarian/business authorities, thus it focuses on the concerns of these authorities with little or no interest in developing the public sphere that may address public issues of concern to Lebanese citizens. Television's news advances the larger agenda of the tribal/sectarian/business authorities to whom the media are bonded. Television officials have a lesser amount of independent judgment. They are more vulnerable to influence by their sponsors and the sectarian/tribal groups to which they belong. Consequently, hate-promoters fill the Lebanese airwaves and journalistic public interest standards are doomed.

Lebanese television today is a mélange of various inconsistent programs, policies and structures, predominantly foreign in orientation and barely relevant to the needs of Lebanese society. The different commercial broadcasting channels have managed to marginalize the government-broadcasting channel, Tele Liban. This channel receives an inadequate financial budget and the plans of its officials to develop its service are regularly frustrated by political authorities in fear that this medium may develop into a serious competitor to the commercial channels that they own or control.

Examining the content of television programs, one gets the impression that television officials suppose that their viewers will adapt to whatever is given to them. This has led television channels to air low quality entertainment programs and talk shows that may entertain the common person but do not appeal to her/his mind or meet her/his intellectual and developmental needs. Thus, we find that in one television channel more than two-thirds of its cultural programs are presented in a foreign language. We also find, for example, that only one-third of the programs directed at children were in Arabic and that the majority of the remaining children's programs were aired without Arabic subtitles.[46]

Lebanese television channels are mainly directed or supervised by the establishment; the establishment being the tribal/sectarian authorities who patronize the different national as well as foreign organizations, and not the government. Television organizations, therefore, often betray their viewers by failing to provide transparent information about issues that concern them, concentrating instead on augmenting and propagating the politicians that patronize them.

Television in Lebanon has succeeded more in social and political destruction than in building national unity and solidarity. It has contributed to the mobilization of the public to take negative action more than bringing about positive action. Television does not endeavor to work toward a unified Lebanon. Instead, it acts as an advocacy medium on behalf of the different political, ethnic and religious minorities, thus encouraging and promoting division within the country. Broadcasting in Lebanon is in need for reorganization in order to cope with the role it is expected to play in the reconstruction of a country that is overwhelmed by divisiveness, sectarianism and corruption. While television channels give their audiences an "overdose" of political discussions and entertainment, there is almost a total absence of public affairs programming with scant investigative reporting about the issues that affect the livelihood of the average Lebanese.

When Lebanese audiences were restricted to just a few terrestrial channels, the programs available to them were controlled by the government censors. With satellite broadcasting, Lebanese citizens are now at the mercy of tens of satellite stations, whose managers bombard them with a large range of alien programs, many of which are of low quality, usually carrying odd values or slanted political news.

Lebanese television also plays a major role in diverting the citizen from her/his genuine problems by directing attention to secondary issues that have no relation to the existing social and political problems of Lebanon. This has resulted in the disorientation of the public and in an inadequate vision of its norms and values. Lebanese television, thus, is contributing to divergence in social consciousness among the different Lebanese groups, even to a discrepancy in the general outlook on social values and possible solutions to the problems facing Lebanese society.

Lebanese television channels have chosen to focus on displaying the incompatible views of different political, ethnic and sectarian currents, but have failed to serve as a responsible forum for debate among these currents. Television has failed to bridge the gaps among citizens and failed in achieving a national consensus, which is basic for any true national development.

Media practitioners ask for more freedom from the government instead of earning this freedom by addressing themselves to the task of moving their society toward its goals. Television institutions cannot guarantee their freedom unless they agree to be held accountable for their role in defending the rights of citizens. Their ethical right for freedom of expression must be indelibly tied to their acceptance of this accountability. Their legal right for this freedom may not be denied as long as they continue to fulfill their ethical role toward society. The moral right of television to freedom of expression has to be linked to its accountability.

The emergence of diverse Lebanese television stations with contradictory premises and outlooks has contributed to the evident contradictions among the Lebanese people. Lebanese television channels have managed to create a false consciousness of Lebanese realities and to an incongruent public participation.

In conclusion, Lebanese television lacks the adequate structures and professionals that would provide the opportunity for this medium to contribute to its society's unity and cohesion, as well as to address issues that are relevant to the everyday life of the average citizen. This medium has a commercial orientation and lacks social responsibility as well as professional ethics.

From Folk to Social Media

Lebanon's Oral Culture

Communication modes are shaped by a society's customs and traditions that originate from norms and values as well as from behavioral and ethical practices that mold the patterns of a society's communication. While modern media play a role in developing the public sphere in Lebanon, it is the traditional face-to-face encounters within folk institutions that have the most impact in this area. Encounters such as those that take place at mosques or churches on Friday and Sunday meetings or discussions at coffee house meetings or female morning "*sobhiya*" gatherings are among the public sphere habitats. It is thus relevant to reflect on the modes of communication within some of the significant Lebanese folk institutions. Such a reflection would elucidate the examination of the role of media within the Lebanese society.

Arab culture is an "oral culture," where word of mouth plays a main role in communicating ideas among different Lebanese social spheres. Indeed, folk media in Lebanon used to play an important role in materializing public attitudes toward community issues. With the introduction of new modern modes of communication, however, the role of the folk media was compromised. The introduction of broadcasting media and the new social media that are characterized by heavy foreign content have contributed to the prevalence of an "Orientalist" perspective among Arab intellectuals[1] and thus to the confusion between "Westernization" and "modernization."

Folk media refers to forms of communication where face-to-face interaction takes place, usually in informal settings. This denotes interpersonal interaction that involves simple forms of relaxed discussions, and somehow more involved practices where interaction is routinized like in religious meetings, community public performances, or social gatherings of friends, peers and family members.

Folk Interaction Channels

Religious and Social Channels

Religious meetings are of the oldest type of folk routes of face-to-face communication. In many Lebanese areas, especially in villages and rural areas, mosques and churches still constitute a major communication outlet for the populace, particularly the youth and single people, who are not usually included in the gatherings of the older and married.[2] It can be reasoned that the recent development by Wahhabi Muslim fundamentalists to fund the building of mosques in Europe and several Arab countries and to provide these mosques with Wahhabi preachers has played a major role in the spread of fanatic and terrorist organizations such as "ISIS."[3]

Friday and Sunday sermons usually play the role of framing local and national events and thus set the agenda of public debate among mosque- or church-goers and are instrumental in bringing about change. For example, in 2013, the Lebanese government had to withdraw a law allowing the performance of civil marriages in Lebanon, as a consequence of wide-ranging mosque sermons calling for opposition to this law.[4] On the Arab regional level, Friday prayer gatherings played a major role in shaping public action during the so-called Arab Spring events in Egypt, Tunisia, Libya and Syria. One can clearly observe the punch of popular activities that took place on Fridays, after the prayer gatherings.

Another important Lebanese folk communication channel is the coffee house, where traditionally men meet, usually after work, to socialize and discuss general public affairs. The coffee house, referred to as "*kahwa*" (café) or "*maqha*" is a place for talks, leisure and playing popular domicile games.

In addition to being a place for entertainment and leisure, coffee houses serve as an important social gathering point and a hub for cultural and political discussions. Beirut cafés were and continue to be venues where people and academics in particular, gather to talk, write, read, entertain one another, or to pass the time. The "café" played a role in shaping and lobbying for social and political change in Lebanon. Arab leaders and thinkers met in Lebanese cafés to discuss the political affairs in their countries. A number of Beirut cafés played a central role in the political and cultural change in the region and as an origin of many radical changes. Some view Beirut cafés as the habitat of rebellious ideas.[5]

A modern version of a Beirut café is perhaps Mat'am Faysal facing the main gate of the American University of Beirut, where it is said that most nationalistic "plots" for political and regime changes took place. Horse Shoe is another famous "modern style" coffee house in Beirut. It was the gathering point for intellectuals, writers, critics and well-known artists like Roger Assaf, Saadallah Wannous and Onsi El-Hajj.[6] Mat'am Faysal and Horse Shoe faded away during the Lebanese Civil War, among many other known coffee houses like City Café and Abou Daoud Café.

With globalization/Westernization stimulating Lebanese communication practices, multinational diner chains and cafés found their way onto Lebanese streets and have managed to introduce new and alien values and norms. These new practices affected the political and cultural scene but the traditional forms of interpersonal interaction were maintained in different new forms. These recent forms can be observed in the formation and continuation of intellectual meeting hubs for students and academics in new styles of cafés. An example of such a new café is T Marbouta in the Hamra Street area in Beirut. This new popular café has a reading room designed to host public events. Social media pages of this and similar cafés are established and spread the word on their upcoming events.

Hamra Street cafés served in the 1960s and 1970s as the heart of political as well as social activities, not only for Lebanon but also for the entire Arab region, and were frequented freely by both men and women. The Civil War diminished this role but the recent Arab Spring and the eruption of civil unrest in the region is reviving it again. Today, many coffee houses exist in Lebanese cities. They host various types of public discussions ranging from general political and cultural discussions to screenings and discussions of movies that address local or national issues. Some of these offer folk leisure items on the menu, like the traditional "*barjees*" and backgammon.

Coffee houses are also the home of another important folk medium, that of the "*hakawati*" (the storyteller). The *hakawati* is a prominent figure in the established coffee houses around whom the regulars gather in the evenings to listen to his exciting narration of stories of Arab legendary heroes. The *hakawati* usually would hold café audience captive for hours and has immense influence in enlivening national pride among his listeners and is usually an essential figure in café gatherings during the fasting month of Ramadan.

While coffee houses are traditionally the meeting place for men, women have their own traditional channel for interpersonal communication; the "*subhiya*" (morning get-together). This is a semi-formal affair governed by detailed rules of etiquette held in a woman's household that gathers a close and rather intimate group of friends and family at set mornings to socialize.[7] Notable women usually designate a set day in the month or week for their *subhiya* get-together.

A *subhiya* gradually shifted from being purely social to a combined social/religious event in which religious readings and performances were led by one woman accompanied by female percussionists, and then followed by individual and collective prayers and lavishly catered meals. These religious gatherings would allow the leading woman, referred to as the "*Shaykha*," to engage the conversation and guide it toward topics and trends of interest to society.[8]

Often a *subhiya* takes a political role and a political activist engages the participants in discussions aimed at propagating social or political views. A *subhiya* has recently become a favorite channel of communication for underground political movements as well as fundamental religious groups.

While this form of gathering occurs for different purposes, all are mostly geared toward reinforcing the woman's place within society. Through community service, Arab woman have underlined the importance of fulfilling social responsibility, and the *subhiya* is the place to discuss such a topic as well as promoting it.[9]

Caricatures, Zajal and Theater

Social discussions at informal gatherings are a source of inspiration for "caricatures," another form of expression that endeavors to escape the authorities' suppression. A caricature is an eighteenth-century satirical art that expresses sociopolitical criticisms in a comic manner.[10] Though they

Figure 5.1 In most of Naji al-Ali's cartoons there stands a small boy viewed from the backside. That small boy is Naji al-Ali himself as a child expelled from his Palestinian homeland. Naji named the character **Hanzala** ... which means "bitterness" in Arabic. The artist saw his Hanzala character as a bold witness to history, and he said that his character was, "my icon which safeguards my soul from committing mistakes ... he is the ever alert conscience." In the cartoon above, Hanzala watches a young Palestinian girl forced to play a macabre game of jumping rope, only the "rope" held by her tormentors is a barbed wire.

Source: See www.art-for-a-change.com/Naji/naji.html.

Figure 5.2 Caricature by the late al-Hayat artist, Mahmoud Kahil depicting children of Lebanese leaders substituting their parents in the parliament. Private collection of the author.

Figure 5.3 Caricature by the late *An-Nahar* artist, Pierre Sadek showing a Lebanese popular character rejecting both of the two opposing Lebanese political fronts. Private collection of the author.

usually appear in traditional media outlets, people's discussions in their social gatherings are the main inspiration for caricature artists.

Generally, caricatures are a very powerful form of expression in the Arab world. A well-known Palestinian caricature artist, Naji al-Ali was murdered for his powerful caricatures. Al-Ali created a very legendary character called "Hanzala," who represented the Palestinian conscious.[11] This form of popular expression has become quite prominent and there are many caricature artists in Lebanon.[12] Among the best known are: Pierre Sadek, Mahmoud Kahil, Armand Homsi, Benoit Debbané, Stavro Jabra, Habib Haddad, Mazen Kerbaje, Lena Merhej, Areej Mahmoud and Christiane Boustani. Sadek was the first caricature artist to create television animated caricatures.

The Lebanese General Security does not censor caricatures prior to their publishing, however, caricature artists themselves impose self-censorship in their drawings. For instance, the Pierre Sadek family reported that Sadek had many personal threats from different people due to publishing powerful caricatures criticizing different political figures in the region.[13] Kahil told the author that his move from Beirut to London during the Civil War was partly to escape pressure.

Zajal is another form of popular performance that depicts a significant element of Lebanese culture and heritage. This folk medium employs colloquial poetry and takes place in the form of "verbal dueling" where topics of public interest dealing with social issues or current political events are addressed. This kind of face-to-face exchange is chanted by a group of men at social or public gatherings, usually held in coffee houses or in the center of the village.

As a rule, *zajal* is improvised and includes commentaries on social, cultural or political matters. Its importance is in its expression of the mood of the people in colloquial Arabic, criticizing or praising the ruling elite or forcefully commenting on current events in down-to-earth language. It is the "common-man's" poetry. This form of folk media was losing ground before a number of television channels began scheduling *zajal* events. The state-owned Tele Liban broadcast recorded old *zajal* events that were held in various villages around Lebanon. However, important *zajal* work is often lost because of its oral nature.

Another effective folk medium in Lebanon is the theater. Arab theater played a vital role in Lebanon during the nineteenth century by emphasizing social-collective identity and representation. Early theatrical productions were in the form of "shadow plays" in which the shadow of actors was displayed. These shadows were conceived to reflect society in a satirical form or to present fictional tales. Another form was the one developed to commemorate the death of Al-Husain, the grandson of Prophet Mohammad. Known as *ta'ziyah* (condolence), this form is still practiced today and it focuses on the issue of righteousness and justice. *Ta'ziyah* is usually performed during the Muslim Shi'ite religious occasion known as *'ashora*.

Marionettes are another theatrical form, which is mostly performed in rural areas. This theatrical form makes use of a puppet that is operated by means of strings attached to its hands, legs, head and body. Often the puppet is put on show inside a wooden box that is known as a "*sandouk el furjeh*" (viewing box) or "*sandouk el 'ajab*" (curiosity box).

Today, Lebanese theater has matured to become a space where all varieties of taboos and subjects are tackled. Several prominent theater playwrights and directors have contributed to the indigenous theater field, among these are: Mounir Abo Debs, Issam Mahfouz, Antoine Kerbage, Berg Vazilian, Maroun Naccash, Nidal el Ashkar and George Khabbaz. Among the established and active academicians who are training students in the theater are Lina Abiad and Sahar Assaf. The Rahbani brothers are celebrated for their musical plays that reflect social and political satire. The diva Fairouz has also acted in several musical plays that are still popular among the different generations.

The Lebanese "Security General" applies prior censorship on theater plays based on a 1977 legislative decree, which "explicitly gives it the right to fully reject or partially approve the staging of a play without directives or guidelines."[14] The decree has been implemented to censor plays that may threaten political or religious authorities or that are judged as nude or indecent.[15] At some point, plays that pass uncensored are often barred, if they are found to be threatening to any of the ethnic or religious groups in the country. For instance, SKeyes reported that a play titled "*Limaza*" (Arabic for "Why") was broadly criticized in 2015 because of an objection by a prominent Catholic authority in the country of a scene in the play that he claimed to be criticizing a Christian ritual.[16]

The 1960s and 1970s witnessed a boom in starting theaters, however, due to the Civil War and lack of funding only a few have survived. Popular theaters that have closed include Piccadilly Theater, Theatro De Beirut, Shoushou Theater, Elisee Theater, and many others.[17]

Theater and Friday sermons are the only folk media that are subject to prior restraint (censorship): theater is censored by the Lebanese "security general" and the Friday sermons by Dar al-Fatwa, the top religious authority in the country.[18] All other folk media can usually communicate messages freely and are rarely subject to accountability.

A successful approach to circumventing official censorship and to appealing to the public has inspired the employment of humor and satire to criticize daily Arab and Lebanese political and social practices in theatrical plays and public shows. This theatrical form has proved to have a strong public appeal and has been thriving since the 1960s. Today, traditional and social media employ comedy to portray serious issues and Lebanese comedians.

Among the well-known Lebanese comedy groups are "le Theatre Chansonniers"; "le Theatre de 10 Heures" and "Comedy Night on the Road." Prominent among the modern Lebanese comedians are Pierre Chamasian, Andre Jadaa, Mario Bassil, Hisham Haddad and Adel Karam. Because of cultural proximity, several Arab artists who employ comedy in their work also have wide appeal in Lebanon. Such artists include Adel Imam and Basem Yousef of Egypt, and Duraid Lahham of Syria.

Social Media Reach in Lebanon

Social Media Landscape

While folk media traditionally play an important role in the development of public opinion and in attitude formation within the different Lebanese groups, this role began diminishing with the entropic proliferation of mass media and the culture of "globalization." The fast spread of social media with their propensity to introduce alien forms of interpersonal interactions through speedy communication channels is threatening the potency of the role of folk media.

According to the 2015 "The Arab Social Media Report," Lebanon is in the top five most active Arab countries across social media networks and achieves the highest rate of female social network users in the region.[19] The report suggests that that the social media is a platform that "shields and enables expression and creativity" for the youth who were among the top groups in social media usage. It also exposed the fact that women in Lebanon are more active on Facebook than those in any other country in the region, with female users of Facebook in Lebanon making up 45 percent of total users.[20]

The Arab Social Media Report (2015) documented that WhatsApp is the most preferred social media channel across the Arab world (99 percent of Internet users in Lebanon). In Lebanon, Facebook is the second most used social media channel (95 percent), followed by YouTube (75 percent), Google Plus (58 percent) and Instagram (49 percent). The report identified communication, entertainment and knowledge as the three cores of social media usage in the region.[21] The March 2018 distribution figures of the social media in Lebanon show a similar picture: 43.16 percent for Facebook, 37.67 percent for YouTube and Twitter has 8.68 percent.[22]

Because Twitter is a relatively recent social media trend, it is not among the top five social media outlets in Lebanon. Its introduction began with a relatively wide use by celebrities and with a shy use by politicians and the general public. The so-called Arab Spring uprisings in Tunisia and Egypt intensified the public use of Twitter as a means of expressing political and ideological positions among the educated and young population. The outbreak of hostilities in Syria and the resulting intense division of the Lebanese public in their perception of these hostilities stirred up the use of Twitter among the politically active. However, the relatively increased use of this social medium did not have a significant impact on the hostilities as its use was mainly within a minority of young and education young population.

The 2017 alleged involuntary sojourn of Lebanese Prime Minister Saad Hariri in Saudi Arabia from where he announced his resignation on the Saudi television channel "al Arabia" enticed a highly volatile Lebanese public opinion. Twitter became an attractive medium for Lebanese politicians, including Prime Minister Hariri to reach out to the Lebanese public. This new tendency allowed politicians to stay relevant and maintain some clout in a politically challenging atmosphere.[23] This medium, however, has not yet acquired a wide national impact and its spread is still restricted.

> These practices are peer based, focused on expression and interaction, and are nonhierarchical in nature by starting political groups online, circulating a political blog, or forwarding and sharing political videos with friends, thus amplifying their voices in the political realm ... They are connected to their friends and family and communicate with them on regular basis.[24]

The number of Twitter users in Lebanon increased from 19,271 users in September 2011 to 111,000 users in March 2013.[25] Interestingly, many Lebanese politicians are active on Twitter, including the former president Michel Suleiman, Prime Minister Saad Hariri, and many parliament and

Table 5.1 Progression and Evolution of Users on the Three Principal Networks until 2013

Mobile Facebook, Twitter, Social Media Usage Statistics in Lebanon (Percentages)

1.	Facebook	95.2
2.	Twitter	3.03
3.	Pinterest	1.02
4.	Google+	0.42
5.	StumbleUpon	0.14
6.	Tumblr	0.13
7.	YouTube	0.03
8.	Reddit	0.02
9.	Other	0.01
	Total Users	100

Source: Arab Social Media Report (n.d.) Facebook in the Arab Region, retrieved in July 2016 from https://icannwiki.org/Arab_Social_Media_Report.

cabinet members.[26] Lebanese Twitter accounts in 2017 were more than 200,000 users, with a 2.8 percent penetration rate.[27]

The growth of smartphones in the past decade suggests the increasing influence of this medium in Lebanese interpersonal interaction. Figures released by an audience research firm IPSOS-STAT shows that Lebanon's smartphone penetration rate rose by 44 percentage points between 2012 and 2016 (from 36 percent in 2012 to 80 percent in 2016). This is the second highest increase among the five Arab countries with available data. The report indicates that 90 percent of smartphone owners in Lebanon had mobile Internet on their device in 2014, up from 74 percent in 2012. The survey also showed that 92 percent of Lebanese use their mobile phone, while watching television. In addition, 12 percent of Lebanese use their computers, while watching television and 4 percent use their tablets.[28]

Wireless Internet was introduced in Lebanon in 2005 as a service administered by the Ministry of Telecommunication. The ministry provides three types of services: dialup services, wireless Internet service and ADSL, which was first accessible in April 2007. Wireless Internet is connected to the client via USB or Ethernet and it provides download rates between 2 Mbit/s and 9 Mbit/s. The number of Internet users in Lebanon has grown rapidly in the past two years after the Telecommunications Ministry and state-run Ogero introduced fast DSL and 3G and 4G service. A fiber optic network is being deployed across Lebanon allowing subscribers to reach a connection speed of 4 Mbit/s and more at home.[29] Voice over Internet Protocol (VoIP) which permits free long-distance voice calling as well video conferencing is illegal in Lebanon. The ministry activates hardware and software equipment to enforce this ban.[30]

Internet Space and Regulation Modes

A cybercrime bureau, attached to the internal security forces in Lebanon, was established in 2006 to investigate Internet-related lawsuits.[31] In 2011, the National Audio-Visual Media Council called on all news websites and blogs in Lebanon to register with it in order "to get an idea of the electronic media landscape in the country prior to passing a new law that would include online publications currently not covered by the most recent media law of 1994." The head of Council declared that online news sites and blogs should draft a code of ethics and a new media law that would include them. He suggested that failure to register could result in the site being banned.[32]

Heated debates on Internet freedom took place in 2012 as a consequence to an announced intention of the then telecommunication minister Walid Daouk to introduce an Internet-guiding law, known as the Lebanese Internet Regulatory Act (LIRA).[33] The circulated text of LIRA restricts the publication of "anything that offends public morals and ethics."[34] The proposed law was strongly opposed by media activists and consequently was withdrawn from circulation and not pursued further.

Social Media Exchange (SMEX) reported that 50 websites were blocked in Lebanon by 2015.[35] These were classified by SMEX into five main categories: poker websites, escorting services, pornographic sites, Israeli websites, breaching copyright and LGBT (Lesbian, gay, bisexual and transgender).

The United Nations Agency for Information and Communication Technologies (ITU) noted an increase in the number of Internet users in Lebanon from around 300,000 users in 2000 (6 percent of population), to more than 3 million users in 2015 (80 percent of population).[36]

The state-owned telecommunication agency "Ogero" has a monopoly over the Internet sector in Lebanon. All Internet service providers, including the state-owned mobile network companies Alfa and MTC are expected to get their capacity bandwidth for providing 3G and 4.5G services through Ogero.[37]

Internet speed in Lebanon is low in comparison to neighboring countries like Syria and Egypt.[38] Yet, the Ministry of Telecommunication is seeking to improve the services. In this direction, it increased the Internet bandwidth and reduced the prices. Moreover, a 2020 Telecom plan was implemented in the country, where 5G Internet services will be available across Lebanon, and a proper fiber optic that covers all areas will be installed.[39]

Bloggers Breaking Barriers

Blogging is an early online activity in Lebanon and blogs have become one of the main media sources for Lebanese youth to access diverse information and various opinions. In spite of their high exposure rates, blogs are not yet an effective course for actual social and political change. Some bloggers have migrated to newspapers, the publication of books, to radio stations or to civil movements that have demonstrated impact on the ground. The Lebanese blogosphere is breaking down the barriers that separate traditional media from electronic media. Blogs have become an alternative media source on many issues, particularly on matters related to the environment, which aren't routinely covered by traditional media.[40]

Imad Bazzi was the first blogger in Lebanon; he started the first blog back in 1998, under the name *Trella.org*.[41] Among the well-known blogs in Lebanon are: *Blog Baladi*, *Gino's Blog*, *HummusNation*, and *Beirutiyat*. In 2005, focus on blogs increased noticeably in light of the assassination of the former Prime Minister Rafik Hariri and the political events that this aroused afterward.[42] By 2010, a survey revealed that several Lebanese blogs have the same daily readership as prominent Lebanese newspapers, an average of 14,000 readers per day.[43] The number of Lebanese blogs exceeded 800 by 2014, which is quite a considerable number, given the population of the country and the quality of Internet service provided.[44]

The cybercrime bureau arrested several bloggers for their posts. *Reporters Without Borders* reported Bazzi's arrest in March 2014 for insulting a former minister.[45] When a local television channel hosted Bazzi to discuss the lawsuit, its broadcast was suspended. Not only were citizens arrested based on blog posts, but also similar cases have arisen based on social media posts. Three citizens were interrogated in 2010 for criticizing the former President Michel Suleiman on a Facebook group, which was deleted.[46] With the absence of social media law, the government bases its prosecution of social media on the Lebanese penal code.

Internet usage in Lebanon is on the increase and the government is attempting to improve the present infrastructure. Interestingly, social media are contributing to the awareness about the folk media activities by spreading the word about various folk media events. Theater plays, coffee house events, as well as religious sermons and lectures are now announced as events on Facebook and other social media outlets.

Conclusion

The ongoing debate about the role of social media is still in its early stages. There are no definitive answers about the extent of the impact and effectiveness of this role. Social interactive media are only one feature among many that influence mass popular movements. There are several other political, economic, social and cultural influences that must be taken into account.

Ideally, social media enables everybody to interact with it and with its audiences. These interactive media facilitate and accelerate the process of social networking. However, there are major obstacles and many cautions to such an interaction. In particular, social media allow different uses that vary in benefit, impact and function on the different population generations. Thus, one needs to focus on the differential roles these media play on the different population generations. For example, the older Lebanese generation was brought up differently than the young: they were raised to think analogically, while the young generation is socialized digitally. Hence, the old cannot keep up with the speed and ease of the young's dealing with the new information technologies. On the other hand, the speedy dealings of the young are challenged with the analogic deliberations of the older generation.

Social interactive media are double-edged swords. They can raise important issues that help set the citizens' agenda for public discussion. On the one hand, they can have a positive impact on public awareness and on the other hand, they can contribute to the erosion of social values or national achievements. One cannot overlook the negative consequences of misusing these social media. For example, the indulgence in the social media may cause the young generation to neglect discussing fundamental life issues facing their society and instead turn to unethical and marginally useless issues.

Social media can elevate or reduce the level of culture in a community for they can develop certain cultural, social and political relations as well as breaking up others. Among the possible consequences of the heavy use of Facebook, for example, may be the damaging of family ties and an increase in alienation. The accelerating development in information technologies resulted in a media revolution and created a new social reality that obliges changing or overhauling the current media policies to adapt to the new technological reality.

One cannot overlook the negative consequences of indulgence in the social media, which may divert public attention from fundamental life and national issues to unethical or marginal inoperable issues. Among the serious consequences of the indulgence in the social media is the weakening of use of Arabic language in interpersonal interaction.

Language comprises, in addition to its vocabulary, views and prejudices that are embedded in the culture's values and norms. The use of the Arabic language in interactive communication, thus, is vital to preserve heritage. Interactive media can develop positive cultural, social and political relations but they can also break up others.

Social media networking has created a new space for dialogue and discussion. These media have the potential of activating the public sphere that generates a new political and social nature. If well designed, interactive communication technology can help the citizen to contribute, via the Internet, to the emergence of a new consciousness that establishes new social development. However, misuse of such technologies can lead to the alienation and loss of the citizen.

Experience has demonstrated that the real difficulty is in what might be called the integration of technology with the social structure. The adoption of social media produces new set of work rules, a new production style and even a new content. These technologies are usually developed to meet the communication needs of countries that are culturally different and might not necessarily agree with Lebanon's cultural mores or lifestyle and thus need to be adapted to Lebanon's needs and necessitates.

Additionally, social media do not operate in a vacuum but within a social reality. They work within the context of social and moral responsibility toward society. These media are an important factor in the formation of mental cognition or awareness of a citizen's perspective to her/his community and to the world. The content provided by these modern interactive channels of communication—be it cultural, recreational or other—contributes to the formation of a new "hyper reality" that may lead to the alienation of the citizen.

For the electronic and social media to be able to play a positive role in dealing with the alienation of the younger Lebanese generation and its incapacity to play an active role in the revival of its society, they need to develop into positive interactive channels for building good citizenship. The social media need to adapt its messages to address Lebanese society's problems and needs. Its messages, thus, should denote content that is culturally and socially relevant. Developing a critical vision that blends the social media with the folk media has a potential for innovation and renewal of the Lebanese society. From such a vision can emerge suitable policies that facilitate the correct use of the social media in the advancement of cultural identity among the Lebanese and safeguarding the society from cultural pollution.

A necessary step in this direction would be to inject common expression into the social media substance. By superimposing folk messages on the electronic and social media, these outlets may become relevant and its content in harmony with collective subject matter. Policy makers and media executives will be in a better position to design relevant plans by incorporating the folk media within their national communication polices.

6

Conclusion

Peculiar Environment

The sharp deterioration of the political and administrative situation in Lebanon, visible in an inability to elect a president for over two years, was also reflected in a serious decline in the state of affairs of its media. By the end of 2016, the situation had reached such an extent that threatened its survival. A prominent paper, *As-Safir*, folded, others (*An-Nahar* and *Al-Mustakbal*) were unable to pay their employees' salaries and television stations (LBCI and Al-Jadeed) were laying off employees. This serious situation impelled the parliamentary information and communication committee to announce, early in January 2017, that it had reached an agreement, after six years of fruitless deliberations, to refer to the parliament's general assembly a 35-page draft law that governs both the print and audio-visual media. The draft law also includes a number of articles dealing with the social media.

While the proposed draft law includes a number of improvements on the existing practices, it is clear that it was a result of a "force majeure" and not a genuine effort to address the ailing media situation in the country. The draft law includes an article abolishing prior licensing of both print and audio-visual media. It merely requires that the different media outlets, including blogs, submit a "letter of intent" to the ministry of information. The draft law also changes the task of the audio-visual media council from being merely advisory and gives it full authority for overseeing the media. If the draft law is approved, the appointment of members of this council would be freed from interference by political authorities.[1] Among the positive changes in the proposed draft law is an article abolishing the imprisonment of journalists and emergency (administrative) suspension as a penalty in press offenses. It also eliminates from the military judicial code crimes and penalties relating to freedom of opinion and expression. This change obliges the military institution to resort to civil courts should it be subjected to a press offence.

On the other hand, the proposed draft law acknowledges the right of general security forces (GSS) to censor publications and leaflets and gives power to the minister of information to prevent entry of any foreign publication to Lebanon, as well as confiscating its copies before a court decision. The draft law enforces prior licensing on Internet broadcasting and maintains the powers of the "Office to Combat Information Crimes." Police stations investigate matters relating to the expression of opinion on the Internet. It also places an unjustified financial burden on prospective publishers by requiring a $200,000 fee on new publications.

The crisis of the Lebanese media is not new. It started in the 1950s with a "laissez-faire" policy when funds poured into Lebanon and its media institutions. The period introduced an increase in the political and economic role of Lebanon in the Arab region. Local and foreign political business interests raced to enter the media scene by financing media outlets. The proposed draft law before the parliament, thus, represents a mere sedative and does not offer a "cure" to the ailing Lebanese media situation.

The folding down of *As-Safir* newspaper was a warning that the press, which Lebanon proudly articulates, as "the Press of the Arabs," needs a brave decision to admit failure of the present order. There is a need to accept the necessity of adopting a new accurate and realistic order.

Lebanon and its media resemble a pregnant woman, who supposes her swollen belly to be a transient tumor; whenever she feels the pains of labor, she takes medications, such as the present proposed draft law, to ease the pain and delay childbirth. This woman has to choose between two possible solutions: giving birth or death. The exit of *As-Safir* was not a problem of a single newspaper but that of a troubled country. It lies in the refusal of many Lebanese to admit Lebanon's need to change its ailing order. The Lebanese media, like Lebanon, are in need of undertaking an "order change." Patchwork and plastic surgery are no longer feasible or even possible options.

The starting point is to accept giving up the sectarian/tribal order that governs Lebanon and its institutions. Alternative structures and the creation of a new system of governance need to be considered. There is need for a new order in which citizens are equal and are not mere members of divergent and rival sects and tribes.

The spread of the Internet and social media has, no doubt, had an important impact on changes that affected the print and audio-visual media. The problem of the Lebanese media, however, goes beyond technological changes. Before the employment of new technology, there is a need to uphold professionalism within a state run by sects and tribes. Media professionals in both print and audio-visual media need to change the present order of their operation. They need to uphold their ethical and social responsibility in the face of an ineffective Press Order, whose work is almost exclusively limited to ceremonial activities and the protection of failing media.

The media community today resembles a private club that is geographically and socially isolated from the people; they write about each other and for each other. Lebanon has a large number of media outlets serving a country with a population of some 4 million, and with annual advertising budgets of no more than $175 million.[2] In order to survive with such a small population size and advertising budgets, the media became organically related to the ruling political and financial system. Thus, they struggle to compete for subsidies rather than for better public service.

To broaden their audience share, they resort to a style of sectarian reporting rather than professional improvement. The Press Order regulates the situation in the print media by measures approved and enforced by a body elected by publishers of 110 existing licensed political papers. This board takes it upon itself to protect the interests of feeble publications, which form the majority of the licensed publications. Professionally successful publications, thus, have to operate within an unfair system that enforces restrictions on their day-to-day operation including determining sale price, size as well as the days of publication per week. There is paradox that the audio-visual media are not organized in a union and that the prevailing media laws are not immediately obvious about their operation, therefore unlike the print media, competition among them for audience share and advertising budgets has no rules.

According to the Dean of the School of Journalism at the American University of Dubai, Ali Jaber, the crisis of Lebanese media is not in the closure of news media outlets; it is in the scarcity of professionalism in these outlets. This, he explained is due to their dependence on subsidies to survive. He revealed that, as a senior executive of one of the leading audio-visual companies, he is in a position to assert that Arab TV market earns less than 15 percent of what it spends. The estimated cost of operating television channels in the Arab region is US$7 billion, with a deficit close to 90 percent.[3]

Addressing the media crisis by maintaining its present structure and by pursuing temporary and transitory financers is merely "plastic surgery." A proper solution requires major structural changes. It requires an "out-of-the-box" solution: taking a courageous decision that may be alien to current media culture. This begins with the government and the Press Order accepting their obligation to implement applicable laws governing the media. This necessitates revoking licenses of newspapers and audio-visual media that are in violation of applicable laws. This entails adopting measures to reduce the number of newspapers and audio-visual media to a manageable and efficient level. A possible measure in this direction would be to merge different media outlets. A merger between these outlets could result in a further reduction in existing ailing media. This merger might take place by uniting media with divergent audiences in a way that would increase the new medium's audience spread, geographically and demography. Consequently, its advertising share of the market would increase. Such a move would make it reasonable for the government to allocate a budget to support the remaining media for a certain period (five years, for example), after which the status of every medium could be assessed in terms of its professional and financial achievement.

The true challenge of the media profession in Lebanon is to appeal to viewers, and to gain readers and not only subsidizers. An examination of the media budgets submitted to the ministry of finance for the past four to eight decades shows continuous financial losses, while one observes the inflated fortunes of the media publishers. The unquenchable yearning of newspaper and television station owners to join the "Ruling Class Club" have provoked them to enjoy a lifestyle of the ruling class. Commenting on the closing of *As-Safir*, a media critic, Hassan Ulaik, asks, "How can a medium survive when its publisher spends $1 million annually from its budget on his personal life?"[4] He contends that the profits of media owners have declined but they are far from being bankrupt. Jamal Ghosn of *Al-Akhbar* newspaper argues that the crisis of the Lebanese press began when the first editor received a bag of money from a president or a prince or king or a businessperson in the "golden era" of the press, therefore the originating scarcity of these bags signals the end of the crisis and not the opposite. The community of journalists today is isolated from the people ... Some papers in Beirut sell less than hundred copies ... The crisis is not in the closure of newspapers, it is in not having "journalism" in the newspapers.... . There are readers, and the press crisis will not end until the press returns to the readers, to their concerns and their problems.[5]

In an editorial about the fate of the press in Lebanon, the publisher of the popular daily *Al-Akhbar* claims that Lebanese media audiences are active and enthusiastic and the press crisis will not end until Lebanese media outlets focus on addressing the people's concerns and problems. He suggests that declining public interest in the Lebanese media is more a result of a pause by the public of media content and the charge that the public lost interest in news media is not accurate. Monitoring audience reaction to media's coverage of breaking news shows great interest in this news. Most television channels have increased their daily news reports from one to several daily, and the electronic websites transmit several breaking news items every hour.[6]

The present state of affairs of the Lebanese media escorted the development of a media system that took the shape of the tribal/sectarian Lebanese system. Each medium chose to "specialize" in addressing and being the spokesperson of one of the political/ethnic/sectarian Lebanese groups instead of serving as a forum for public debate and national unity. The media failed to build bridges between citizens and create a national consensus. Each Lebanese medium, thus, has narrowed its audience to a "political/sectarian class" that decides on the headlines of its articles. Decisions about its news agenda are made by an economic, financial, industrial and professional class; and religious authorities have veto power over what is to be published or broadcast. The result was that Lebanese media became a sectarian/tribal media rather than a national media. The peril of the Lebanese press is in its moral degeneration and trivial or corrupt content.

The media today faces great professional and managerial challenges and the Lebanese political system provides no answers. The government seems to consider the course and fate of the Lebanese press as only marginally related to its role.

Professional Failure

The media in Lebanon tend to focus on political and official news at the expense of news dealing with the everyday problems of the average citizen.[7] The coverage of political events by these media is often sensational and is lacking in sober assessment as well as in credible and investigative reports. According to the former Prime Minister Salim el-Hoss, "the media in Lebanon are no longer a mirror of reality; rather, the news event in these media has become a point of view."[8]

The Lebanese media are going through multifaceted crises that have contributed to their downfall and failure to reinstate their institutions financially and professionally, as well as to reclaim the leading role which they had occupied in the 1950s and 1960s in the Arab region. This is mainly because the media pay primary attention to structural developments at the expense of moral and professional ethics, which have contributed to the spread of a culture dominated by a market perspective and by a lack of social responsibility. The result was confusion by media institutions as to their role in society that focuses on seeking material profit as well as social and political influence.

The demise of the Lebanese media institutions is, in the first place, due to their failure to perform their role as responsible overseers (watchdogs), who protect public interest and defend the right of individuals from being exploited by political and business bosses and institutions. The average Lebanese, therefore, finds in her/his media only disorienting and confusing messages that divide an already fragmented society.

One of the main reasons why the Lebanese citizens have lost faith in their media, and consequently do not perceive them as credible, is that these media have been ineffective as channels to improve the conditions of the people. They have failed to promote a civil society that can shape good citizens. The Lebanese media have failed to reexamine their role in a changing society that was torn by a destructive and long civil war. As a result, one still observes this civil war in the messages of the different Lebanese media institutions.

The Lebanese media concentrate on presenting conflicting orientations of the different political, ethnic and sectarian groups in the country. They have failed to serve as a forum for responsible debate between these orientations.

They have also failed to build bridges between the citizens and to develop a national accord without which Lebanon cannot move into a sustained development.

The proper professional and ethical structures, that are essential for a climate of fruitful debate between the different factions in the country and the government is lacking in Lebanon's media. Perhaps the main reason for this professional and ethical deficiency is in the inability of the Lebanese media to focus on developing their independent financial means and hence being financially viable.

Mistaken Impression of Freedom

The problem facing the Lebanese media lies in a wrong visualization of freedom: a vision that emphasizes private interests and gives little notice to social responsibility. Censorship is no longer the appropriate scheme to reflect on the subject of freedom of expression in Lebanon. The correct approach is to focus on the issue of human rights, and in particular, the right of the citizen to communicate—the right that gives this citizen the opportunity to improve her/his livelihood and become conscious of, as well as practice, true democracy.

While democracy requires an attitude of openness by the government, it also requires the active participation of citizens in discussions and decisions concerning their livelihood. Only if the media can guarantee that the views of the conflicting groups are accessible to the public will the media's freedom of expression achieve this goal.

The often-repeated statement by media spokespersons that "the media are only mirrors of reality and are not responsible for the negative political climate in the country" is not precise and is too simplistic. While it is true that the content of the media originates from the people and the government, yet the media play an active role in "polishing" this content. Through their gatekeeping role, the media determine what information the public discusses by selecting what information the public receives. The media, therefore, set the agenda for public discussion.

In formulating democratic media policies, the citizen must be the focus of attention—and not the media or the journalist. Media protection does not inevitably imply the protection of the individual or society. There is a need for checks that will guarantee access to relevant and accurate information for all citizens, even those who have no media outlets. The freedom of the press thus becomes a legal right only inasmuch as it guarantees the right of the citizen to receive accurate information about public issues.

Media professionals cannot demand freedom to report if their practice violates public interest and transgresses the right of individuals to obtain accurate information that provides them with the opportunity to play an active role in building a proper and enlightened civil society. Public interest needs to be placed ahead of the private rights of journalists and the media. The state needs to legislate and develop policies that facilitate setting up public media channels that can serve as a model to the private media.

The core problem of Lebanese media is in the inability of the state to introduce clear plans and policies that bond the different social institutions, including media institutions, with the overall goals of society. The basic responsibility of the state is to involve citizens in the affairs of their country and unite them therein. In the absence of this essential governmental role, the Lebanese media will continue to fail in preparing their audiences for democratic participation.

The Lebanese media have failed to contribute to national development. None of the Lebanese media outlets speaks for all of Lebanon; instead, they have braced and encouraged division in the society with each medium serving as a voice for a religious, sectarian or ethnic faction. An essential starting point for a fruitful and effective involvement of the media in national development is to constitute a balance between public, private and government interests.

Additionally, the Lebanese media have contributed to the destabilization of its society by creating political confusion and spreading moral disorder at a time when Lebanon was in serious need for national unity to repair the material and moral damages resulting from the Civil War. The content of the Lebanese media contributes to the alienation of the Lebanese individual instead of facilitating her/his participation in the affairs of society. This sense of alienation is a result of providing the citizen with media content that has little or no relation to her/his society.

What is offered to the Lebanese citizen by the media outlets is beyond her/ his scope. These media outlets do not deal with matters that are of concern to the citizen but to the political or economic power groups behind these channels. Should this citizen accept the content presented, she/he would feel a stranger to social values, and even to her/himself.

The real problem of the Lebanese media institutions lies in their tendency to dismiss information and views that do not agree with their patrons. Here lies the danger of fragmenting the society into highly polarized groups. The media today spend more time avoiding information that disagrees with their patrons and intended audiences than they spend collecting information about public issues and presenting these issues objectively regardless of the position of the patrons.

Democratic principles that are spelled out in declarations of human rights mandate that the media should serve the people and not the contrary. Thus, it is no longer acceptable to exploit the principle of "freedom of expression" to justify giving the media a special status that makes them above other social institutions.

The people have become the target of media messages while ethically they should be the origin of these messages. Their civic interests should be the main factor affecting news selection. The citizen, not the media, should be the center of attention and the protection of the media no longer implies the protection of the public or society. Public interest needs to be above that of the private interests of the media and its practitioners.

The moral right of the media for freedom of expression has to be linked to their accountability. The main mission of the media is to serve the people before serving the authorities or economic authorities. The media should not continue to serve as tools in the hands of people of influence while the common person is forbidden to play any role except that of an observer and consumer.

The Lebanese public is more concerned with its livelihood than with the news and views of politicians. This is perhaps the reason why Lebanese media audiences are declining. By reassessing their role in society and by snubbing the commercial domination and agitations by the sectarian and tribal political factions, the Lebanese media will be able to revive themselves. The success of these media depends on accepting their social responsibility. Only then can Lebanon have media of adequate professional standard and credibility.

The relative freedom that the Lebanese press enjoys has not been transformed into a correct democratic practice. Effective accountability thus, is not achievable. In the absence of a properly functioning central government, tribal/sectarian authorities dominate in the management of the country's affairs and in the operation of its media. Consequently, Lebanon does not have a truly free press.

Re-Feudalization of the Public Sphere

Additionally, the adoption of entertainment values by a mercantile management outlook has prompted the Lebanese media to focus on scandals, fabricated sources, fictional events and the overall tabloidization of mainstream news. Wealth, power and sectarianism are intimately intertwined in the Lebanese media, and knowledge plays no mediating role. As a result, Lebanon faces a media muddle that allowed foreign elements to meddle with its media. The public is ignorant of how media affairs are handled. Because of this ignorance, they have little or no effect on influencing media performance. Consequently, we are today witnessing a media situation that in fact contributes to the re-feudalization of the public sphere.

The Lebanese situation is characterized by a lack of balance in the way Lebanese media handle the three basic forces that operate on this sector and interact within it. These forces are: 1. the interest of the public sector; 2. the interest of the tribal/sectarian (political) institutions of the state; and 3. the interest of the private sector. While we observe that state institutions and many private sector institutions influence and operate on the media to serve their interests, we note the absence of the public interest in Lebanese media content. What we find today is a distinct imbalance between public interest and the interest of the political, financial and economic forces in the country. While the free-flow of accurate information is essential for a well-informed public, we find that the public sphere is grossly distorted and "restructured" by today's media.

The government is unable to implement or even draft communication plans and policies that are founded on public interest. This situation has allowed Lebanese media institutions to advocate conflicting values and identities that further divide the population politically as well as socially. Unrestrained media channels are crowded with political leaks, void of professional ethics and pay little attention to cover basic public concern events. And while people are indeed agitated by the news coverage on their media outlets, they nevertheless no longer trust these outlets as it has become clear that they are controlled by a select few and that there is virtually no genuine exchange of views in the media's sphere.

What is lacking is the ability of the Lebanese media to deliver transparently socially and politically functional ideas to the public. What we see in Lebanon is a social system that gives opportunities and advantages to people based on their wealth and seniority within a tribal/sectarian system. The concentration of control over these powerful media is by a select few who are driven by narrow tribal/sectarian interests that carry the potential for damaging the democratic process.

The Lebanese media are dominated by a market mentality culture that gives little thought to social responsibility. Therefore, there is confusion between the freedom of the media to inform the people, their freedom to propagate tribal/sectarian dogma and their freedom to seek material profit. Attention to societal needs, in terms of content directed at addressing such needs, figures little, if at all. Little attention is given to the development of an environment of genuine dialogue between the ruling authorities and the public on the one hand, and among the people themselves on the other.

The Lebanese media are mostly advocacy voices for both national political groups and regional and international authorities. Each medium clearly sets a different agenda for the discussion of public issues and news developments by its audiences. Moreover, since these media are patronized and/or managed by feudal sectarian authorities, they contribute to the fragmentation of the Lebanese society. Each medium addresses itself to audiences that are essentially of the same demographic characteristic.

Freedom to Communicate

The description of where the media are within the Lebanese society is necessary for any meaningful projection of goals as to where this society intends to go and why. For "without a clear analysis and articulation of existing structures and influences upon communication we cannot plan ... in any meaningful or realistic way." [9] A former Lebanese prime minister described the Lebanese citizen as one "having a decent mind but evil hands ... who, for a while, preferred to use his hands rather than his mind." [10] The Lebanese media are among the most advanced in the Arab region in terms of professional resources. Their competence and expertise, however, rest more in their practiced skill than in the ethical aspect or the requirements of the profession.

Generations of Lebanese media professionals have struggled for their freedom to report and to criticize. They were successful in attaining a level of freedom better than that achieved by professionals in neighboring countries. However, they underscore their freedom and under-rate their responsibility to their profession and to society. They thus handle the affairs of their profession as they handle a business firm, not as a public service. They also pay more attention to structural and technological changes than to upholding the ethics of their profession.

Freedom of the press means the ability of the media to be "free to serve its society" through articulating a social consensus with respect to values and goals. [11] While Lebanese media are relatively free from government controls they are, however, not free to serve the call of their profession or that of their society. This lack of freedom "to serve," or lack of social responsibility, is due to disorientation in the societal and professional mission of the media practitioner and not only to government restrictions.

The recent ushering of social media into Lebanon, with their potential to spread information within seconds, carried hope for a free and genuine interpersonal dialogue. The introduction of social media was viewed by some as "an effective wake-up tool" and "a catalyst for change." [12] Bloggers and citizen journalists were now actively using the social media to report about general affairs. Political and social uprisings in the region became an important source of their reports. However, innuendos and malicious misrepresentation were carried in many of these reports. The government was unprepared to introduce policies to regulate the social media and consequently reacted arbitrarily to what it considered inappropriate. When coverage of the events in Syria by bloggers and "citizen journalists" exposed that numerous "eyewitness" reports or videos were prepared in foreign locations, public confidence in social media as information media was shaken. An active blogger ran the following in one of her blogs:

As a journalist with over two decades of experience ... I am always shocked by the fact that there is a significant portion of young men and women who know full well the repercussions of sensationalism ... but go ahead and resort to it anyways. Speaking with some of them, I was surprised by the extent to which they defended these methods as totally justified, arguing that new media demands it because we live in a competitive time that requires us to attract the highest number of followers possible.[13]

The central problem facing media in Lebanon is not that of government meddling, for this interference is carried out within the "rules of the game" of Lebanese politics. Primarily, it is that of both government and media institutions lacking adequate structures and authorities that would tolerate the media's contribution to their society's unity and cohesion as well as to address issues that are relevant to the everyday life of the average citizen. Instead, principal attention is given to commercialism at the expense of professionalism and social responsibility.[14]

Lebanese media institutions do not embrace their social responsibility obligations as much as they adhere to the society's unwritten sectarian norms. This sectarian bondage results in an inability to maintain independence or to operate freely. Consequently, they fail to develop widespread audiences that span over all existing sectarian and ethnic boundaries in the country. This contributes to their inability to be financially self-sufficient and, thus, to their continued bondage to the sectarian norms and, hence, they go around in a vicious circle.

The situation of the Lebanese media is that of disoriented media in a fragmented society. It illustrates the need for planning and for the establishment of policies that would regulate the media operation within the Lebanese society. The serious difficulty facing the media in Lebanon is in the lack of communication plans based on sound policies that properly integrate the media institutions within society and that coordinate the function of these media with other social institutions in the attainment of overall societal goals and plans.

If the media in Lebanon were evaluated based on their contribution to societal development, we would be faced, in the cases of print media, radio, television and social media with a quadrupled failure. The Lebanese media are unable to establish a balance between the public sector, the government and the business sector. A balance based on the respect of the interest of each would allow the media to operate properly and contribute to societal development.

The Lebanese media have constituted a platform for every political, ethnic or religious group. The main contradiction is in the inability of any single medium to constitute a genuinely open platform for opposing groups or diverging interests. They have often encouraged and reinforced divisions within society.

As managers of public commodities, the Lebanese media have discredited the image of business and brought into the open the contradictions between an economic reasoning based on profit and the logic of social welfare and political democracy, which often necessitates making sacrifices that business people are not ready to undertake. Lebanese media have continuously overstepped the limits of society's mores and public taste. As a result, messages in the Lebanese media often stimulate entropic practices, mainly deviant and anomic behavior.

The problem for the Lebanese media is that they lack adequate structures that would enable them to give the public what it "needs." Identifying what constitutes a threat to society and addressing civic necessities requires achieving national accord.

The Lebanese media, in short, have failed to facilitate the citizenry's participation in the affairs of their society; thus, they have contributed to their alienation. This alienation takes place by making the citizenry feel that they are distant and separate from the political process in society. Lebanese citizens cannot find a relationship to real life problems in the content of their media. They realize that what the media communicate to them about what is happening in their society is beyond their reach. They further realize that the content of their media has no relationship to their social reality. Should they accept the content of the messages, which the Lebanese media are presenting them, they find themselves revolting against their own values and norms, thus becoming strangers to their society.

Moreover, the Lebanese media are oriented to serve the power groups to which they are bonded. Therefore, they divert the attention of the common person from real social and political problems to marginal problems that are usually of concern to the authority the media is serving or that which is exported from outside. Genuine concerns of the public interest are very low on the list of priorities of media officials. Lebanese media institutions do not facilitate participation of the public in political and social affairs of their society. On the contrary, they often impede this participation. These media view the public through the situation of centers of power. The media fail to address themselves to public interest and to the needs of a truly democratic society. They also fail to defend the public against power abuses in their society.

An improvement in the present media conditions requires not only technological advancement but also, and most importantly, a change in the public, as well as professional, outlook to the role of media in society. The Lebanese media need to be regarded as a planning (strategic) tool to influence and move the public. Essential media improvements are in the route of making these media address themselves to the task of moving their society toward its goals rather than maintaining the troubling status quo. This requires both the improvement of the human element in charge of these media and the establishment of policies that direct media efforts toward societal goals. It requires communication policies that are based on the findings of social research, particularly problem and/or policy-oriented research.

Confessional divisions and contradictions are perhaps among the most serious problems facing the Lebanese society. Research findings by this author suggest that Lebanese citizens have stronger loyalty to their demographic community than to their country as a whole, and that they do not seek or expect solutions to their problems from the central government.[15] They expect these solutions from their "confessional group" or "social class."

The differential media, and consequently information exposure in Lebanon is widening the differences of the "image of the world" in the minds of different Lebanese confessional and ethnic groups. Such differences are possibly leading toward conflicting patterns of social consciousness, even different value systems within the same society.

Differences in media exposure and consumption, particularly in as far as media content is concerned, may introduce yet another division within the Lebanese society. In addition to confessional differences and the failure of the media to provide enough attention to real and conceived problems of their society, we may be moving toward widening "class" differences. The findings by this author suggest that the consumption of television programs differs among the rich and educated on the one hand and the poor and uneducated on the other. The rich and educated watch mainly foreign television programs and read "trustworthy" newspapers, while the poor and uneducated watch local and Arabic television programs, and usually read popular magazines rather than reliable papers.[16]

Lack of National Policies and Plans

The failure of the traditional mass media—print media, radio and television—to address issues that concern the average Lebanese is a result of a lack of policies and planning for societal development. It is a result of a faulty approach to development—the approach of superficially imitating the developed world with little consideration for societal needs.[17] Failure to address societal issues may also be attributed to the media's tendency to ignore the social aspects of development, while giving primary attention to material aspects by equating development with industrialization, Westernization and with technological innovation.

Like most of the newly emerging Western-oriented developing countries, Lebanon attempted to model its institutions after those of the Western world. Thus, priority was given to the improvement of communication technology rather than attention to the quest for satisfactory human interaction, dialogue and exchange of ideas through revolutionizing the communication process at the personal, group, national and international levels.

The embrace of the revolution of the communication technology unprepared perforce requires embracing the values associated with these technologies. By merely providing information, one does not necessarily achieve the targeted effect. In many cases, the adoption of new technologies leads to the destruction, or disruption, of useful traditional communication systems.

In quest of building a modem nation fortified by national pride, officials often adopt unnecessary or extremely costly technologies at the price of burdening society and ignoring other basic social development needs. This is usually done upon the ·advice of foreign "experts," who either represent companies or governments that have vested interests in having their clients adopt certain technologies or who are ignorant of the cultural background of the society they are advising. Sometimes, they may be familiar with the general physical structure of the society but not with the social or cultural values and ideals, tending therefore, to base their advice on their own cultural backgrounds.

Government officials often give priority of expenditure to the establishment of fashionable or admired media technologies, such as the Internet and social media, before they are prepared for the proper functioning of these technologies. These technologies are often designed for alien cultures and values; thus, they allow uses that are often not in harmony with national culture and traditional media. They do not operate in a vacuum but within the social reality of alien societies, thus they result in producing new social realities that are not congruent with the society's developmental needs.

This is at the expense of ignoring the development of other basic but less recognized institutions, such as the folk media and the traditional physical communication channels. Investing in new information technologies is at the cost of breaking important cultural norms and the development of new values that contradict with existing ones.

Lebanon, thus adopted television in 1959 before it had developed the supporting physical and social institutions that are required to ensure proper and socially useful functioning of this medium. The result was broadcasting heavily imported television programs and the weakening of the folk media and various traditional values and norms.

Examples of poor planning and of waste are plentiful: a few years ago, Lebanon purchased an expensive electronic mail sorting machine. The machine remained idle because the country did not have trained technicians to operate it. After securing trained technicians, the officials realized that streets and buildings in Lebanon are not numbered and that the Lebanese were in the habit of locating their residences by placing them nearby key locations rather than streets names. Earlier the government, in an effort to "modernize" the traffic system in the capital city, replaced the properly functioning old tramline system of transportation with "modern" bus lines. Large buses, the same as those used in Paris, were purchased. These proved hardly suited to the narrow streets of the city, thus creating serious traffic problems.

One finds numerous similar examples in almost all developing countries. These countries often adopt new technologies that are not really needed or purchase obsolete technologies that are dumped on them by developed countries at heavy costs. A more serious aspect of this adoption is that technology is not value-free; it is not neutral. The adoption of technology results in the introduction of the values of advanced societies, and thus in value conflicts whereas the developing society is badly in need for social stability to cope with development.

Not only do some developing countries adopt obsolete or irrelevant technologies, they often adopt irrelevant issues. The media of developing countries often show immense concern for problems faced by the Western world that are irrelevant or of little concern to developing communities. The situation is aggravated by the media giving little or no concern for basic problems of the developing society and by ignoring rural areas as well as minority and deprived groups.

The lack of proper analysis of the social environment and goals of society usually results in the failure of technology to solve human communication problems. Little attention is given to the development of indigenous skills and to self-reliance, or to the reduction of inequalities: of opportunity, of resources, of information access and of capability.[18] To mobilize technology for the service of developing Lebanese media, therefore, it is necessary to regard it as a planning instrument.

Meaningful plans for media development need to give equal attention to both material and nonmaterial (human) resources. Lebanese officials tend to concentrate their efforts at introducing "structural" changes, which are material changes. Moral (ethical) changes receive little or no attention. No matter how valid or appropriate the structure is, it is doomed if the moral order is inadequate. In the final analysis, the driver is more important than the car, and the one who plans the technology determines its output.

The disease in the present Lebanese media situation was moral before it became structural. Similarly, the structural changes needed in the Lebanese media situation should ensure the democratization of communication as well as address the need for the establishment of a moral order under which the mass media operate. Without such a moral order, democratization is meaningless and multiple standards will continue to apply.

The advancement of Lebanese media institutions requires the development of plans that are drawn in light of both material and nonmaterial societal needs. It is presumptuous to hold an a priori assumption that such needs require freeing the media institutions from government or business interests.

Within the context of genuine and dynamic policies and plans, stemming from the needs of society, government and business interests may at times be needed and even helpful in the development of the media. Sound and effective communication policies and plans are those based on the needs of the society, as determined by careful and "problem oriented" research.

What Lebanon truly needs is openness to social, political and cultural diversity, not necessarily to the media per se. To be truly democratic, the media must come closer to its citizens. There is an immediate need to develop a mutual relationship of influence between the media and the citizen. It is far from helpful to the cause of democracy to have the media in the hands of influential politicians and/or business people, while the average citizen is exclusively delegated the role of the consumer or spectator.

The diversity of media institutions does not necessarily lead to democracy. Political representation is the necessary ingredient for democracy. Actually, the present diversity of Lebanese media institutions along sectarian/tribal allegiances is one of its major troubles. A truly workable move toward media reform in Lebanon would be to reduce the highly inflated number of media outlets (print and audio-visual) that presently operate along sectarian/tribal lines. The reduction of the number of media outlets in Lebanon is a necessary first step to permit each medium to provide content diversity as well as achieve national audience reach.

In quest to modernize along Western lines, thus, Lebanese communicators concentrate their efforts on establishing a media system free from governmental control. Calls for government regulation of the affairs of the media were branded as either socialist or dictatorial. This parochial focus on freeing the media from government intervention contributed to ignoring, or paying little attention to, other sources of media control, such as those operating in Lebanon: foreign or local political and business interests. Controls by political and business interests that manage the media directly or indirectly are indeed serious.

Freedom of the press does not reside exclusively in *freedom from government* or business controls but, in the *ability to respond* to the needs of the people and to seek dignity through dialogue. In this context, if the government, through proper and constructive regulation, and the business sector, through proper and legal financial support, contribute to making the press free from nonprofessional interference in its affairs and, therefore, responsible to its society, then interference by these agencies may very well be justified—even welcome.

What Lebanon and other developing countries need are alternative approaches to solving communication problems. Lebanon needs approaches that emerge from, and are based on, genuine societal needs. It needs a vigorous flow of information within a meaningful communication process. In order to overcome the dangers of the fragmentation of its society because of the Civil War, it urgently needs approaches that bring together otherwise diverse groups.

Establishing alternative approaches to solving communication problems necessitates taking into consideration that there are various forces operating on the media from outside, through social and business institutions. A plain preview of the media from within media institutions, therefore, is not sufficient. The different Lebanese groups need more access to the different channels of communication by ensuring a free and balanced flow of information among the various segments of society. As an essential element of the political structure of the country, the media can make a powerful contribution to the functioning of democratic institutions by giving people the means to participate in political life.

To be able to contribute to their society's unity and cohesion, the Lebanese media institutions need to adopt an innovative outlook to their profession and end the shallow and superficial devotion to the neoliberal critical outlook,[19] which has contributed to the present media disorientation. Setting national communication plans is a basic requirement to guide the establishment of communication policies. The formulation of communication policies and plans need to be founded on the overall goals of the society, which takes into consideration the society's social, cultural and economic conditions as well as its political ideology. This formulation requires "public acknowledgment and deliberate choice; they cannot be left entirely to the initiative of engineers, lawyers, or other specialists."[20] The starting point, therefore, is to establish a national communication policy council that will serve as a forum for discussions and identify priority areas as well as suggest ways for the implementation of plans and the setting up of policies.

Setting the Limits of Political Publications: Legislative Decree No. 74 of April 13, 1953

The Lebanese President
Based on the Lebanese Constitution
and on the law of October 15, 1952
and at the suggestion of the Minister of Information
and after approval of the Council of Ministers
Decrees the following:

Article I—Until the number of all political periodicals in all Lebanese territories becomes twenty-five political daily or periodical publications including at least fifteen Arabic daily publications, no new license for a political daily or periodical will be given except for those who own two licenses of the type of the requested new license and who agree to permanently let go of the old licenses.

And when the number of publications drops, in the manner set forth in the preceding paragraph, no new license will be given except to whoever owns one license that permanently ends publication.
It is prohibited for a publication to establish a branch or an independent branch.

Article II—this Decree goes into effect immediately after its publication in the Official Gazette.
Beirut, April 13, 1953
Issued by the President of the Republic
 Signed: Camille Chamoun
 Prime Minister
 Signed: Khaled Chehab
 This legislative law is still in force. At the time of its enactment, the number of Lebanese political publications was 45. Today the number is 110!

Appendix 2

Licensed Lebanese Political Publications

	Name of Publication English	Name of Publication Arabic	Owner
1	*Daily Star*	ديلي ستار	The Daily Star Company
2	*Le Monde*	لي موند	The Middle East Publications Company
3	*L'orient*	لوريان	Alaurian Company
4	*Magazine*	ماجازين	The Eastern Institute for Printing and Publishing
5	*Revue du Liban*	ريفو دي لبنان	Press Development Company
6	*Al-Adab*	الأداب	Suhail Idriss
7	*Al-Adeeb*	الاديب	Al-Heni Company
8	*Al-Osbou Al-Arabi*	الاسبوع العربي	The Eastern Institute for Printing and Publishing
9	*Al-Afkar*	الافكار	Al-Afkar for Press, Publication and Public Relations
10	*Al-Aman*	الامان	Islamic Foundation for Press, Printing and Publishing
11	*Al-'Anba'*	الانباء	Walid Junblatt
12	*Al-Intikad*	الانتقاد	Al-Duha Company for Journalism and Media
13	*Al-Insha'*	الانشاء	Dar Al-Inshaa for Journalism, Printing and Publishing
14	*Al-Anwar*	الانوار	Dar al-Sayyad Company
15	*Irarat*	ارارات	Masis for Journalism and Publication
16	*Iztak*	ازتاك	Iztak
17	*Balagh*	بلاغ	Dar al-Balagh Company
18	*Bayrak*	بيرق	Press Development Company
19	*Beirut Al-Masa'*	بيروت المساء	Mohsen Alsayed Ali Ibrahim
20	*Tamadan*	تمدن	Dar al-Bilad for Printing and Media in the North
21	*Jareda*	جريدة	Jameel Kamel Mrowa
22	*Hadeeth al-Mosawer*	حديث المصور	George Sijaan and Arej Saadeh

23	*Harmoon*	حرمون	Al-Hadath Company for press and Advertising
24	*Horiya*	حرية	Dar al-Takadom al-Arabi for Press, Printing and Publishing
25	*Hawadeth*	حوادث	Al-Hawadeth Company
26	*Hayah*	حياة	Al-Markaziyeh Company for Printing and publishing, media and distribution
27	*Khawater*	خواطر	Emil Hayek
28	*Dabour*	دبور	Dar al-Dabour Company
29	*Diyar*	ديار	Al-Nahda Company
30	*Rayah*	راية	Dar al-Raya Company
31	*Rakeed*	رقيب	Manar for Publishing, Advertising and Printing
32	*Zartong*	زارتونغ	Zartong Company
33	*Zahlet el-Fatah*	زحلة الفتاة	The heirs of Shokri Bakhash
34	*Safeer*	سفير	Talal Ibrahim Salman
35	*Shiraa*	شراع	Federal Institution for Printing and Publishing
36	*Shark*	شرق	The heirs of the journalist Khayri Kaaki
37	*Shark Awsat*	شرق اوسط	United Arab Company for Press
38	*Shaab*	شعب	Mohammad Amin Dugan
39	*Sada al-Balad*	صدى البلد	The Lebanese Institute for Media and Documentation
40	*Sada al-Jonoub*	صدى الجنوب	Al-Enmaa Company for Press
41	*Sada Lebanon*	صدى لبنان	Mohammad Baalbaki
42	*Sayaad*	صياد	Dar al-Sayad for Press, Printing and Publishing
43	*Tareeq*	طريق	The heirs of Anton Thabet
44	*Asr*	عصر	Bekaa for Press and Publication Skaff & Co.
45	*Awasef*	عواصف	Ahmed Hussein
46	*Kefah al-Arabi*	كفاح العربي	Abu Dhor al-Ghafari Company for Printing and Press
47	*Lewa'*	لواء	Abdul Ghani Salam
48	*Mustaqbal*	مستقبل	United Arab Press
49	*Najwa*	نجوى	Al-Masera Company
50	*Nahar*	نهار	Al-Nahar Company
51	*Action*	اكشن	Rimoun Daou
52	*L'appel*	لا بيل	Nedaa al-Watan Newspaper Company

53	*Le jour*	لي جور	Lugar Company
54	*Le matin*	لي ماتن	The United Arab Company for Press
55	*El-Etihad el-lebnani*	الاتحاد اللبناني	The heirs of Zidan
56	*Al-Ahad*	الاحد	The Journalists Siham and Sabah and Abir Taha
57	*Al-Ahrar*	الاحرار	Press Printing and Publishing
58	*Al-Akhbar*	الاخبار	Lebnaniyeh al-Arabia for Press
59	*Ela al-Amam*	الى الامام	The heirs of Naseeb Hanna Nimr
60	*Bilad*	بلاد	Islamic Unity House Company
61	*Binaa'*	بناء	National for Press Company
62	*Bayyan*	بيان	Al-Bayyan Company for Press and Publication
63	*Beirut*	بيروت	Al-Watanieh Institute for Press, Printing and Publishing
64	*Telegraph Beirut*	تلغراف بيروت	Joseph Louis Tonji
65	*Thabat*	ثبات	Sameer Nasri Atallah
66	*Thakafet el-wataniyeh*	ثقافة الوطنية	The Lebanese Arab Company for Media
67	*Jadeed*	جديد	Jadeed for Publishing and Media
68	*Jumhour al-Jadeed*	جمهور الجديد	Al-Mostakela Institute for Media
69	*Jumhouriya*	جمهورية	Dar al-Jumhouriya Company
70	*Jihad*	جهاد	Talal Ibrahim Salman
71	*Hadeeth*	حديث	The United Arab Company for Press
72	*Haraka*	حركة	Dar Movement for Press and Publication
73	*Hewar*	حوار	Al-Hewar Company
74	*Hayah al-Dawliyeh*	حياة الدولية	Al-Ahlia Company for Studies and Research
75	*Dastour*	دستور	Ali Balout
76	*Donya*	دنيا	Awni Khayri al-Dein Kaaki
77	*Raed*	رائد	Beirut Foundation for Press and Publication
78	*Rabeta al-Sharkiyah*	رابطة الشرقية	President Kamel Ahmed al-Assad
79	*Rased*	راصد	Morabet for Press, Printing and Publishing
80	*Rakeeb al-Ahwal*	رقيب الاحوال	The Independent Media Institute company
81	*Rowad*	رواد	Rimoun Daou
82	*Refay*	ريفاي	Dar Alarifay for Press and Publication

83	*Zaman*	زمان	Amal for press, publishing and advertising
84	*Seyasa*	سياسة	Al-Motahida Company for printing and publishing
85	*Sho'la*	شعلة	Charles Hanna al-Khoury Ayyoub
86	*Shams*	شمس	Dar al-Shams for Press and Publication
87	*Sabah el-Khair*	صباح الخير	The heirs of Anaam Tawfiq Ra'd
88	*Sada al-Shamal*	صدى الشمال	Lebnaniyeh for publishing, media and press printing
89	*Safaa'*	صفاء	Wataniyeh for Press and Publication
90	*Sout al-Oroba*	صوت العروبة	United Arab for press
91	*Sout al-Fayhaa*	صوت الفيحاء	Noun Company
92	*Tayar*	طيار	Dar al-Sayyad Company
93	*Asefa*	عاصفة	Press Development company
94	*Irfan*	عرفان	Zaid al-Zain
95	*Amal*	عمل	The Lebanese Phalanges Party
96	*Kalam al-Sareeh*	قلم الصريح	Al-Etihadiyeh for Printing and Publishing
97	*Kol Shi'*	كل شيء	Kol Shi Company for Press
98	*Kawkab*	كوكب	Kawkab for Press, Publishing and Media
99	*Lesan al-Mahal*	لسان المحال	Al-Wataniyeh Company for Media
100	*Masees*	ماسيس	The heirs of the Journalist Barseekh Toboseann
101	*Majales al-Mosawara*	مجالس المصورة	Dar al-Majales Company for Printing and Publishing
102	*Mharar*	محرر	Alf Company for Publishing
103	*Nedaa'*	نداء	The Lebanese Arab for media
104	*Nedaa al-Watan*	نداء الوطن	Nedaa al-Watan Newspaper company
105	*Nahda*	نهضة	The heirs of Nadim Abou Ismail
106	*Hadaf*	هدف	Al-Ameh Company for the Press and Media
107	*Houda*	هدى	The heirs of Ahmed al-Sabe'
108	*Wadi*	وادي	Markaziyeh for Printing, Publishing and Media
109	*Wakt*	وقت	Prestige Company for Media and Publishing
110	*Youm*	يوم	Waleed, Khaled, Mazen and Wafik al-Tibi

Source: Lebanese Press Order, June 2016.

Appendix 3

List of Radio Stations

(Broadcasting times specified here are local. "24h" indicates that the station broadcasts 24 hours a day)

Source: Jack FitzSimons, "VHF/FM RADIO STATIONS IN LEBANON."
www.qsl.net/g4jfs/stnlist.htm.

Political Category Stations

NBN [89.0–89.4](89.3) Adnan al-Hakim Street, Block A (or P.O. Box 13–6633, Chouran) Beirut. Tel: 01 841 020 Fax: 01 841 029 Email: info@nbn.com. lb Internet: www.nbn.com.lb 24h Currently carrying the program "Risala Radio" Rue Barbour, Beirut. Tel: 01 667 200 Fax: 01 667 300 Email: info@ risalaradio.com Internet: risalaradio.com

Nidaa al-Maarifa (The Call of Knowledge) [91.1–91.5] (91.1, 91.3, 91.5) Shaykh Ahmad Iskandarani Centre, Bourj Abi Haidar, Beirut. Tel: 01 667 601 Email: darnash@lynx.net.lb Internet: www.nidaa.fm Al-Ahbash; Association of Islamic Philanthropic Projects

Radio Liban; Radio Lebanon [96.0–96.4] (96.2) Studio 7, Ministère de l'Information, Rue Emile Edée, Sanayeh, Beirut. Tel: 01 756 185 Fax: 01 347 489 Internet: www.96-2.com French, English, Armenian 24h. Also relays Radio France International 12 hours a day. Arabic Service [98.1–98.5] Radio Liban Building, Rue Lyon, Sanayeh (or P.O. Box 4848), Beirut. Tel: 01 343 217 0530 0130 mono. Also on 837kHz ID: "Huna Iza'at Loubnan"

Radio Liban Libre "Loubnan al-Horr" [102.3–102.7] (102.3, 102.5, 102.7) Kebbe Building, Adonis, Zouk Mosbeh (or P.O. Box 110, Zouk Mekhael, Jounieh). Tel: 09 225 577 Fax: 09 218 235 Email: info@rll.com.lb Internet: www.rll.com.lb 24h mono

Radio of the Light "Izaat al-Noor" [91.8–92.2] (91.7, 91.9, 92.2) Al-Noor
Building, Abdel Nour Street, Haret Hreïk (or P.O. Box 25–197, Ghbeiry)
Beirut. Tel: 01 543 555. Fax: 01 450 771 Email: alnour@alnour.com.
lb Internet: www.alnour.com.lb 0600-0030 Prior *to being licensed this*
station was permitted to operate due to the continuing Israeli occupation of
Southern Lebanon and Hezbollah's operations of resistance.

Radio Orient "Izaat al-Shark min Beirut" [88.3–88.7] (88.3, 88.7) Australia
Street, Rawche (or P.O. Box 13-60 52, Schouran) Beirut. Tel: 01 791 466/7
Fax: 01 869 772/3 Email: radioorient@future.com.lb Internet: www.
radioorient.com.lb 24h

Voice of Lebanon "Saout Lubnan" [93.2–93.6] (93.1, 93.3, 93.5, 93.6) Bashir
Gemayel Avenue (or P.O. Box 165271) Beirut. Tel: 01 323 458 Fax: 01 219
290 Email: info@vdl.com.lb Internet: www.vdl.com.lb 0550-0120

Voice of the Nation "Saout el-Watan" [93.9–94.3] Borj Abi Haidar (or P.O.
Box 14/5439) Beirut. Tel: 01 300 997 Fax: 01 647 044 Email: makassed@
makassed.org.lb

Voice of the People "Saout al-Sha'ab" [103.7–104.1] (103.7, 104.0) Jabal
el-Arab Street, Wata el-Mousaitbeh (or P.O. Box 14/5425) Beirut. Tel: 01 311
809 Fax: 01 313 605, 0600-0100

Voice of Tomorrow "Saout al-Ghad" [96.7–97.1] (96.7, 96.9, 97.1, 98.0)
Amaret Chalhoub, Jounieh-Beirut Highway, Jemejian bldg (Daihatsu bldg.),
4th floor Tel: 01 881 222 Fax: 01 881 999 Email: info@sawtelghad.com
Internet: www.sawtelghad.com Some separate programs for Syria from the
Deïr al-Achayer transmitter on 97.1MHz

Voice of Van "Vana Tsain" [94.6–95.0] (94.7, 95.0) 2nd Floor, Shaghzoyan
Centre, Borj Hammoud (or P.O. Box 80–860) Beirut. Tel: 01 267 657 Fax: 01
241 272. Armenian, Arabic 24h Email: info@voiceofvan.net Internet: www.
voiceofvan.net

Voice of Beirut Unity (108.0) Borj Abi Haidar, Beirut. Tel/Fax: 01 707 047

Voice of Liberty "Saout al-Horriya" (89.7, 89.9, 90.1) 5th floor, Garden
Center Building, Tele Liban, Tallet el-Khayat, Beirut. Tel: 01 797
864 Fax: 01 864 800 Email: info@sawtalhorria.com Internet: www.
sawtalhorria.com 24h

Voice of Unity Licensed by the Cabinet (October 2000). Operates in North
Lebanon. Islamic Tawheed.

Entertainment Category Stations

Saout al-Bachaer [95.3–95.7] (95.3, 95.5, 95.7) Mabarrat Association Building, Bir Hassan Street (P.O. Box 25/83) Beirut. Tel: 01 853 805 Fax: 01 857 389 Email: albachaer@albachaer.com Internet: www.albachaer.com 0630-2400 (Voice of Faith) *Some separate programs for Syria from the Deïr al Achayer transmitter on 95.3MHz*

Al-Qur'an al-Kareem Radio "Dar al-Fatwa Izaat al-Qur'an al-Kareem min Lubnan" [89.7–90.1] (93.9, 94.1, 94.3) Dar al-Fatwa Building, Ibn Rouchd Street, Aisha Bakkar, Beirut. Tel: 01 795 700 Fax: 01 795 149 Email: quranradio@darelfatwa.gov.lb Internet: www.darfatwa.gov.lb 24h

Saout al-Mahaba; The Voice of Charity; La Voix de la Charité [105.8–106.2] (87.5, 104.4, 105.8, 105.9, 106.0,106.1, 106.2, 107.7) Couvent St Jean, Fuad Chehab St., P.O. Box 850, Jounieh. Tel: 09 918 090 Fax: 09 930 272 Email: marhaba@radiocharity.org Internet: www.radiocharity.org Arabic, French, English, Armenian 24h mono Also relays Vatican Radio programs (and is relayed by Vatican Radio). *Unlicensed but broadcasts with Cabinet approval*

Saout el-Mada [92.5–92.9] (92.5, 92.7, 92.9) 2nd floor, Mirna el-Chalouhi Centre, Sin el-Fil (P.O. Box 90–1346) Beirut. Tel: 01 488 001 Internet: www. sawtelmada.com Email: info@sawtelmada.com Launched May 2009. Allied to the Free Patriotic movement. These frequencies were originally licensed to France FM

Jaras Scoop FM [100.9–101.3] (100.9, 101.1, 101.3) 4th Floor, Antablian Bldg, Henry Saab Street, Hazmiyé. Tel: 05 958 881 Fax: 05 958 883 Email: radio-scope@radio-scope.com Internet: www.radio-scope.com www.jarasfm.com

Light FM [90.4–90.8] (90.5, 90.7) 3rd Floor, Private Club building, Dekwaneh, Cityrama, Sin el-Fil, Beirut. Tel/Fax: 01 513 517 Email: lightfm@ radiolightfm.com Internet: www.radiolightfm.com stereo

M.B.S. (Master Broadcasting Station) [107.2–107.6] (107.2, 107.5) 1st Floor, St Paul building, facing La Cite, Haret Sakhre, Jounieh. Tel: 09 912 911 Fax: 09 635 933 Email: radiombs@yalla.com.lb *Some separate programs for Syria from the Deïr al Achayer transmitter on 107.2MHz*

Melody FM [99.5–99.9] (99.5, 99.7, 99.9) 3rd Floor, Habib Centre, Sin el Fil Highway, Beirut. Tel: 01 510 850 Fax: 01 510 854 Email: info@ melodyholding.com Internet: www.melody.fm

Mix FM [104.4–104.8] (104.4, 104.5, 104.7) VdL Building, Alfred Naccache
Avenue (or P.O. Box 16–6815) Achrafieh, Beirut. Tel: 01 333 288 Fax: 01 217
788 Email: info@mixfm.com.lb Internet: www.mixfm.com.lb stereo

Nostalgie [87.6–88.0] (87.7, 88.0) 1st Floor, Studiovision Building, Naccache,
Metn. Tel: 04 444 088 Fax: 04 444 000 Email: nostalgie@nostalgie.com.lb
Internet: www.nostalgie.com.lb 24h

NRJ Lebanon [98.8–99.2] (95.1, 98.8, 99.1) Studiovision Building, Naccache,
Metn. Tel/Fax: 04 444 000 Email: info@nrjlebanon.com Internet: www.
nrjlebanon.com 24h stereo

Pax Radio [103.0–103.4] (103.1, 103.3, 103.4) 6th floor, Sea Sweet
building, Fuad Chehab Avenue, Mkallès, Beirut. Tel/Fax: 01 480 077
Email: paxradio@hotmail.com Internet: www.paxradio.net 24h stereo

Radio Delta [101.6–102.0] (101.7, 101.9, 102.0, 103.4) 5th Floor, Hitachi
Centre, Jdeideh Highway, Beirut. Tel: 01 495 222. Fax: 01 498 333
Email: radiorotanadelta@radiorotanadelta.com Internet: www.radiodelta.fm
Arabic 24h mono

Radio Liban Star "Noujoum Loubnan" [100.2–100.6] (100.2, 100.5)
Zakhem Building, Beit Meri el Metn. Tel: 04 872 832 Fax: 04 872 444
Email: noujoumloubnan@hotmail.com

Radio One [105.1–105.5] (105.1, 105.5) Zakhem Building, Beit Meri el-Metn.
Tel: 04 872 111 Fax: 04 972 818 Email: info@radioone.fm Internet: www.
radioone.fm 24h stereo

Radio Scope (Bekaa) (100.0) facing Tal-Shiha Hospital, Tal-Shiha, Zahlé.
Tel: 08 806 200 Fax: 08 822 730 0600-2400. There are two Radio Scopes;
one serving only Zahlé and another national service. These are no longer
operated by the same company.

Radio Sevan (90.8, 101.3, 101.5) Ground Floor, Khederlarian Building,
Khashadourian Street, Mar Mikhael, Beirut. Tel: 01 567 161 Fax: 01 567 186
Email: info@radiosevan.com Internet: www.radiosevan.com Armenian

Radio Strike [97.4–97.8] (97.4, 97.7) 2nd floor, Abi Jaber Building, Al-Saideh
Street, Sin El-Fil, Beirut. Tel: 01 510 517 Fax: 01 510 519 Email: radiostrike@
radiostrike.com Internet: www.radiostrike.com 0800-2400

Sound of Music "Saout al-Moussika" [106.5–106.9] (106.5, 106.7, 106.9) 7th
Floor, Wadih Nasrallah Centre, Rue Al-Anwar, Jdeideh, Beirut. Tel: 01
878 819 Fax: 01 602 222 Email: info@sawtelmousika.com Internet: www.
sawtelmousika.com 0630-0200 stereo

Voice of Stars "Saout al-Noujoum" (95.9, 107.8, 108.0) 7th Floor, Kracht Building, near Saidet al-Intikal Church, Ghazalieh Street, Sioufi, Achrafieh, Beirut. Tel/Fax: 01 339 100 24h ID: Email: info@sawtelnoujoum.com Internet: www.sawtelnoujoum.com

Other (Unlicensed) Stations

Aghani (98.9) Internet: www.aghaniaghani.com/ Arabic

Al-Fajr (Radio Dawn) (100.7, 104.9, 107.7) Islamic Propagation Centre, Aisha Bakkar, Beirut. Tel: 01 751 157 Email: info@fajrradio.com Internet: www. fajrradio.com Islamic fundamentalist group Al-Jamaʾa al-Islamiya

Arabic Voice "Saout al-Arabi" (96.5) Borj Abi Haidar, Beirut

Arabic Voice of Beirut "Saout Beirut Lubnan al-Arabi" (108.0) Bourj abi Haidar, Beirut

Green Lebanon R "Lubnan al-Akhdar" (107.4) Adib Ishac Street, Beirut. Tel: 01 219 980

Irtiqaa Way Radio (87.5, 96.3, 96.5, 98.5) Internet: www.irtiqaaway.com

Islamic Reunification Radio "Izaʾat al-Tawhid al-Islami" (95.0)

Nida al-Iman (89.2)

Parliament of the Shiʿite Council "Al-Majless al-Shiʿii" (105.2) ID:

Radio City (89.7) Beirut

Radio Liban Culture (88.5, 92.3) Central College, Jouneih. Tel: 09 910 669 Email: radiolibanculturerlc@gmail.com

Radio New Power (93.8) Beirut

Radio Sawa (87.7) Email: comments@radiosawa.com Internet: www. radiosawa.com Using one of Radio Nostalgie's frequencies.

Virgin Radio (89.5) Jal al-Dib highway, Beirut. Email: info@ virginradiolebanon.com Internet: www.virginradiolebanon.com

Voice of Freedom "Saout al-Horriah" (104.7) Kleiaat

Voice of Islam "Saout al-Islam" (89.5) *unlicensed Muslim religious station. Irregular*

Voice of Love "Saout al-Hobb" (101.2) Kleiaat ID

The 1994 Audio-Visual Law: Law Number 382

(The author's edited and corrected version of the translation by *ARAB AD* magazine)

Chapter 1

Terms and Objectives

Article 1: The objective of this law is to organize Radio and Television transmission by means of any techinque or method or device, regardless of its condition or name, and to organize the rules and all matters related to this transmission.

Article 2: The terms used in the text of this law have the following meaning:

Radio transmission: Transmission via electromagnetic waves, or any other means, that can be received by an audience.

Television transmission: The transmission over the air of moving or still pictures that are either accompanied by voice or not, via electromagnetic waves or any other system, that can be received by an audience.

Channel: The frequency niche used by a television institution for television transmission.

Wave: The frequency niche used by a radio institution for radio transmission.

Television or radio transmitter: All kinds of transmitter devices, stationary or mobile, and relays and transposers and all networks, whether on earth or in space that can directly continue television and radio transmission.

Retransmission: Receiving radio or television programs wholly or in part, regardless of the technical means, which the licensed institution uses to transmit these programs to the audience, and transmitting them instantly or at a later time without change.

Television institution: Any entity that organizes and transmits television programs to an audience, or that transmits programs unchanged to a third party.

Radio institution: Any entity that organizes and transmits radio programs to an audience, or that transmits programs unchanged to a third party.

Program: All the service elements provided by the institution, as mentioned in the previous section.

Advertisements: The commercials that are directed to the public within the time-frame granted to the advertiser, for the purpose of promoting a product or service, or buying it, or renting it, or to propagate a certain issue or opinion or inducing any other effect the advertiser wishes to induce.

Literary, artistic, musical, scientific right owner: Any real person or entity that creates an achievement of a literary, artistic musical or scientific nature. Or that acquires the investment rights of such an achievement.

Chapter 2

Article 3: Audio-visual media are free enterprises. The freedom of the media is to be practiced within the framework of the constitution and the applied laws. The right to utilize an airwave or channel is not by any means an exclusive concession and after the end of the rent contract, no compensation right ensues of any kind and the rent duration is determined by the license. The television or radio institution has no right to sell its rental rights, wholly or in part, or to lease them or waive them, directly or indirectly. In the event of any violation of the above, the institution will be forced to cease transmission immediately.

Article 4: It is intended by audio-visual media, any process of television and radio transmission that is made available to the public, or specific segments of it, via signals or pictures or sounds or writings of any sort that are not characterized by personal communication nature, through channels and frequencies and transmission devices or technologies.

Article 5: The setting up of television or radio institutions inside Lebanese territory or in its national waters is subject to prior licensing.

Article 6: It is prohibited for any person or entity, without prior licensing, to import or manufacture or assemble or use any transmission device or relay any audio or visual transmission. The authorities will confiscate all devices, parts and equipment that are imported or manufactured or used or being assembled without prior licensing. Whoever violates the articles of this law shall be subject to the penalties set in the Lebanese laws.

Article 7: The following should be taken into consideration when granting a license.

First:

1. The technical and professional potentials and specifications of the transmission and relay equipment via the allocated channels and frequencies.
2. The work conditions and operational requirements: human resources, programs, locations, installations, equipment, studios and institutions.
3. The ability of the institution to sustain its operational expenditure, at least for the first year of licensing.

Second: The commitment of the institution to respect of human character and the freedom of others and their rights and the diversity of opinions and points of view and the objectivity of the news bulletins as well as the maintenance of public order and national defense necessities and requirements of the public interest.

Third: The commitment of the institution to national industry needs that are related to national audio-visual production.

Fourth: The commitment of the institution requesting a license to produce the volume of local productions that are specified by the statement of conditions for each radio and television category.

Fifth: The commitment of the institution not to retain any financial gain that did not originate from its operations, whether directly or indirectly.

Sixth: The commitment of the institution not to transmit whatever may promote relations with the Zionist enemy.

Seventh: The commitment of the institution to apply the general laws, in a way that does not conflict with this law.

Article 8: Granting licenses should take into consideration the rights to channels and airwaves that are available to Lebanon according to international concords relating to the distribution of channels and airwaves. These channels and airwaves will be determined and distributed in accordance to international technical criteria and standards that guarantee a clear and superior transmission.

A technical committee is formed, the Audio-Visual Transmission Organization Board, that works in conjunction with the Minister of Information and the National Audio-Visual Council. The Board is formed of:

- ** The Director General of Investments at the Ministry of Telecommunications,
- ** The Director General of the Ministry of Information,
- ** A representative from the Defense Ministry,
- ** Four qualified communication engineers appointed by a government decree upon the recommendation of the Ministers of Information and Telecommunications,
  - **** The Technical Director of Radio Lebanon
  - **** The Technical Director at Tele Liban
  - **** And technical representatives from other television and radio institutions.

This Board will study all the technical aspects relating to television and radio transmissions, and submit the required recommendations to the Minister of Information and members of the committee.

Article 9: The State is the sole and exclusive owner of all television channels, radio airwaves and frequencies. These may not be sold or leased.

The audio-visual institution can utilize the channel or airwave by renting it during the period of the license according to the applied laws and regulations. The right to utilize an airwave or channel is not by any means an exclusive concession. At the end of the rent contract, no compensation right ensues of any kind and the rent duration is determined by the license. The television or radio institution has no right to sell its rental rights wholly or in part, or to surrender the rent, directly or indirectly to another group. In the event of any violation of the above, the institution will be obliged to cease transmission immediately.

Chapter 3

The Classification of Television and Radio Institutions

Article 10: Television institutions are categorized according, to the following:

First Category: Television institutions that transmit visual programs, including news and political programs, and that covers all of the Lebanese territory.

Second Category: Television institutions that transmit visual programs, except news and political programs, and that cover all of the Lebanese territory.

Third Category: Television institutions that transmit coded signals.

Fourth Category: that can only be received by subscribers who possess the necessary technical equipment.

Article 11: Radio institutions are categorized according to the following:

First Category: Radio institutions that transmit different kinds of programs including news, political programs that cover all the Lebanese territory,

Second Category: Radio institutions that transmit different kinds of programs except news and political programs and that cover all the Lebanese territory.

Third Category: Radio institutions that transmit coded signals that can only be received by subscribers who possess the necessary technical equipment.

Fourth Category: International radio institutions that transmit via satellites and whose coverage exceeds the Lebanese territory.

Chapter 4

Manner of Setting Up the Institution

Article 12: The television or radio institution is set up in the form of a Lebanese anonymous company that cannot own more than one television and one radio institution.

Article 13: All the shares in this institution have to be nominal and the shareholders have to meet the following conditions:

- ** The real shareholder has to be a Lebanese citizen, legally eligible and not convicted of any crime or violation, or deprived of his civic rights.
- ** The entity shareholder has to be strictly a Lebanese company, whose by-laws do not permit it from passing over these shares to non-Lebanese persons or companies.
- ** A real person or entity is not allowed to own directly or indirectly more than 10 percent of the total company shares. The husband or wife and all direct relatives are considered to be one person or entity.

Article 14: Founders of such an institution are required to own at least 35 percent of its capital and are not allowed to sell their shares before five years from the day of issuing the license.

The institution is required to publish in the official gazette a list of all its shareholders with their relatives' shares at the time of issuing the license. In case shares are bought or sold, the company should republish this list in the same manner.

Article 15: All the shares' movements in the television and radio institutions are subject to prior licensing. Any selling or buying or passing over of shares that is done with no prior licensing is considered null and void.

A penalty is imposed on whoever commits an illegal action, of the sort mentioned above, or participates in it, that consists of the value of the shares that were sold or passed over and of a jail sentence from six months to three years, and the confiscation of the shares by the state, which can sell them according to the applied laws.

The rules of this article also apply to actions committed by an intermediary, who is considered liable for the fine mentioned above.

Any agreement or contract pertaining to the above-mentioned offences is considered null and void and no compensation of any kind ensues there from.

Chapter 5

Licensing

Article 16: Licenses are granted to the television and radio institutions in accordance with a decree issued by the government after consulting NCOAVM.

Article 17: An agency is formed under the name **The National Council of Audio-Visual Media** (NCOAVM) that comprises ten members appointed jointly and equally by the government and parliament.

Article 18: Members of this council are selected from among Lebanese people of intellect, literature, science and technical specialization who are not employed by the state, the municipalities or any public agency.

Article 19: In addition to other functions mentioned previously in this law, the National Council of Audio-Visual Media carries the following functions:

1. The consideration of license applications submitted to the government and referred to it by the Ministry of Information. When necessary, this council can seek the advice of information specialists.
2. Making sure that the applications meet the legal requirements.
3. Submitting recommendations in which they state whether any license application should be approved or rejected. This recommendation is published in the official gazette as soon as the Minister of Information deposits it in the governmental system and before any decision is made by the government regarding the application.
4. The National Council of Audio-Visual Media has to make its recommendation and present it within 45 days from the date it has received the application.
5. The government, through the Minister of Information, will place the license application and all the required documents and technical information at the disposal of the National Council of Audio-Visual Media.

Article 30:

- —The NCOAVM's term is three years, renewable.
- —In the event of any membership vacancy, for any reason, a new member will be appointed in the same manner adopted to appoint the previous member, and within one month, for the rest of the term.

Any member who fails to attend three consecutive sessions with no valid excuse is considered as resigned.

Article 21: Members of NCOAVM are prohibited from engaging in any other business that conflicts with the nature of their work for the Council.

Article 22: The NCOAVM legislates its modus operandi and the government approves it.

Article 23: The member's compensation schemes are specified by the government.

Article 24: Any decision issued by the government can be reviewed before of the State Jury in case any legal licensing law was broken.

Article 25: All the exemplary conditions are to be prepared and listed by one or more specialized committees depending on the nature of the subjects. This committee is formed by a decree issued by the government, and the committee can seek the advice of specialists and technicians of its choice.

This exemplary condition logbook is accredited by a government decree after consulting the higher media council.

Article 26: The duration of the license is 16 years, renewable, provided the institution applies three years prior to the expiry date of the license.

Article 27:

First: The license fee payable by the television or radio institution is determined as follows:

1. Television institutions of the first and second categories: L£250 million.
2. Radio institutions of the first category: L£125 million.
3. Radio institutions of the second degree: L£50 million.

Second: The yearly rental fee payable by television and radio institutions is determined as follows:

1. Television institutions of the first and second categories: L£1 million.
2. Radio institutions of the first degree: L£20 million.
3. Radio institutions of the second degree: L£15 million.

Chapter 6

The Management and Duties of Institutions

Article 28: Each television or radio institution must appoint a program director. First degree institutions that transmit news bulletins and political programs must appoint a director in charge of such programs.

The director has to be a Lebanese citizen for more than ten years, enjoys legal competence, not convicted in any crime or misdemeanor, and ready to work in a full-time capacity for the institution.

Article 29: The television or radio institution must publish in the official gazette and in three local newspapers and in the commercial register the names of its chairman, and board members, and has to also provide the public with a list of all shareholders.

Article 30: Television and radio institutions have to transmit national orientation programs, educational, health, intellectual and tourist programs at the rate of one hour a week. These programs are to be aired free of charge and upon the request of the Ministry of Information in the air times determined by the conditions logbook. Materials required for transmission are either supplied by the ministry or from the institutions' archives.

Article 31: Any person or entity has the right to defend himself against any allegations transmitted by any television or radio institution.

The institution in question has to transmit this defense under the same technical conditions that the allegations were transmitted in, and in a fashion that ensures the same audience.

It is up to the Minister of Information to request the transmission of any correction or negation of any news item that has to do with any public interest or administration according to the norms specified under the publication law.

The right of defense has to be exercised during the specified periods, and according to the law, and under the penalties mentioned in the publication laws and their amendments.

Article 32: The license decree is issued after verifying that the institution has abided by the required conditions. The licensed institution is given a one-year period, from the date it is informed by the government, to put itself into operation according to the legal conditions, and the government can extend this period if it deems it necessary, and it loses its rights to obtain a license should it fail to request from the Ministry of Information to verify that the institution has abided by the legal, technical and financial licensing conditions, before the one-year period.

Article 33: The television and radio institutions bear the legal responsibility that ensues legally from any malpractice in its operations.

Chapter 7

Article 35:

1. In the event the institution does not abide by the requirements of this law and other laws, the following procedure is applied.

First violation: Based on the recommendation of the National Council of
   Audio-Visual Media, the Minister of Information orders a three-day
   suspension of the institution in question.

Second violation: based on the Minister of Information's recommendation,
   originating from the recommendation submitted by the National Council of
   Audio-Visual Media, the government orders the institution in question to
   stop its transmission for a minimum period of three days and a maximum
   period of one month.

The National Council for Audio-Visual Media meets under its own initiative or if summoned by the Minister of Information.

The Minister of Information can waive the Council's recommendation should the Council fail to meet within 48 hours after the minister issues the summons.

All the decisions mentioned under this article are subject to revision before a special Court that studies the case within a period of one year according to the applied laws. In the event that the procedure inflicted on the institution is not constitutional, the institution can claim up to LL10 million for every day of non-transmission and the radio institution LL3 million and that is as a maximum.

2. In addition to what preceded in Item 1 above, all the penalties mentioned in the general penalties law and in the publication law and in this law and others are applied to the violations committed by television and radio institutions. These penalties will be applied in their maximum form as mentioned in Article 257 of the penalties law.

The sentence television and radio institutions is added wherever needed in the mentioned laws and transmission is considered equal publication, which is mentioned in Article 209 of the penalties.

Chapter 8

Advertisements

Article 36: The television and radio institutions should refrain from airing any advertisement that might misinform the consumer, harm his health or interests, and that includes any violation of public morals.

Article 37: Advertisements should be prepared clearly and easily and in a manner different, audio-visually from the programs during which they are aired. It is not allowed for newscasters to appear or be heard in an advertisement.

Article 38: Advertisements are to be aired between each program and, can be aired during a program, provided that the unity and value of the program are intact, and in a manner not harmful to the owners of the program's literary and artistic rights.

Article 39: It is mandatory that each institution establishes or deals with a media concessionaire (*regie*) that solicits advertisements and that manages its advertising affairs.

It is not allowed for the advertising management in a television or radio institution and the advertising agencies to contract their advertisements to one medium exclusively.

It is forbidden for the owners of a television or radio institution or their *regies* and their spouses and children to have shares in more than one establishment. Also, full-time employees in a *regie* are not allowed to work in similar establishments. A *regie* can only serve one television and one radio institution.

Article 40: All matters related to the subject of advertisements that are not mentioned in this law are to be regulated by a special law.

Chapter 9

Tele Liban

Article 41:

1. The exclusive rights originally granted to Tele Liban to utilize all television channels is cancelled. Tele Liban is granted the right to transmit on all VHF channels, and one program on the UHF channels, assigned by the technical organization that will distribute channels to the licensed institutions.
2. Tele Liban has no right thereof in any form for compensation of any kind, with the exception of the compensation mentioned above.
3. The government has the right to organize Tele Liban's operation by special government decrees issued on the basis of recommendations submitted by the Ministers of Finance and Information.

Chapter 10

Institution Income Audit

Article 42: At the end of every six months, the licensed institution has to submit to the Ministry of Information a statement of its investment account. This account includes only the sums and income that originate from the institution's business operations under the legal and technical consensus. The ministry in question has to audit this account and verify the income from advertisements, production sales.

In the event that the institution falls under financial deficit that does not exceed three-quarters of its capital as submitted in the previous statement, the Minister of Information can grant the licensed institution a period of six months at the end of which the institution is obliged to submit its accounts. If after this period the income did not cover half of this deficit, the Minister of Information has the right to request the publications court to issue a verdict by which the institution is obliged to cease transmission for a period decided by the court but not exceeding one year.

Should the deficit turn out to exceed three-quarters of the institution's capital, the Minister of Information has the right to refer the institution to a specialized jurisdiction in order to decide on ceasing transmission immediately and without prior notice, for a period not exceeding one year. It is meant by financial deficit: the accumulated financial deficit.

Article 43: After the suspension period expires, the institution cannot resume transmission unless it proves that it has acquired the necessary funds required to cover the whole deficit, in which case it has to submit the source of funds and the method by which they were acquired. The Minister of Information can request more clarification and evidence, and consequently can make a decision to allow the institution to resume transmission in light of that evidence and statements submitted by the institution clarifying the sources of the funds and their authenticity, and after ensuring that the institution was not engaged in any action that could conflict with the public interests.

Article 44: Any violator of Articles 42 and 43 previously mentioned in this law, or any of them is penalized by a jail sentence varying from three months to one year. And by a fine of LL10 million to LL30 million, or both penalties.

Article 45: In the event the institution achieved a financial gain that could not be legally explained, the Minister of Information can request the publications court to issue an order to stop the institution's transmission for a period ranging from three to six months.

The court has to also impose a fine on the institution in question equivalent in value to double the amount of the unexplained financial gain.

In the event that it was proven that the gain was obtained with the intention to serve another state, or any foreign or local institution, in a manner that conflicts with the public interests or that affects the political system or that stirs up sectarian conflicts or encourages havoc and acts of turmoil, the penalty would be six months to two years jail sentence and a fine ranging from LL50 million to LL100 million.

The court can rule that the institution ceases transmission for a period ranging from six months to two years and can also rule to cancel the license issued to this institution indefinitely.

Article 46: The mechanism by which the institution's income audit is carried out is determined by a decree issued by the government based on recommendation of the Minister of Information.

Chapter 11

Censorship on Television and Radio Institutions

Article 47: By request from the Ministry of Information, the National Council of Audio-Visual Media practices censorship over television and radio institutions.

Chapter 12

Article 48: All the rulings of the law of commerce that do not conflict with the rulings of this law are applied.

Article 49: If necessary, the details required in the application of this law are specified by government decrees based on recommendations submitted by relevant ministers.

Article 50: Television and radio institutions are granted a period of two months prior to putting this law into effect to present license applications after the Ministry of Information announces that it is receiving them. The government can grant additional extension periods to complete the application file.

These institutions remain operative until the license decree is issued and resume their operation accordingly thereof; or are given a period of time to liquidate their assets in case their applications were rejected.

Article 51: All the television and radio institutions are exempted from fines, taxes and fee of any kind before this law came into force.

Article 52: All the previous legislation that contradicts or conflicts with this law are annulled.

Article 53: This law becomes effective immediately after its publication in the official gazette.

Appendix 5

Amendments of the 1962 Publications Law

Legislative Amendments of the Publication Law of 1962

(Translated from Arabic by the author; a number of minor articles have been omitted.)

Decree No. 104 Date June 30, 1977

The President of the Republic

Based on the Constitution

Based on Law No. 2/76 Date December 30, 1976 (granting the government the right to issue legislative decrees)

Based on Publications Law, issued on September 14,1962

After consultation with the State Consultative Council

At the recommendation of the Minister of Information

After the approval of the Council of Ministers on June 30, 1977

legislates the following:

Part I Publication Crimes

Chapter 1: False or Erroneous News

Article 1: Articles 51 to 70 of the Press Law, issued on September 14, 1962 are annulled and replaced by the following provisions:

Article 2: If a publication published an article based on erroneous or false information it is required to publish a correction in accordance with the provisions of this legislative decree.

Article 3: in accordance with the provisions of Article 25 of this decree, if the published article would disturb the public peace, the officials of the publication are subject to a penalty of: imprisonment ranging from six months to a year and a half, and a fine ranging from 5,000 to 15,000 Lebanese liras, or either.

It someone was sentenced under the preceding paragraph of this article and then committed the same offense or another that falls under the same paragraph before the lapse of five years, the penalty will be doubled, and the publication will be closed for 15 days. If this was repeated, the publication will be closed for 30 days, and if it was repeated for the third time, the publication loses its license.

If the news was false without disturbing the public, the officials are to be penalized by imprisonment from three months to six months and a fine of 3,000 to 10,000 Lebanese liras, or one of these penalties, and as well as they will be required to compensate the injured party.

In all the cases described in this article, punishment may not be less than the minimum of a fine, and the court in determining the judgment should take into account all the material and moral damages whether direct or indirect resulting from the offense.

Chapter 2: Right of Reply and Correction

Article 4: If a publication published articles or false or erroneous news about an official body, the Minister of Information can request the Responsible Director to publish a correction or denial of the item, in the place of publication of the false article or news and using the same type size. If the publication refuses to publish the correction, it is punished by a fine of 1,000 to 5,000 Lebanese liras, and the Minister of Information can issue a decision to suspend the publication. The Minister of Information can revisit his decision and allow the publication to be resumed on condition that it publishes the correction in the first issue after its continuation.

Article 5: The same procedure specified in the previous article applies to every foreign publication distributed in Lebanon, if the publication does not comply then the publication is prevented from entering the Lebanese territory by a decision of the Minister of Information.

Article 6: If a publication publishes a news item or article that makes reference to a particular person directly or indirectly, this person has the right of reply, and of prosecuting the publication.

Article 7: If the response exceeds the space of the initial false article or news item, then the publication's Responsible Director may ask the person replying to pay for the extra lines, or delete them.

If the possessor of the right of reply has died, his right transfers to his heirs; heirs also have the right to respond to every article or news published about the deceased after his death.

Article 8: Legal persons may benefit from the provisions of Articles 6 and 7.

Article 9: The responsible director may refuse to publish the reply or correction or uncertainty in the following situations:

1. If the publication has already corrected the article or news in a proper manner.
2. If the reply or correction is indistinguishably or vaguely signed.
3. If it is written in a language other than the language used in the initial article or news item.
4. If the words used in the correction display the publication in an immoral or unprofessional way, in variance with the law.
5. If the correction is received after thirty days from the publication of the initial article or news item.

Article 10: if the responsible director refused to publish the reply, citing the reasons set forth in the preceding article, the person may file a request to the judge to make a ruling, which is to be published within three days.

The judge issues a ruling and recalls the concerned persons within a week. If the judge's ruling is that the response is to be published, this is to appear in the first issue after the ruling and the cost of legal fees and expenses are to be paid by the publication owner and its Responsible Director.

Article 11: If a publication does not act according with the judge's ruling, the Responsible Director is to be punished by imprisonment from one month to three months and a fine of 1,000 to 5,000 Lebanese liras, in addition to the obliged fine for each day of delay in publishing the ruling.

Chapter 3: Restrictions

Article 12: All publications are prohibited from publishing the following:

1. Proceedings of a criminal investigation before its announcement in a public hearing, secret trials as well as trials dealing with divorce and annulment, immigration and paternity proceedings of the Council of Ministers, and the secret proceedings held by the Chamber of Deputies or its committees. The decisions and reports of these committees may be published after being deposited at the Bureau of the Council of Ministers unless a committee decides otherwise.
2. Proceedings of investigations and forensic inspection by the Central Inspection Department, except for decisions and communications issued by the Department.
3. Letters, papers or files belonging to one of the public administrations tagged under the phrase "secret." If persons or entities were harmed by such dissemination, they have the right to prosecute before the judiciary.
4. Proceedings of legal proceedings, which are prohibited to be published by court.
5. Reports, books, letters, articles, news, images that are contrary to public morality.

Each violator of the provisions of this article shall be punished by imprisonment from three months to one year and a fine of 5,000 Lebanese liras, or either. The offender may not be punished by less than the minimum fine. The court in determining the personal rights should take into account the material and moral damages whether directly or indirectly resulting from the commission of the offense.

Article 13: It is not permissible for nonpolitical publications to publish news or investigations or photos or comments of a political nature.

Any violation of the provisions of this article subjects the offender to a fine of 500 to 1,000 Lebanese liras. The punishment may not be less than the minimum fine. In case of repetition of the violation within a year, the Publications Court can cancel the license and prevent the license holder from issuing a new one for the next three years.

Article 14: Publishing the names of those who refuse to subscribe to a publication will be fined by up to 1,000 Lebanese liras. A subscription fee will be in effect only if there was a proof of a subscription request. No person is required to return a publication sent to him without a request.

Article 15: Advertising an underwriting to compensate for payments of fines and fees and damages incurred on those convicted of a felony or a misdemeanor is prohibited. Any violation of the provisions of this article shall be punished by imprisonment of up to six months and a fine of up to 10,000 Lebanese liras or by one of these penalties.

Chapter 4: Exaggerations

Article 16: Whoever threatens a person, through publications and advertisements or any form of images, to expose a matter or reveal information about him that defame his dignity or honor, or that of his relatives, so that he may achieve an illegal benefit is to be punished by imprisonment of six months to two years and a fine of 10,000 to 15,000 Lebanese liras or either, in addition to a payment of compensation to the injured party. The punishment may not be less than the minimum fine, and the court should take into account the material and moral damages whether directly or indirectly resulting from the commission of the offense.

The penalties in the first paragraph of this article are also applicable to journalists who attempt to intimidate Lebanese guests. If the violators are impersonators of the press profession, the penalty is doubled and the appropriate legal authorities may put them under immediate arrest until the outcome of their trial.

If someone who spent a sentence based on one of the first and second paragraphs of this article commits the same offense or one that falls under the same paragraph before the lapse of five years, the penalty stipulated in the first paragraph is doubled, in addition to the suspension of the publication for fifteen days. In case of a second repetition of the offense, the suspension period will be three months. Upon the third repetition, the publication license will be permanently revoked.

Chapter 5: Slander and Libel

Article 17: Any form of libel, slander and vilification that is not covered in this law is subject to the provisions of the Penal Code. Legal complaints against such offences may not be accepted after the lapse of three months from the date of publication of the offending item for residents within Lebanon and six months for residents outside.

Article 20: Libel offenses are punished by imprisonment from one to six months and a fine of 1,000 to 3,000 Lebanese liras, or either. In case of repetition of the offense, the penalty may not be less than the minimum specified fine.

Article 22: Libel or slander of a person because of the execution of his job is punishable by imprisonment from one to six months and a fine of 3,000 to 5,000 Lebanese liras, or either. In case of repetition of the offense, the penalty may not be less than the minimum fine.

If the person subject to the offense is a public official, the punishment will be from three months to a year and if this person is a judge on the bench, the punishment will be from one to two years and a fine of 5,000 to 10,000 Lebanese liras, or either. In case of repetition of the offense, the penalty may not be less than the minimum fine.

Cases of libel and slander should be raised by the offended person.

Chapter 6: Defamation of Presidents

Article 23: If a publication printed material that is considered to be defamatory or libelous of a head of a foreign state, the public legal authorities will pursue the matter without the need of a complaint by the offended head of state.

The Appeals Attorney-General can suspend the publication for a period not less than three days but not more than ten days, confiscate the issues of the publication and refer the publication to the court which may decide to continue the suspension until the court ruling and may enforce a punishment of imprisonment for a period of one to three years and a fine of 10,000 to 25,000 Lebanese liras, or one of these punishments.

The punishment may not be less than a one-month imprisonment and the minimum payment.

If a publication that was sentenced in accordance to this article commits the same crime, or one that falls under the limitations of this article, after the lapse of less than five years, the publication will be suspended for six months. Upon the third violation, the punishment will be the permanent suspension of the publication.

Chapter 7: Incitement to Commit Crimes, Stirring Public Opinion and Endangering Safety of the State

Article 24: Anyone who publishes or advertises in the print media incitements to commit a crime will be punished according to the provisions of Article 218 of the Penal Code. Any written call to commit or promote a crime is judged to be an incitement.

Article 25: If a publication prints what may be considered to be a slander to a recognized religion in the country or what may incite sectarian or racial prejudice or disturb the public peace in a way that exposes to danger the boundaries or unity and safety of the state, or cause the distortion of its foreign relations in a way that subjects it to external risks, the Appeals Attorney General is entitled to temporarily suspend the publication for a period of not less than one week and not more than one month, to confiscate its issues and to refer it to the legal authorities. The court may decide to continue the suspension of the publication until the outcome of the trial. In this case, the temporary suspension of the publication may not exceed on year. The court may impose imprisonment of one to three years and a fine of 10,000 to 25,000 Lebanese liras, or either.

If a publication that was sentenced in accordance to this article commits the same crime, or one that falls under the confines of this article, after the lapse of less than seven years, the punishment will be doubled and the publication will be suspended for six months. Upon the repeated violation, the publication will be the permanently suspended.

Chapter 8: Responsibility for Publication Crimes

Article 26: The penalties imposed as a result of publication crimes fall on the publication's Responsible Director and the author of the article as the main actors. They will be subject to the Penal Code provisions on participation or intervention in a criminal act. The owner of the publication shall share the civil responsibility for the personal rights entailed and for the legal fees but does not assume criminal responsibility unless his actual involvement in the committed crime is proven.

The immunity enjoyed by a member of the parliament during the duration of his mandate does not relieve the Responsible Director or owner of the publication from liability in the event of publishing statements and declarations by a member of parliament if these fall under the provisions of the publication laws.

Article 27: The responsibility for publication crimes that are not outlined in the preceding article falls on the original author as a main actor and on the publisher as an accessory. If the writer or publisher are not known, the responsibility falls on the printing press and its owner shall incur the civil responsibility.

The provisions of the second paragraph of Article 26 apply to the cases set in the first paragraph of this article.

Owners of printing plants, publishing and distribution firms assume civil responsibility for personal rights and legal fees that are incurred on their employees by the publication courts.

Publications that are suspended or whose license is revoked by a legal action may not be issued in any other form under the name of another newspaper by borrowing its license or confusing the display of its name, in one way or another, that may suggest to the reader that he is reading the suspended publication. In such a case, the issues of the publication will be confiscated by a decision of the Minister of Information and the publication involved in the complicity will be suspended for a period ranging from one to three months.

Chapter 9: Court Proceedings

Article 28: The Court of Appeals considers all cases involving publication crimes and its rulings are subject to the review of the Court of Cassation in its capacity as the appellate reference.

Pretrial detention is not permissible in publication offenses except in the circumstances set out in Articles 23 and 25 of this above Legislative decree.

Article 29: If a case requires judicial inquiry, the investigating magistrate must undertake it and must transmit the case to the Court within a period not exceeding five days.

Article 30: When a case is referred to the court directly or by a decision of the investigator, the court must proceed with the trial within a period of five days at most and its ruling must be issued within a period not exceeding one month from the date of referral of the case.

The time limit for appealing the decision is ten days and five days for contesting it. The court must deposit with the Ministry of Information summaries of its decisions.

Article 31: All articles of the criminal code that do not conflict with this legislative decree or the Publications Law of September 12, 1962, apply.

Chapter 10: Publication of Court Rulings

Article 32: The provisions of the Penal Code, and all other Lebanese laws that are in contradiction with this legislative decree, are considered void. Consideration is to be given in rulings on infractions that were committed before the enactment of this legislative decree where the provisions of the earlier applicable laws are more tolerant.

Article 34: Texts contrasting with the provisions of this legislative decree in the Penal Code and other Lebanese laws are canceled. The interests of a suspect for acts committed prior to the issuance of the provisions of this legislative decree shall be taken into account, if sanctions contained in its articles include milder sanctions.

Article 35: The following is an amendment to Article 10 of the Press Law dated September 14, 1962:

Impersonating a journalist for whatever reason is punishable by imprisonment from six months to one year and with a fine of 1,000 to 5,000 liras. In all cases, the punishment may not be less than the minimum imprisonment and a fine (the rest without modification).

Part II Censorship of Publications

Article 38: Censorship of publications and information media are subject to the following provisions:

Article 39: In exceptional cases, that is, if the country or an area of it is exposed to danger resulting from an external war or an armed revolt or disorders or disastrous events, the government may, upon a decision taken at a meeting of the Council of Ministers, based on a recommendation by the Minister of Information, subject all publications and media channels to prior restraint. Such a decision should stipulate the manner of regulation of the censorship and the authority entrusted to implement it.

Censorship will be lifted by a decree issued by the Council of Ministers upon the suggestion of the Minister of Information.

The decree to impose prior restraint and that to lift it are not subject to any kind of appeal including revocation requests before the State Consultative Board.

Article 42: Ruling by the Publications Court on the subject of censorship is in no way subject to review.

Article 43: Administrative decisions to suspend a publication or confiscate its issues are not subject to any form of annulment or lawsuits.

Part III Jurisdiction over the Publication Revenues

Article 44: Subject to the provisions of Article 41 of the Press Law, issued on September 14, 1962, which requires the owner of a publication to keep three account ledgers, as stipulated in Article 16 of the Trade Law, the owner of the publication is obliged by the following:

Article 45: Submit to the Ministry of Information current account reports every six months. The current account should not include accounts or funds that are not related to journalism in its professional and legal sense.
The ministry should make sure that what is stated in the account is accurate.

If there is a fiscal deficit, and if this deficit does not exceed three-quarters of the publication's capital according to its recent budget, the Minister of Information may give the publication a period of six months to adjust its accounts. If at the end of this deadline the net income did not cover half of this deficit, the Minister of information has the right to request that the Publications Court suspend the publication for a period left to its discretion provided it does not exceed a year.

If the deficit exceeds three-quarters of the publication's capital, the Minister of Information may request the Publications Court to take a decision to suspend the publication immediately for a period not exceeding one year.

By fiscal deficit is meant accumulated deficit.

Article 46: After completing the suspension period, the publication may not resume publishing except if its owner can prove securing the necessary funds to cover the entire amount of the deficit, and in this case, to prove the source of those funds and how they were obtained. The Minister of Information may request further clarifications and evidence and may decide on the resumption of publication in the light of the evidence presented by the owner.

Article 47: Any violation of the provisions of Articles 45 and 46 is punished by imprisonment from three to six months, and a fine of 1,000 to 3,000 Lebanese liras, or either, as well as by the immediate confiscation by the Appeals Public Prosecution of issues, if published despite of the suspension decision.

Article 48: In addition to the above, if the Minister of Information finds that a publication made an illegal profit, he may request the Publication Court to issue a court order to suspend the publication for a period ranging between three and six months, and to fine it with an amount of twice the amount it has received. If it is determined that the profit obtained was in order to serve the interests of a State or a foreign authority in a way that contradicts public interest or to prejudice the political system or incite sectarian grudges or incite unrest and riots, the penalty shall be from six months to two years and a fine of 10,000 to 100,000 lira. The court may issue a decision to suspend the publication for a period ranging between six months and two years, and may decide to annul its license permanently.

Article 49: The details of the implementing the inspection of publications incomes will be set by a decree by the Council of Ministers upon the proposal of the Minister of Information.

Article 50: All provisions contrary to the articles of this decree or consistent with its content are canceled.

Article 51: This legislative decree shall be effective upon its publication in the Official Gazette.

Baabda on June 30, 1977,
Issued by President Elias Sarkis
Minister of Information, Signed: Salim Hoss
Prime Minister, Signed: Salim Hoss

Amended

On May 18, 1994 the government of Prime Minister Rafik Hariri issued law No. 330 that included amendments to basic articles of Decree 104 which abolished withdrawing publication licenses as a punitive measure, and to set a time limit for a publication's suspension as well as reducing the duration of imprisonment prescribed in Article 23, and to raise the ceiling of fines to be proportionate with the purchasing power of the Lebanese lira (now 50–100 million Lebanese liras, instead of a maximum of 20,000 liras), and to abolish the principle of administrative detention in all publication crimes. Also to reduce the time limit for judicial referrals, and to abolish all imprisonment penalties set in all articles: 3 (paragraph 3), 11, 2 and 47 of the Decree. The amendments do not affect the articles dealing with the inspection of the income of publications.

Notes

1 Background

1   This census, which was conducted by the French mandate, was the basis of the confessional arrangement in Lebanon, and no census has been conducted after that date for fear of upsetting this arrangement.

2   This is an estimated figure for the resident population in Lebanon in 2007, according to the Living Condition Survey result, that was based on 6,686 interviewed households in Lebanon; see Lebanese Central Administration of Statistics, www.cas.gov.lb/index.php/key-indicators-en (accessed on March 28, 2018).

3   This estimate from the US Bureau of the Census was updated on January 20, 2018; see CIA World Facebook, www.indexmundi.com/lebanon/population.html (accessed on March 28, 2018).

4   See World Bank estimate, https://data.worldbank.org/indicator/SP.POP. TOTL?locations=LB (accessed on March 28, 2018).

5   No official census has been conducted in Lebanon since then, for fear of changing this agreement.

6   Labib Zuwiyya Yamak, "Party Politics in the Lebanese Political System," in Leonard Binder (ed.), *Politics in Lebanon* (New York: John Willey, 1966), 163.

7   Ibid.

8   In October 2017, a Lebanese minister, Jibran Basil, blocked the appointment of forest guards who had passed the qualification exams on the grounds that the Muslims who passed the exam outnumbered the Christians; see http://aliwaa.com. أخبار-لبنان/المانشيت/التوافق-يصطدم-ب-حمادة-والتعيينات-بالمادة-95/lb.

9   Confronted by such a constitutional violation during a parliamentary hearing in March 2018, Prime Minister Sad Hariri responded that he will conduct "political consultations" to resolve the violation pointed out.

10   Singular of "*zu'ma*."

11   It can be argued that Lebanon does not have a "government" in the modern sense but rather a ruling group based on a coalition of sectarian/tribal chieftains each attending to the needs of his own group.

12   Samir A. Makdisi, "An Appraisal of Lebanon's Post-War Economic Development and a Look to the Future," *The Middle East Journal* (Summer 1977): 267–270.

13   Lebanese Ministry of Agriculture, "Ministry of Agriculture Strategy, 2015–2019," November 2014, 7, www.agriculture.gov.lb/Arabic/NewsEvents/

Documents/MoA%20Strategy%202015-19%20-%20English-for%20printing.pdf (accessed November 5, 2015). No, the "7" should be removed. It is included by mistake.

14 Ibid.

15 Lebanese Ministry of Agriculture, "Ministry of Agriculture Strategy, 2015–2019." Lebanon is a major food importer with local production satisfying only 20 percent of domestics' consumption.

16 While the president had the power to appoint the prime minister and to veto decisions, he now appoints the prime minister after mandatory parliamentary consultations and has to sign all parliamentary decisions or return them for further deliberations within a specified limited period of time.

17 An international tribunal was appointed by UN Security Council resolution to look into the assassination of Hariri.

18 See Wikipedia, https://ar.wikipedia.org/wiki/2011_الاحتجاجات_اللبنانية.

19 See *Al-Akhbar*, http://english.al-akhbar.com/node/2548.

20 "Sahafat al-watan ath-thani wa kadiyat al-ʿilam fi lubnan" ["The Press of the Second Nation and the Media Problems in Lebanon"], *Al-Usbuʾ al-Arabi*, No. 602, December 21, 1970.

21 Jürgen Habermas, *The Structural Transformation of the Public Sphere: An Inquiry into a Category of Bourgeois Society*, trans. Thomas Burger (Cambridge, MA: MIT Press, 1991).

22 Michael Hardt and Antonio Negri, *Empire* (New Haven, CT: Harvard University Press, 2001).

2 The Print Media: Unceasing Challenges

1 Nabil Dajani, "Arabic Books," in Noha Mellor, Khalil Rinawwi, Nabil Dajani, and Muhammed I. Ayish, *Arab Media: Globalization and Emerging Media Industries* (Cambridge: Polity Press, 2011), 29.

2 Ibid., 29–30.

3 Ami Ayalon, *The Press in the Arab Middle East: A History* (Oxford: Oxford University Press, 1995), 166–173.

4 Ibrahim Abdo, *Sabah el-Khayr* magazine, October 1958.

5 Antoine K. Dabbas and Nakhle Richo, *Tarikh at Tibaʾa al Arabiyyah fi al Mashrik* [*History of Arabic Printing in the Orient*] (Beirut: Dar an Nahar, 2008), 114–115.

6 Ibid., 208, 109–112.

7 Dajani, "Arabic Books," 34.

8   Khalil Sabat, *Tarik at-Tiba'afish-Shark al-Arabi* [*The History of Printing in the Arab East*], 2nd edn (Cairo: Dar al-Ma'arif bi-Masr, 1966), 35–38.

9   Ibid., 38.

10 Sabat, *Tarik at-Tiba'afish-Shark al-Arabi*, 54; and Ussama Makdisi, *Artillery of Heaven: American Missionaries and the Failed Conversion of the Middle East* (Ithaca, NY: Cornell University Press, 2009).

11 I am concerned here only with "popular" (unofficial) newspapers published by Arabs in the Arab World. In 1827, Mohammed Ali Pasha published the first official Arabic newspaper *Journal al-Khidawi* (Later, in 1828, to be named *Al-Wakaae' al-Misriyah*) in Egypt and Rizkallah Hassoun el-Halabi published a popular Arabic newspaper *Mir'at al-Ahwal* in Istanbul in 1855. The American missionaries in Lebanon irregularly issued a religious publication, *Majmu' al-Fawa'id* as early as 1851 which continued until 1855, after having published only three issues on an irregular basis. It was designed solely to promote their missionary work. None of their contributors were Arabs. Another irregular publication, *A'mal al-Jam'yyah as-Suriyah* dealing with the sciences and crafts, was published in 1852 by the Syrian Society, which was sponsored by the American missionaries. *Hadikat al-Akhbar* appeared first under the name *Al-Fajr al-Muneer* (The Enlightening Dawn), but its founder decided that the latter was "an uncommon name" and changed it.

12 Yusuf Ibrahim Yazbek, *Tarikh as-Sahafa al-Lubnaniyah* [*History of the Lebanese Press*], in *Al-I'lam fil Hayat al-Hadirah* [*Information in the Present*] (Beirut: Institute of the Press, Lebanese University, 1969), 136.

13 Ibid., 125.

14 Shamsud din Rifa'ie, *Tarik As-Sahafa As-Suriyah* [*History of the Syrian Press*], Vol. 1 (Cairo: Dar al-Ma'arif bi Masr, 1969), 58.

15 Adib Mroueh, *As-Sahafa al-Arabiyah* [*Arab Journalism*] (Beirut: Dar al-Hayat, 1961), 171.

16 Abdul Latif Hamza, *Al-I'lam Lahu Tarikhuh wa Mathahibuh* [*Information has Its History and Its Doctrines*] (Cairo: Dar al-Fikr, al-Arabi, 1965), 111.

17 Ibid., 112; and Rifa'ie, *Tarik As-Sahafa As-Suriyah*, 73.

18 Yazbek, *Tarikh as-Sahafa al-Lubnaniyah*, 123.

19 Although Egypt saw the first official Arabic newspaper, *Journal el-Khidawi*, its first popular paper, *Wadi en-Nil* did not appear until 1866.

20 Tom J. McFadden, *Daily Journalism in the Arab States* (Columbus: Ohio State University Press, 1953), 2–3.

21 Viscount Philippe de Tarrazi, *Tarikh as-Sahafa al-Arabiyah* [*History of the Arab Press*], Vol. 2 (Beirut: al-Matba'a al-Adabiya, 1913), 7; and Rifa'ie, *Tarik as-Sahafa as-Suriyah*, 112.

22 Rifa'ie, *Tarik as-Sahafa as-Suriyah*, 133–142.

23 Uthman Nuri, *Hayat Abdul Hamid wa Siyasatuhu [The Life and Policy of Abdul Hamid]*, Vol. 3 (1914), 286.

24 *Al-Manar*, Vol. 15, Section 10 (1912): 796–797.

25 McFadden, *Daily Journalism in the Arab* States, 4.

26 May Shaheen reports that two famous Egyptian journalists declared, in 1944, that "We Egyptians are not used to being publishers and editors of newspapers. We are only used to being reporters. Publishing is the business of the people of ash-Sham (Syria and Lebanon) and not ours." In Shaheen, *Shari' as-Sahafa [The Press Street]*, 2nd edn (Cairo: Dar al-Ma'arif bi Masr, 1957), 62–63.

27 Rifa'ie, *Tarik as-Sahafa as-Suriyah*, 209.

28 Amer Mashmushi, "Towards a New Press Union," in Hilmi Malouf (ed.), *National and Modern Development of the Communication Sector* (Beirut: Lebanese University, 1979), 146.

29 See the series of 13 articles titled: "Confessions of Aref el-Ghrayyeb," in *As-Sayyed* magazine, August 27, 1970 to March 18, 1971; and Iskandar Rayashi, *Al-Ayam al-Lubnaniyah* (Beirut: Sharikat at-Tab' wan-Nashr al-Lubnaniyah, 1957 and Beirut: *Kabl wa Ba'd*, Matabi' al-Hayat, 1953).

30 For details of this period, see Lebanese Press Union, *Al-Mu'tamar as-Sahafi [The Press Conference]* (Beirut: Lebanese Press Union, 1949).

31 Publications in Lebanon are licensed in three horizontal categories: daily, weekly, and monthly or quarterly; and in two vertical categories: political and non-political. Non-political publications are expected to deal only with non-political matters. Some nonpolitical publications, however, managed to publish political material but were not checked by the government, either because of a lack of proper control, or because of the power of the publisher's position in the country.

32 Press Law of September 14, 1962, Article 1.

33 Ibid., Articles 10 and 22.

34 This clause in the law was included because several of the practicing journalists at the time did not have either a high school or university degree.

35 Ibid., Article 62.

36 Ibid., Articles 60 and 63. Appendix X includes the text of the law on this subject.

37 This act, however, proved to be only a technical hurdle. Foreigners, wishing to own shares in papers could do so easily by registering their shares under the name of Lebanese citizens, after concluding secret agreements.

38 See Appendix 5: Legislative Amendments of the Publication Law of 1962.

39 *As-Safir*, January 16, 1984.

40 The value of the Lebanese pound dropped from £3 to the US$ in 1982 to close to L£2,400 in 1992.

41 The price of the paper in the 1950s was 10 piasters; there are 100 piastres in a Lebanese Lira.

42 Ibrahim Salameh, "As-Sahafah al Lubnaniyyah fil Madi wa fil Musttakbal" ["The Lebanese Press: Past and Present"], *Ath-Thakafah al-Arabiyah* 10 (1967): 173–175.

43 In the early 1950, newspapers were sold for one-tenth of a Lebanese Lira. Today the price ranges from 1,000 to 2,000 Liras. Several newspapers used to come out in 32 pages now their size ranges usually from 8 to 16 pages.

44 Several leading papers, including *An-Nahar* and *Al-Mustakbal*, have been forced to lay down many employees and are not able to regularly pay the salaries of the remaining employees.

45 This figure is based on my own field research. This figure does not include "bulk subscriptions" by governments, which are more of a political subsidy. Circulation figures are usually guarded secrets in Lebanon. When released, they are often quite exaggerated. In the 1960s and early 1970s, some newspapers' circulation could reach 60,000 during their peak period.

46 Baha Abu-Laban, "Factors in Social Control of the Press in Lebanon," *Journalism Quarterly* 43(3) (1966): 514.

47 A freeze on licensing new political publication was imposed in 1952. Consequently, the license, which usually costs less than US$20, forces a publisher to purchase an existing license on the black market.

48 This author had access to an official Ministry of Information payment voucher in the early 1970s for services rendered. The voucher lists "secret" payments to several prominent journalists.

49 Georges Corm, "The Lebanese Economy: Crisis Highlights Features of Lebanon," *National Defense Magazine* 47 (January 2004), www.lebarmy.gov.lb/ar/content; and Georges Corm, *Fi naqd al-iqtisad li-ray'i li-'arabi* [*In the Criticism of the Arab Rent Economy*] (Beirut: Center for Arab Unity Studies, 2011).

50 Republic of Lebanon, Ministry of Finance, Public Debt Directorate, "General Debt Overview," August, 2017, www.finance.gov.lb/en-us/Finance/PublicDebt/PDTS/Documents/General%20Debt%20Overview%20Updated%20as%2031%20August%202017.pdf.

51 Gibran Hayek, editor publisher of *Lisan ul-Hal*, a leading afternoon Beirut paper, at a seminar on the "Freedom of the Press in Lebanon," Club of the Alumni Association of the American University of Beirut, January 24–25, 1974.

52 Dr. Edmond Rabbat, at the "Freedom of the Press in Lebanon" seminar.

53 Lebanese American University, "Professional Ethics, Media Legislation & Freedom Expression in Lebanon," March 1–2, 2002.

54 *Ad-Diyar* daily newspaper, November 3, 2012, "Who Governs Lebanon Security Officials or State or Justice Officials: A Security Source Threatens Revenge and Says Let He Who Has Ears to Listen," front page.

55 *An-Nahar*, March 1, 1967.

56 *The Daily Star*, March 4, 1967.

57 Salim Laouzi, "Mabadi' Said Frayha al Wataniyyah" ["The Nationalistic Principles of Sa'id Frayha"], *Al-Hawadith* 18(882) (1973): 28.

58 *Al-Anwar*, September 7, 1973.

59 The Lebanese Minister of Information, Albert Mansour, during a discussion following the presentation of a paper by Talal Salman, editor and publisher of *As-Safir* newspaper, on "The Role of the Lebanese Press in Protecting Freedom and the Dangers of the Politicization and Monopolization of Advertising," at the international forum "Gateways to Reconstruction" organized by the Lebanon Chapter of the International Advertising Association, Beirut, Bristol Hotel, September 19–20, 1990.

60 Abu-Laban, "Factors in Social Control of the Press in Lebanon," 514.

61 Wilton Wynn in a private conversation.

62 A number of papers, however, went around such limitations and appeared seven times a week, either by defying the union or by purchasing or renting additional licenses, and using their logotypes once a week (see Figure 2.x).

63 *An-Nahar*, December 9, 1972.

64 *Al-Anwar*, December 15, 1972.

65 *Al-Hawadith*, March 23, 1973.

66 Acts of retaliation from neighboring Arab countries include closing the borders, shifting from regular transit routes, preventing nationals from visiting Lebanon during the tourist season, and so forth.

67 Yet, although the granting of new licenses was discontinued in 1952, Lebanon today has 110 political publications.

68 See *An-Nahar*, February 23, 1976, 3.

69 Nabil Dajani, "The Lebanese Media Scene," in A. Sreberny and R. L. Stevenson (eds.), *Mapping International News: Theory and Research* (Cresskill, NJ: Hampton Press, 2001); Nabil Dajani, "World News in the Lebanese Media," (in Arabic) *Bahithat* 6 (2000); Nabil Dajani, "The Analysis of the Press in Four Arab Countries," in *The Vigilant Press* (Paris: UNESCO, 1989: and UNESCO, "Foreign News in the Media," *Reports and Papers on Mass Communication* 93 (Paris, 1985).

70 Lebanon Corruption Report, www.business-anti-corruption.com/country-profiles/lebanon, updated: August 2016; and Alexander D.M. Henley, "Religious Authority and Sectarianism in Lebanon," Carnegie Endowment for International Peace, https://carnegieendowment.org/2016/12/16/religious-authority-and-sectarianism-in-lebanon-pub-6648.

71 *As-Safir* ceased its print publication in January 2017, but I am including it here because its publisher is regularly coming out online with editorial comments and there are efforts to reinstate it.

72 Henry Mukhiber, *As-Sahafa, al-Itha'a at-Talevisyun, wal-Ra'i al-'Am* e [*Print Media; Radio, Television and Public Opinion*], unpublished monograph submitted at the Third Conference of the Political Science Association, May 1963.

3 Radio Broadcasting

1 *Al-Itha'a* [*Broadcasting*], September 1938, as quoted in Fayek Khuri, *Al-Itha'a al-Lubnaniyah* [*Lebanese Broadcasting*] (Beirut: Sader Press, 1966), 14.

2 Nabil Dajani, *Lebanese Media Habits*.

3 Fayek Khuri reports that the power of transmission was half a kilowatt only in its experimental stage, which began in April 1938, see Khuri, *al-Itha'a al-Lubnaniyah*. Before its official inauguration, the power was increased to 2.5 kilowatts by utilizing local equipment.

4 Ibid.

5 Hasan al-Hasan, *Public Opinion, Information, and Public Relations* (Beirut: ad-Dar al-Lubnaniyah lil-Nashr, n.d.); and Khuri, *al-Itha'a al-Lubnaniyah*.

6 Al-Hasan, *Public Opinion, Information, and Public Relations*, 168.

7 In September 1971, the ministry was named "Ministry of Information" in compliance with a decision by the Arab governments to unify the name of this ministry.

8 Al-Hasan, *Public Opinion, Information, and Public Relations*, 170; and Adel Butros, *Communication Law* (Beirut: Feghali Press, 1991), 41.

9 In August 1991, the Minister of Information proposed that the pirate radio stations should pay 5 percent of their income from advertising to the budget of Radio Lebanon in return for getting licenses by the government. The Council of Ministers shelved the proposal.

10 See "Interpreting the Figures of Lebanon's 2015 Draft Budget," *Information International Monthly* magazine, July 2, 2015, http://monthlymagazine.com/ar-article-desc_3779_.

11 For a discussion of rebel stations in Lebanon, see Douglas A. Boyd, "Unofficial Radio and National Dissolution: The Lebanese Experience," unpublished paper, Department of Communication, University of Delaware, Newark, September 1982.

12 Butros, *Communication Law*, 40–41.

13 Lebanese government, council of deputies, *Wathikat al-Wifak al-Watani*, section on communication in Article 1, 1990.

14 *Monday Morning*, November 1–7, 1982, 22.

15 Albert Mansour, the Lebanese Minister of Information, at a press conference, *An-Nahar*, August 9, 1991.

16 Lebanese government, council of deputies, *Wathikat al-Wifak al-Watani*, section on communication in Article 1, 1990.

17 Lebanese government, council of deputies, *Wathikat al-Wifak al-Watani*.

18 Lebanese Ministry of Information, *Nadwat I'adat Tanzim al-I'lam fi Lubnan*, Beirut, May 1991.

19 Human Rights Watch, "Implementation of the Broadcasting Law," www.hrw.org/reports/1997/lebanon/Lebanon-03.htm.

20 *The Washington Post*, January 31, 1997.

21 Jack FitzSimons, "VHF/FM RADIO STATIONS IN LEBANON," www.qsl.net/g4jfs/stnlist.htm. See list in Appendix.

22 In 2011, Sawt Lubnan was split into two stations with the same name, as a consequence of a dispute each representing one side of the dispute, between the party's leadership and the heirs to the station's post-war director.

23 *Trombetta, Lorenzo, Lebanon—Media Landscape, European Journalism Centre (EJC) 2018*, MediaLandscapes.org and Lebanon's Media Landscape: An Overview, March 23, 2017 / August 8, 2017, https://fanack.com/lebanon/society-media-culture/lebanon-media/

24 "Religious Media, Why Does It Matter?" www.lb.undp.org/content/lebanon/en/home/ourwork/crisispreventionandrecovery/successstories/Religious-Media-why-does-it-matter.html.

25 Albert Mansour, Lebanese Minister of Information, at a press conference, *An-Nahar*, August 9, 1991.

4 Television

1 The first noncommercial television station in the Arab world is the Iraqi government television station in Baghdad, which was established in 1957.

2 Early Lebanese Tele Orient productions were in classical Arabic so as to sell in Arab Gulf states that had difficulty comprehending the Lebanese Arabic dialect.

3 This coordination was reestablished when a new government was formed under the regime of President Elias Sarkis, broken again early during the regime of President Amin Gemayel, and finally reestablished with the end of the Civil War when President Elias Hrawi reunited the army and took hold of the affairs of the country.

4 "Research Bureau Limited," *Middle East Media Survey*, 1974, Op. Cit.

5 "Report on the Study in Lebanon," in Communication in the Community, *UNESCO Reports and Papers on Mass Communication*, No. 87, Paris, 1982.

6 In 1982, CLT acquired 8 percent of the stock of Tele Orient, thus its share of Tele Liban increased to 33 percent.

7 *As-Safir*, "Contracting TV Ads are bad for employees and company ..." October 25, 1988, 5; and "Officials and Labor Opposition Force the Cancellation of Deal to Contract TV Ads," November 3, 1988, 5.

8 Communication in the Community, Op. Cit.

9 Tele Liban benefited from an old arrangement between CLT and the French government to receive free French programs. LBC adopted a similar arrangement when it aired exclusively French programs on a special UHF channel (33). No advertising was allowed, however, on these programs.

10 "Research Bureau Limited," *Middle East Media Survey*, 1974, Op. Cit.

11 Nabil Dajani, "Mass Media and Social Consciousness in a Lebanese Community," in J. Halloran (ed.), *Communication in the Community* (Paris: UNESCO, 1980).

12 Tele Liban officials requested financial compensations of L£1 billion (at the time equivalent to US$40 million) from *LBC*, half a billion from *Al-Mashrek*, and L£10 million from *NTV*.

13 *As-Safir*, "Televangelists Expand to Lebanon through two TV Stations," July 12, 1987, 11.

14 This service deteriorated when the political power of the Maronite Lebanese Forces that controlled *LBC* was curtailed with the implementation of the Taif Agreement by the government of President Hrawi.

15 Statement by the Lebanese Minister of Information, Albert Mansour, to the Voice of Lebanon radio, *Ad-Diyar* newspaper, December 15, 1991.

16 Zahera Harb, *Channels of Resistance in Lebanon: Liberation propaganda, Hezbollah and the media* (London: I.B. Tauris, 2011), p. 103.

17 *An-Nahar*, August 9, 1991, 3.

18 Ibid.

19 The new terms allowed an upcoming political power, Rafik Hariri to purchase these shares. Later, when Hariri became prime minister he sold his shares to the government at a substantial profit.

20 "The Story of the Decree Which Raised a Storm: How It was, How It Became, and How It was Issued," *As-Safir*, January 15, 1992.

21 Ibid.

22 "Is the Press Facing a New Battle for Its Freedom?" *An-Nahar*, January 21, 1992, and "A Dangerous Proposal," *As-Safir*, January 11, 1992.

23 *As-Safir*, "A Dangerous Proposal."

24 Ibid.

25 "The Issue of Information Raises More than One Question," *As-Safir*, January 13, 1992.

26 *As-Safir*, February 12, 1992.

27 Official Gazette, Law No. 382, special supplement to issue No. 45, November 10, 1994. See translated text of law in Appendix X.

28 "Terms of Conditions for Licensing Television Broadcasting," Chapter 5, general rules. See also, "Terms of Conditions for Licensing Television Broadcasting," *An-Nahar* newspaper, February 2, 1996, 6, and "Terms of conditions for licensing political and nonpolitical television broadcasting," *Al-Liwaa* newspaper, February 5, 1996, 3.

29 Official Gazette, No. 47, September 16, 1996, 3315–3319.

30 Al-Manar's website describes its mission as follows:

> Lebanese TV channels have been overwhelmed by a trend of movies and programs that can only be described as immoral. At the time when the Lebanese—such as any people coming out of a devastating war—needed what could erase the effects of that conflict and work on building the personality of good citizenship, numerous TV channels have been broadcasting programs that would decay one's ethics and provoke his or her instincts in addition to instigating violence and identifying with western living patterns which are quite remote from our Islamic and Eastern values and culture.

See www.almanar.com.lb.

31 See "The information scandal shows, with detailed names, that the freedom of the Lebanese is in the hands of the politicians." *Ad-Diyar* newspaper, October 5, 1996. 1.

32 *As-Safir* newspaper, March 6, 2000.

33 Habib Battah, "Lebanese Number of Viewers per TV Brand," www.khazen. org/index.php?option=com_content&id=2469:lebanese-number-of-viewers-per-tv-brand-sa-lebanese-media-background-lbc-ntv-mtv-future-otv-nbn-tl&Itemid=213.

34 Findings of a 1998 study by the author of the media habits between two groups (political elites and workers) in the capital of Lebanon, Beirut, show that all the elite members have television sets and 98 percent of the workers have at least one television set.

35 Findings of the 1998 study by the author revealed that 90 percent of the Lebanese elites have cable access compared to 44 percent of the blue-color workers; "World News in the Lebanese Media," (in Arabic) *Bahithat* 6 (2000).

36 Peter Speetjens, "Pirate's Paradise: When Stealing Is the Norm," *Journal of Middle East Broadcasters* (4) (November–December 2005).

37 Al-Jazeera sport channels took the opportunity of the "World Cup" tournaments to oblige providers to accept its terms.

38 According to surveys conducted by the Pan Arab Research Center (PARC) during the period December 1996–January 1997, and by the Middle East Research and Consultancy (MERC) during the period March–April, 1997.

39 Donald R. Browne, "Television as an Instrument of National Stabilization: The Lebanese Experience," *Journalism Quarterly* 52 (1975): 692–698.

40 Ibid., 21.

41 Riad Taha at a press conference on September 6, 1973.

42 Report of the International Independent Investigation Commission Established Pursuant to Security Council Resolution 1595 (2005), Article 16, Beirut, October 19, 2005.

43 See http://civilsociety-centre.org/party/social-movement-responding-lebanese-garbage-crisis.

44 See also Marwan Kraidy, "State Control of Television News in 1990s Lebanon," *Journalism and Mass Communication Quarterly* 76(3) (1999): 485–498. Michael Johnson, "Political Bosses and Their Gangs: Zu'ama and Qabadayat in the Sunni Quarters of Beirut," in Ernest Gellner and John Waterbury (eds.), *Patrons and Clients in Mediterranean Societies* (London: Duckworth, 1977), suggests that governments in Lebanon are run by a coalition of political bosses (*zu'ama*), who are assisted by tough guys (*quabadayat*). When the law is in conflict with the interest of these *zu'ama*, it is superseded.

45 See Nabil Dajani, "Managing the Crisis of Public Services in West Beirut," in Nabil Beyhum (ed.), *Reconstruire Beyrouth* (Paris: Etudes Sur Le Monde Arabe No. 5, 1991), 195–208; and Dajani, *The Vigilant Press*, 75–88.

46 Nabil H. Dajani, *Disoriented Media in a Fragmented Society: The Lebanese Experience* (Beirut: American University of Beirut Press, 1992), 140.

5 From Folk to Social Media

1 See Halim Barakat, *The Arab World Society, Culture & State* (Berkeley, CA: University of California Press, 1993).

2 Michael Gilsenan, "Lying, Honor, and Contradiction," *HAU: Journal of Ethnographic Theory* 6(2) (2016): 497–525.

3 It can also be reasoned that Christian fundamentalism in the United States thrived among members of fundamentalist churches.

4 Lebanese National News Agency (NNA) (2013). "Friday Sermons: To Close the Discussion on Civil Marriage," January 25, 2013. Retrieved in July from http://nna-leb.gov.lb/ar/show-news/15515/nna-leb.gov.lb/ar.

5 M. Haikal, M. Ghraizi and K. Hajj Mohammad Ali, "Coffee House Meetings," term paper (Beirut: American University of Beirut, n.d.).

6 N. Hammoud, "When Horse Shoe is on Newspaper Leftovers," *Al-Mustaqbal* newspaper, August 14, 2003. Retrieved in July 2016 from www.almustaqbal.com/v4/Article.aspx?Type=np&Articleid=24261.

7 A. Sajoo, *A Companion to Muslim Cultures* (London: I.B. Tauris, 2011).

8 Fudwa El Guindi, "The Veil Becomes the Movement," in Haideh Moghissi (ed.), *Women and Islam: Critical Concepts in Sociology: Social Conditions, Obstacles and Prospects* (London: Taylor & Francis, 2005), 70–91.

9 A. Salvatore, *Religion, Social Practice, and Contested Hegemonies Reconstructing the Public Sphere in Muslim Majority Societies* (New York: Palgrave Macmillan, 2005).

10 N. Aucar, F. Feghaly and L. Homsi, "Caricatures: An Embodiment of the Lebanon's Illusory Freedom of Expression," term paper (Beirut: American University of Beirut, 2013).

11 Ian Black, "Drawing Defiance," *The Guardian*, March 10, 2008.

12 H. Shobokshi, "Honoring Pierre Sadek," *Ash-Sharq al-Awsat*, December 29, 2012. Retrieved July 2016 from http://english.aawsat.com/2012/12/article55239336/honoring-pierre-sadek.

13 Aucar, Feghaly and Homsi, "Caricatures."

14 N. Saghieh, R. Saghieh and N. Geagea, *Censorship in Lebanon: Law and Practice* (Beirut: The Censorship Observatory, 2010).

15 New Human Rights, Lebanon, Report on Censorship in Lebanon (March 2003). Nouveaux Droits de l'Homme Liban. Retrieved in July 2016 from http://a[efliban.org/sites/default/files/NDH%20Report%20Censorship.pdf.

16 SKeyes, "Provocation against Lina Khoury's Play for Offending Christian Rituals" ["Hamlat Tohrid Ala Masrahiyyat Lina Khoury Bi Hijjat Ihanataha Lil Toqos al-Masihiyya"]. *Samir Kassir Eyes*, December 10, 2015. Retrieved in July 2016 from www.skeyesmedia.org/ar/News/Lebanon/5541.

17 N. Tohme, "Lebanese Theater: From Prominence to Decadence," *Aljazeera*, January 26, 2012. Retrieved in July 2016 from www.aljazeera.net/home/print/f6451603-4dff-4ca1-9c10-122741d17432/7d8c17d9-b969-4855-bb81-44d5cc664928.

18 A. Sarkis, "Beirut Mosques are Censored and Its Sermons Recorded," *Al Joumhouria*, February 19, 2015. Retrieved in July 2016 from www.aljoumhouria.com/news/index/213453.

19 Arab Social Media Report, 2015, "Twitter in the Arab Region." Retrieved in July 2016 from www.arabsocialmediareport.com/Twitter/LineChart.aspx?&PriMenuID=18&CatID=25&mnu=Cat.

20 Hashem Osseiran, "Lebanese Women Lead the Social Media Wave," *The Daily Star* English daily, June 27, 2014.

21 Arab Social Media Report, 2015. Arab Social Media Influencers Summit.

22 Lebanon—"Social Media Stats Lebanon," Statcounter Global Stats, July 2017–July 2018, http://gs.statcounter.com/social-media-stats/all/lebanonLebanon.

23 Bassem E. Maamari and Hala El Zein, "The Impact of Social Media on the Political Interests of the Youth in Lebanon at the Wake of the Arab Spring," *Social Science Computer Review* 32(4) (2013): 496–505.

24 Ibid.

25 Ibid.

26 F. Shoukeir, "Twitter Politicians: Minimally Care for Reaction with the Public" ["Siyasiyo Twitter: Akher Hammahom al-Tafaʿol maʿa al-Shaeb"]. *Al-Akhbar*, May 5, 2014. Retrieved in July 2016 from http://al-akhbar.com/node/205792.

27 "Twitter Arab World—Statistics Feb 2017," *WEEDOO*, March 22, 2017, https://weedoo.tech/twitter-arab-world-statistics-feb-2017/.

28 "Lebanon: 2016 TV Audience Measurement," *Ipsos*, March 1, 2017, www.ipsos.com/en/lebanon-2016-tv-audience-measurement. The survey's results are based on face-to-face interviews with about 2,500 persons in Lebanon during the fourth-quarter of 201; and "Lebanon: 2016 TV Audience Measurement," *Ipsos*, March 1, 2017, www.ipsos.com/en/lebanon-2016-tv-audience-measurement.

29 Wikipedia, "Telecommunications in Lebanon," https://en.wikipedia.org/wiki/Telecommunications_in_Lebanon, Lebanon ranks 80th on the netindex.com (as of January 12, 2014).

30 Imad Atalla, "Lebanon is Stifling Your Digital Freedom," *The Daily Star*, June 8, 2010.

31 H. Zayadin, "Lebanese Government Moves to Control Expression in the Online Realm," *Ifex*, March 28, 2014. Retrieved in 2016 from www.ifex.org/lebanon/2014/03/28/bloggers_facing_threats/.

32 Matt Nash, "Media Council Moves to Regulate News Websites," October 30, 2011, https://now.mmedia.me/lb/en/reportsfeatures/media_council_moves_to_regulate_news_ websites.

33 Magda Abu-Fadil, "Activists, Bloggers Stop Lebanese Internet Regulation Act, for Now," *The Huffington Post*, October 4, 2012.

34 Khodr Salameh, "Lebanese Internet Law Attacks Last Free Space of Expression," *Al-Akhbar* English daily, March 6, 2012. Retrieved in July 2016 from http://english.al-akhbar.com/node/4997.

35 Social Media Exchange (SMEX), "Mapping Blocked Websites in Lebanon 2015." March 26, 2015. Retrieved July 2016 from www.smex.org/mapping-blocked-websites-in-lebanon-2015/.

36 Internet World Stats, "Usage and Population Statistics. Lebanon," n.d. Retrieved in July 2016 from www.internetworldstats.com/me/lb.htm.

37 H. Chakrani, "Lebanon: Telecom Chief Doctors Documents," *Al-Akhbar* English, July 26, 2013. Retrieved in July 2016 from http://english.al-akhbar.com/content/lebanon-telecom-chief-doctors-documents.

38 M. Ayton, "Lebanon's Illegal Internet Boom Sparks Crackdown and Calls for Reform," *Middle East Eye*, April 11, 2016. Retrieved in July 2016 from www.middleeasteye.net/news/boom-illegal-internet-providers-sparks-crackdown-lebanon-502165956.

39 Lebanese National News Agency, "Harb: 2020 Plan Started, Fiber Optic will Cover All Lebanon," March 17, 2016. Retrieved in July 2016 from http://nna-leb.gov.lb/en/show-news/58627/nna-leb.gov.lb/en.

40 Tony Saghbini, "Lebanon's Bloggers are Pioneers in the Arab World," *The Daily Star*, October 8, 2010.

41 V. Abu Ghazaleh, "Lebanese Bloggers Still Have Niche." *Al-Monitor*, March 16, 2014. Retrieved in July 2016 from www.al-monitor.com/pulse/culture/2014/03/lebanon-bloggers-challenge-traditional-media.html.

42 Zayadin, "Lebanese Government Moves to Control Expression in the Online Realm."

43 Saghbini, "Lebanon's Bloggers are Pioneers in the Arab World."

44 Abu Ghazaleh, "Lebanese Bloggers Still Have Niche."

45 Reporters Without Borders (2014). Legal Harassment and Harsh Verdicts for Media Information Providers. *Reporters sans frontières*. Retrieved in July 2016 from https://rsf.org/en/news/legal-harassment-and-harsh-verdicts-media-and-information-providers.

46 D. Nasser and T. Chaaban, "Censorship across Social Media Platforms in Lebanon," Term Paper, American University of Beirut, Spring 2013.

6 Conclusion

1 See النّهار موقع على الخبر هذا إقرأ: www.annahar.com/article/506485.

2 A 2012 report by Deloitte and Touche suggests that advertising revenues in Lebanon reached $145.1 million and were projected to reach some $175 million in 2015. www.ifpinfo.com/ifpinfo-news.php?news_id=214#.WIMzsPVOIWw.

3 Ali Jaber at an American University of Beirut seminar discussion on "Arab Media and Society," November 2013.

4 Hassan Ulaik, "Not a Crisis of Lebanese Media," *Al-Akhbar*, December 31, 2016.

5 Jamal Ghosn, "The Half-Filled Glass in the 'Crisis' of the Press," *Al-Akhbar*, October 1, 2016.

6 Ibrahim el-Amin, "Challenges of the Press are Professional, Managerial, and Ethical: The Responsibility of the State is to Protect Employees before Institutions," *Al-Akhbar*, January 11, 2017.

7 See the author's published studies on the subject: Nabil H. Dajani, "Foreign Images in the Lebanese Media" (in Arabic), in *Bahithat* 6, Beirut (1999–2000): 64–96; "The Analysis of the Press in Four Arab Countries," in *The Vigilant Press* (Paris: UNESCO, 1989), 75–88; and *Disoriented Media in a Fragmented Society: The Lebanese Experience* (Beirut: American University of Beirut Press, 1992).

8 From a private discussion with Prime Minister Salim el-Hoss, October 2000.

9 Alan Hancock, *Communication Planning for Development* (Paris: UNESCO, 1981), 18.

10 Salim el-Hoss, at a public lecture, November 26, 1979.

11 Altaf Gauhar, "Free Flow of Information: Myths and Shibboleth," *Third World Quarterly* 1(3) (July 1979): 68. [Emphases mine].

12 Shada Wehbe, "Effect of Social Media in Lebanon: A Powerful Force for Change," *Social Media Tag*, www.socialmediatag.com/news/social-media-lebanon-effect-change/.

13 Diana Moukalled, "Sexuality and Social Media in Lebanese Politics," *Fikra Forum*, March 8, 2017, The Washington Institute, www.washingtoninstitute.org/fikraforum/view/this-is-a-vulgar-video-clip-but- it-is-a-good-launching-pad-for-a-discussion.

14 See Dajani, *Disoriented Media in a Fragmented Society*, 132.

15 Nabil Dajani, "Media and Social Consciousness in a Lebanese Community," *Journal of Global Communication Research*, December 2004; and "The Analysis of the Press in Four Arab Countries," in *The Vigilant Press* (Paris: UNESCO, 1989).

16 Ibid.

17 After 16 years of a civil war in which sectarianism was a major element, one does not find serious attention by the different media to portray purposely a Muslim and a Christian together.

18 Hancock, *Communication Planning for Development*, 12–14.

19 See Kaarle Nordenstreng, "Being (Truly) Critical in Media and Communication Studies: Reflections of a Media Scholar between Science and Politics," *Javnost: The Public* 23(1) (2016): 89–104.

20 UNESCO, *Meeting of Experts on Communication Policies and Planning.* COM / MD/24 (Paris, 1973), 12.

Bibliography

Abdo, Ibrahim (1958) *Sabah el-Khayr* magazine, October.

Abu-Fadil, Magda (2012, October 4) "Activists, Bloggers Stop Lebanese Internet Regulation Act, for Now." *The Huffington Post.*

Abu Ghazaleh, V. (2014, March 16) "Lebanese Bloggers Still Have Niche." *Al-Monitor.* Retrieved in July 2016 from www.al-monitor.com/pulse/culture/2014/03/lebanon-bloggers-challenge-traditional-media.html.

Abu-Laban, Baha (1966) "Factors in Social Control of the Press in Lebanon." *Journalism Quarterly* 43(3): 510–518.

Al-ltha'a magazine, September 1938, as quoted in Khuri, Fayek, al-ltha'a al-Lubnaniyah (Lebanese Broadcasting), Sader Press, Beirut, 1966.

Alterman, Jon (1998), *New Media, New Politics: From Satellite Television to the Internet in the Arab World.* Washington, DC: Washington Institute for Near East Policy.

Alterman, Jon (2002) "The Effects of Satellite Television on Arab Domestic Politics." *Transnational Broadcasting Studies Journal* 9 (Spring).

Al-Usbu' al-Arabi (1970, December 21) "Sahafat al-watan ath-thani wa kadiyat al-'ilam fi lubnan" ["The Press of the Second Nation and the Media Problems in Lebanon"], No. 602.

Al-Zubaidi, Layla, Fischer, Susanne and Abu-Fadil, Magda (2004) *Walking a Tightrope: News Media & Freedom of Expression in the Arab Middle East.* Beirut: Heinrich Böll Stiftung.

An-Nahar (2017, January 6) "Proposed Media Law Accomplished."

Arab Social Media Report (2015) "Twitter in the Arab Region." Retrieved in July 2016 from www.arabsocialmediareport.com/Twitter/LineChart.aspx?&PriMenuID=18&CatID=25&mnu=Cat.

Arsan, A. (2013) *Interlopers of Empire: The Lebanese Diaspora in Colonial French West Africa.* New York: Oxford University Press.

Atalla, Imad (2010, June 8) "Lebanon is Stifling Your Digital Freedom." *The Daily Star.*

Aucar, N., Feghaly, F., and Homsi, L. (2013) "Caricatures: An Embodiment of the Lebanon's Illusory Freedom of Expression." Term paper. Beirut: American University of Beirut.

Ayalon, Ami (1995) *The Press in the Arab Middle East: A History.* Oxford: Oxford University Press.

Ayish, Muhammad (2002) "The Impact of Arab Satellite Television on Culture and Value Systems in Arab Countries: Perspectives and Issues." *Transnational Broadcasting Studies Journal* 9 (Spring).

Ayton, M. (2016, April 11) "Lebanon's Illegal Internet Boom Sparks Crackdown and Calls for Reform." *Middle East Eye.* Retrieved in July 2016 from www.middleeasteye.net/news/boom-illegal-internet-providers-sparks-crackdown-lebanon-502165956.

Barakat, Halim (1993) *The Arab World Society, Culture & State.* Berkeley, CA: University of California Press.

Black, Ian (2008, March 10) "Drawing Defiance." *The Guardian.*

Boyd, Douglas A. (1982) "Unofficial Radio and National Dissolution: The Lebanese Experience." Unpublished paper, Department of Communication, University of Delaware, Newark, September.

Browne, Donald R. (1975) "Television as an Instrument of National Stabilization: The Lebanese Experience." *Journalism Quarterly* 52(4) (Winter).

Butros, Adel (1991) *Communication Law.* Beirut: Feghali Press.

Chakrani, H. (2013, July 26) "Lebanon: Telecom Chief Doctors Documents." *Al-Akhbar English.* Retrieved in July 2016 from http://english.al-akhbar.com/content/lebanon-telecom-chief-doctors-documents.

Corm, Georges (2004) "The Lebanese Economy: Crisis Highlights Features of Lebanon." *National Defense Magazine* 47 (January), www.lebarmy.gov.lb/ar/content.

Corm, Georges (2011) *Fi naqd al-iqtisad li-ray'i li-'arabi* [*In the Criticism of the Arab Rent Economy.* Beirut: The Center for Arab Unity Studies.

Dabbas, Antoine K. and Richo, Nakhle (2008) *Tarikh at Tiba'a al Arabiyyah fi al Mashrik* [*History of Arabic Printing in the Orient*]. Beirut: Dar an Nahar.

Dajani, Nabil (1985) "Foreign News in the Media." *Reports and Papers on Mass Communication* 93. Paris: UNESCO.

Dajani, Nabil (1989) "The Analysis of the Press in Four Arab Countries." In *The Vigilant Press, Reports and papers on mass communication* 103, Paris: UNESCO.

Dajani, Nabil (1991) "Managing the Crisis of Public Services in West Beirut." In Nabil Beyhum (ed.), *Reconstruire Beyrouth.* Paris: Etudes Sur Le Monde Arabe No. 5, 195–208.

Dajani, Nabil (1992) *Disoriented Media in a Fragmented Society: The Lebanese Experience.* Beirut: American University of Beirut Press.

Dajani, Nabil (1999–2000) "Foreign Images in the Lebanese Media." *Bahithat* 6: 64–96 [in Arabic].

Dajani, Nabil (1999–2000) "World News in the Lebanese Media." *Bahithat* 6: 64–78 [in Arabic].

Dajani, Nabil (2001) "The Changing Scene of Lebanese Television." *Transnational Broadcasting Studies Journal* 7 (Fall/Winter).

Dajani, Nabil (2001) "Freedom of Expression and Communication in Lebanon: Elite and Popular Press." *Journal of the Social Sciences* 29(4) (Winter) [in Arabic].

Dajani, Nabil (2001) "The Lebanese Media Scene." In A. Sreberny and R. L. Stevenson (eds.), *Mapping International News: Theory and Research*. Cresskill, NJ: Hampton Press.

Dajani, Nabil (2001) "Lebanese Television: Caught between Government and the Private Sector." In Joe Atkins (ed.), *Journalism as a Mission: Ethics and Purpose from an International Perspective*. Ames, IA: Iowa State University Press.

Dajani, Nabil (2002) "The Role of the Lebanese Media: Who Does the Media Really Serve?" *Lebanon Journalism Review* 1 (Spring).

Dajani, Nabil (2006) "The Re-Feudalization of the Public Sphere: Lebanese Television News Coverage and the Lebanese Political Process." *Transnational Broadcasting Studies* 16 (Spring).

Dajani, Nabil (2006) "Television in the Arab East." In Janet Wasko (ed.), *A Companion to Television*. Chichester: Blackwell Publishing, 580–600.

Dajani, Nabil (2010) "Arab Media and the Building of Public Opinion: The Missing Role." In *The Media and the Reform March in the Arab World, The Arab Anti-Corruption Organization*. Beirut: Center for Arab Unity Studies [in Arabic].

Dajani, Nabil (2011) "Arabic Books." In Noha Mellor, Khalil Rinawwi, Nabil Dajani and Muhammed I. Ayish (eds.), *Arab Media: Globalization and Emerging Media Industries*. Cambridge: Polity Press.

Dajani, Nabil (2012) "Technology Cannot a Revolution Make: Nas-Book not Facebook, in 3 Years since the Spring." Kamal Adham Center for Television & Digital Journalism, 2014; also in *Arab Media and Society* 15 (Spring).

Dajani, Nabil (2012–2013) "The Young Generation, Interactive Media and Society." *Global Media Journal* 16 (Fall/Spring).

Dajani, Nabil (2013) "Ethics and the Media: The Lebanese Experience." *Arab Media and Society* 18 (Summer).

De Tarrazi, Viscount Philippe (1913) *Tarikh as-Sahafa al-Arabiyah* [*History of the Arab Press*], Vol. 1-3, Beirut: al-Matba'a al-Adabiya. and Vol. 4, al-Matba'a al Amerciyah, 1933, Beirut.

El-Amin, Ibrahim (2017, January 11) "Challenges of the Press Are Professional, Managerial, and Ethical: The Responsibility of the State Is to Protect Employees before Institutions." *Al-Akhbar*.

El-Tounsy, Abbas (2002) "Reflections on the Arab Satellites, the Palestinian Intifada, and the Israeli War." *Transnational Broadcasting Studies Journal* 8 (Spring/Summer).

El Zein, Jihad (2017, January 14) "The Vulnerability of the Lebanese Press: Margins I see as Texts." *An-Nahar.*

Fakhreddine, Jihad (2000) "Pan-Arab Satellite Television: Now the Survival Part." *Transnational Broadcasting Studies Journal* 5.

Fanack (2017, March 23–August 8) "Lebanon's Media Landscape: An Overview." *Fanack.com*, https://fanack.com/lebanon/society-media-culture/lebanon-media/.

Fisk, Robert (2009, October 22) "End of an Era for Lebanon's Free Press." *The Independent.*

Fisk, Robert (2009, October 24) Robert Fisk about the press in Lebanon. Training Center for Journalism and News Agencies in Lebanon.

Gauhar, Altaf (1979) "Free Flow of Information: Myths and Shibboleth." *Third World Quarterly* 1(3) (July): 53–77.

Ghanem, E. (2016, April 16) "Will the True Culprits Surface in Lebanon's Infamous Internet Racket?" *Al-Monitor.* Retrieved in July 2016 from www.al-monitor.com/pulse/originals/2016/04/lebanon-internet-scandal-israel-corruption-illegal-stations.html.

Ghareeb, Edmund (2011) "New Media and the Information Revolution in the Arab World: An Assessment." *Middle East Journal* 54(3): 395–418.

Ghosn, Jamal (2016, October 1) "The 'Half-Filled' Glass in the Lebanese Press Crisis." *Al-Akhbar.*

Gilsenan, Michael (2000) *Sheikhs and the Inner Secrets, in Recognizing Islam.* London: I.B. Tauris.

Gilsenan, Michael (2016) "Lying, Honor, and Contradiction." *HAU: Journal of Ethnographic Theory* 6(2): 497–525.

El Guindi, Fudwa (2005) "The Veil Becomes the Movement." In Haideh Moghissi (ed.), *Women and Islam: Critical Concepts in Sociology: Social Conditions, Obstacles and Prospects*, Vol. 2. London: Taylor & Francis, 70–91.

Habermas, Jürgen (1991) *The Structural Transformation of the Public Sphere: An Inquiry into a Category of Bourgeois Society*, trans. Thomas Burger. Cambridge, MA: MIT Press.

Hafez, Kai (2001) *Mass Media, Politics and Society in the Middle East.* Cresskill, NJ: Hampton Press.

Haikal, M., Ghraizi, M. and Hajj Mohammad Ali, K. (n.d.) *Coffee House Meetings.* Term Paper, Beirut: The American University of Beirut.

Halloran, J. (ed.) (1980) "Mass Media and Social Consciousness in a Lebanese Community." Communication in the Community. Paris: UNESCO.

Hammoud, N. (2003, August 14) "When Horse Shoe Is on Newspaper Leftovers" ["*Hina Yakhroj Horse Shoe Min Qasasat al-Jaraed*"]. *Al-Mustaqbal*. Retrieved in July 2016 from www.almustaqbal.com/v4/Article.aspx?Type=np&Articl eid=24261.

Hamza, Abdul Latif (1965), *Al-I'lam Lahu Tarikhuh wa Mathahibuh'* [*Information Has Its History and Its Doctrines*]. Cairo: Dar al-Fikr al-Arabi.

Hancock, Alan (1981) *Communication Planning for Development*. Paris: UNESCO.

Harb, Zahera (2011) *Channels of Resistance in Lebanon: Liberation Propaganda, Hezbollah and the Media*. London: I.B. Tauris.

Hardt, Michael and Negri, Antonio (2001) *Empire*. New Haven, CT: Harvard University Press.

Al-Hasan, Hasan (n.d.) *Public Opinion, Information, and Public Relations*. Beirut: ad-Oar al-Lubnaniyah lil-Nashr.

Henley, Alexander D.M. (2016, December 16) Religious Authority and Sectarianism in Lebanon. Carnegie Endowment for International Peace, https://carnegieendowment.org/2016/12/16/religious-authority-and-sectarianism-in-lebanon-pub-66487.

IWS (Internet World Stats) (n.d.). "Usage and Population Statistics: Lebanon." Retrieved in July 2016 from www.internetworldstats.com/me/lb.htm.

Johnson, Michael (1977) "Political Bosses and Their Gangs: Zu'ama and Qabadayat in the Sunni Quarters of Beirut." In Ernest Gellner and John Waterbury (eds.), *Patrons and Clients in Mediterranean Societies*. London: Duckworth, 207–224.

Kalb, Marvin and Socolovsky, Jerome (1999) "The Emboldened Arab Press." *Harvard International Journal of Press Politics* 4(3): 1–4.

Kamalipour, Yahya R. (ed.) (1995) *The US Media and the Middle East: Images and Perception*. Westport, CT: Praeger.

Kamalipour, Yahya R. and Mowlana, Hamid (eds.) (1994) *Mass Media in the Middle East: A Comprehensive Handbook*. Westport, CT: Greenwood Press.

Al-Kasim, Faisal (1999) "Crossfire: The Arab Version." *Harvard International Journal of Press Politics* 4(3): 93–97.

Khatib, Lina (2006) *Filming the Modern Middle East: Politics in the Cinemas of Hollywood and the Arab World*. London: I.B. Tauris.

Khazen, Jihad (1999) "Censorship and State Control of the Press in the Arab World." *Harvard International Journal of Press Politics* 4(3): 87–92.

Khuri, Fayek (1966) *Al-Itha'a al-Lubnaniyah* [*Lebanese Broadcasting*]. Beirut: Sader Press.

Kraidy, Marwan (1999) "State Control of Television News in 1990s Lebanon." *Journalism and Mass Communication Quarterly* 76(3): 485–498.

Kraidy, Marwan M. (2010) *Reality Television and Arab Politics: Contention in Public Life*. Cambridge: Cambridge University Press.

Laouzi, Salim (1973) "Mabadi' Said Frayha al Wataniyyah" ["The Nationalistic Principles of Sa'id Frayha"]. *Al-Hawadith* 18(882).

Lebanese American University (2002) "Professional Ethics, Media Legislation & Freedom of Expression in Lebanon." March 1–2, Beirut.

Lebanon Corruption Report (2016) www.business-anti-corruption.com/country-profiles/lebanon updated: August 2016.

Lebanese Ministry of Agriculture (2014) "Ministry of Agriculture Strategy (2015–2019)." November, www.agriculture.gov.lb/Arabic/NewsEvents/Documents/MoA%20Strategy%202015-19%20-%20English-for%20printing.pdf (accessed November 5, 2015).

Lebanese National News Agency (NNA) (2013, January 25) "Friday Sermons: To Close the Discussion on Civil Marriage" ["Khotab al-Jomaa: Li Tayy Malaf al-Zawaj al-Madani Ila al-Abada"]. National News Agency. Retrieved in July 2016 from http://nna-leb.gov.lb/ar/show-news/15515/nna-leb.gov.lb/ar.

Lebanese National News Agency (2016, March 17) "Harb: 2020 Plan Started, Fiber Optic will Cover All Lebanon." Retrieved in July 2016 from http://nna-leb.gov.lb/en/show-news/58627/nna-leb.gov.lb/en.

Lebanese National News Agency (2017, January 6) "Information Committee Completed Discussions on a Modern Media Law."

Lebanese Press Union (1949) *Al-Mu'tamar as-Sahafi* [*The Press Conference*]. Beirut: Lebanese Press Union.

Maamari, Bassem E. and El Zein, Hala (2013) "The Impact of Social Media on the Political Interests of the Youth in Lebanon at the Wake of the Arab Spring." *Social Science Computer Review* 32(4): 496–505.

McFadden, Tom. J. (1953) *Daily Journalism in the Arab States*. Columbus, OH: Ohio State University Press.

Makdisi, Samir A. (1977) "An Appraisal of Lebanon's Post-War Economic Development and a Look to the Future." *The Middle East Journal* (Summer): 267–270.

Makdisi, Ussama (2009) *Artillery of Heaven: American Missionaries and the Failed Conversion of the Middle East*. Ithaca, NY: Cornell University Press.

Mashmushi, Amer (1979) "Towards a New Press Union." In Hilmi Malouf (ed.) *National and Modern Development of the Communication Sector*. Beirut: Lebanese University.

Mawlana, Hamid, Gerbner, George, and Schiller, Herbert I. (eds.) (1992). *Triumph of the Image: The Media's War in the Persian Gulf—A Global Perspective*. Boulder, CO: Westview Press.

Moghissi, H. (2005) "The Veil Becomes the Movement." In *Women and Islam: Critical Concepts in Sociology: Social Conditions, Obstacles and Prospects.* London: Taylor & Francis.

Moukalled, Diana (2017, March 8) "Sexuality and Social Media in Lebanese Politics." *Fikra Forum*, The Washington Institute, www.washingtoninstitute.org/fikraforum/view/this-is-a-vulgar-video-clip-but-it-is-a-good-launching-pad-for-a-discussion.

Mroueh, Adib (1961) *As-Sahafa al-Arabiyah* [*Arab Journalism*]. Beirut: Dar al-Hayat.

Mukhiber, Henry As-Sahafa (1963) "Al-Itha'a at-Talevisyun, wal-Ra'i al-'Am e Print Media" ["Radio, Television and Public Opinion"]. Unpublished monograph submitted at the Third Conference of the Political Science Association, May.

Nash, Matt (2011, October 30) "Media Council Moves to Regulate News Websites." https://now.mmedia.me/lb/en/reportsfeatures/media_council_moves_to_regulate_news_websites.

Nasser, D. and Chaaban, T. (2013) "Censorship across Social Media Platforms in Lebanon." Term Paper, American University of Beirut.

New Human Rights, Lebanon (2003) "Report on Censorship in Lebanon." (March). Nouveaux Droits de l'Homme Liban. Retrieved in July 2016 from http://aleffliban.org/sites/default/files/NDH%20Report%20Censorship.pdf.

Nordenstreng Kaarle (2016) "Being (Truly) Critical in Media and Communication Studies: Reflections of a Media Scholar Between Science and Politics." *Javnost: The Public* 23(1): 89–104.

Nuri, Uthman (1914) *Hayat Abdul Hamid wa Siyasatuhu* [*The Life and Policy of Abdul Hamid*] 3: 286.

Osseiran, Hashem (2014, June 27) "Lebanese Women Lead the Social Media Wave." *The Daily Star* English daily.

Rayashi, Iskandar (1953) *Al-Ayam al-Lubnaniyah*. Beirut: Sharikat at-Tab' wan-Nashr al-Lubnaniyah, 1957 and Beirut: *Kabl wa Ba'd*, Matabi' al-Hayat.

Reporters Without Borders (2014) "Legal Harassment and Harsh Verdicts for Media Information Providers." *Reporters sans frontières*. Retrieved in July 2016 from https://rsf.org/en/news/legal-harassment-and-harsh- verdicts-media-and-information-providers.

Republic of Lebanon (2017) "General Debt Overview." Ministry of Finance, Public Debt Directorate, August, www.finance.gov.lb/en-us/Finance/PublicDebt/PDTS/Documents/General%20Debt%20Overview%20Updated%20as%2031%20August%202017.pdf.

Republic of Lebanon, Ministry of Finance, Debt and debt Market reports. Retrieved from www.finance.gov.lb/en-US/finance/PublicDebt/Pages/DebtReports.aspx.

El-Richani, Sarah (2016) *The Lebanese Media: Anatomy of a System in Perpetual Crisis*. New York: Palgrave Macmillan.

Rifa'ie, Shamsud din (1969) *Tarik As-Sahafa As-Suriyah* [*History of the Syrian Press*], Vol. 1. Cairo: Dar al-Ma'arif bi Masr.

Rugh, William, A. (1979) *The Arab Press: News Media and Political Process in the Arab World*. Syracuse, NY: Syracuse University Press.

Rugh, William A. (2004) *Arab Mass Media: Newspapers, Radio, and Television in Arab Politics*. Westport, CT: Praeger.

Sabat, Khalil (1966) *Tarik at-Tiba'afish-Shark al-Arabi* [*The History of Printing in the Arab East*], 2nd edn. Cairo: Dar al-Ma'arif bi-masr.

Saghbini, Tony (2010, October 8) "Lebanon's Bloggers are Pioneers in the Arab World." *The Daily Star*. Retrieved in July 2016 from www.dailystar.com.lb/Opinion/Commentary/2010/Oct-08/120271-lebanons-bloggers-are-pioneers-in-the-arab-world.ashx.

Saghieh, N., Saghieh, R., and Geagea, N. (2010) *Censorship in Lebanon: Law and Practice*. Beirut: The Censorship Observatory.

Sajoo, A. (2011) *A Companion to Muslim Cultures*. London: I.B. Tauris.

Sakr, Naomi (2001) *Satellite Realms: Transnational Television, Globalization and the Middle East*. London: I.B. Tauris.

Sakr, Naomi (2002) "Arab Satellite Channels between State and Private Ownership: Current and Future Implications." *Transnational Broadcasting Studies Journal* 9 (Fall/Winter).

Sakr, Naomi (2007) *Arab Television Today*. London: I.B. Tauris.

Salameh, Ibrahim (1967) "As-Sahafah al Lubnaniyyah fil Madi wa fil Musttakbal" ["The Lebanese Press: Past and Present"]. *Ath-Thakafah al-Arabiyah* 10, 173–175.

Salameh, Khodr (2012, March 6) "Lebanese Internet Law Attacks Last Free Space of Expression." *Al-Akhbar English*. Retrieved in July 2016 from http://english.al-akhbar.com/node/4997.

Salvatore, A. (2005) *Religion, Social Practice, and Contested Hegemonies Reconstructing the Public Sphere in Muslim Majority Societies*. New York: Palgrave Macmillan.

Sarkis, A. (2015, February 19) "Beirut Mosques are Censored and Its Sermons Recorded" ["Masajed Beirut Wa Dawahiha Moraqaba … Wa Khotab Al Mashayekh Tosajjal"]. *Al-Joumhouria*. Retrieved in July 2016 from www.aljoumhouria.com/news/index/213453.

Saud, Ghassan (2017, January 11) "An Nahar Crisis, the Tweini Family Eats Sour Grapes." *Al-Akhbar*.

Schleifer, Abdallah (2000) "Does Satellite TV Pay in the Arab World Footprint: Exploring the Economic Feasibility." *Transnational Broadcasting Studies Journal* 5 (Fall/Winter).

Shaheen, May (1957) *Shari' as-Sahafa* [*The Press Street*], 2nd edn. Cairo: Dar al-Ma'arif bi Masr.

Shobokshi, H. (2012, December 29) "Honoring Pierre Sadek." *Asharq al-Awsat.* Retrieved in July 2016 from http://english.aawsat.com/2012/12/article55239336/honoring-pierre-sadek.

Shoukeir, F. (2014, May 5) "Twitter Politicians: Minimally Care for Reaction with the Public" ["Siyasiyo Twitter: Akher Hammahom al-Tafa'ol ma'a al-Shaeb"]. *Al-Akhbar.* Retrieved in July 2016 from http://al-akhbar.com/node/205792.

Singal, Jesse (2016) "'Citizen Journalism' Is a Catastrophe Right Now, and It'll Only Get Worse." *Intelligencer,* New York Magazine, October 19, 2016. http://nymag.com/selectall/2016/10/citizen-journalism-is-a-catastrophe-itll-only-get-worse.html.

SKeyes (2015, December 10) "Provocation against Lina Khoury's Play for Offending Christian Rituals" ["Hamlat Tohrid Ala Masrahiyyat Lina Khoury Bi Hijjat Ihanataha Lil Toqos Al Masihiyya"]. *Samir Kassir Eyes.* Retrieved in July 2016 from www.skeyesmedia.org/ar/News/Lebanon/5541.

SMEX (Social Media Exchange) (2015, March 26) "Mapping Blocked Websites in Lebanon 2015." *Social Media Exchange.* Retrieved in July 2016 from www.smex.org/mapping-blocked-websites-in-lebanon-2015/.

Tohme, N. (2012, January 26) "Lebanese Theater: From Prominence to Decadence" ["Al-Masrah al-Lobnani: Min Arriyada Lil Tarajoa"]. *AlJazeeraNet.* Retrieved in July 2016 from www.aljazeera.net/home/print/f6451603-4dff-4ca1-9c10-122741d17432/7d8c17d9-b969-4855-bb81-44d5cc664928.

Trombetta, Lorenzo, Lebanon—Media Landscape, European Journalism Centre (EJC) 2018, MediaLandscapes.org.

Ulaik, Hassan (2016, December 31) "Not a Crisis of Lebanese Media." *Al-Akhbar.*

UNESCO (1982) Reports and Papers on Mass Communication, "Report on the Study in Lebanon." *Communication in the Community* 87, Paris.

UNESCO (1985) "Foreign News in the Media." Reports and Papers on Mass Communication, No. 93, Paris.

United Nations Development Programme (n.d.) "Lebanon: Religious Media, Why Does It Matter?" www.lb.undp.org/content/lebanon/en/home/ourwork/crisispreventionandrecovery/successstories/Religious-Media-why-does-it-matter.html.

Al-Usbu' al-Arabi (1970, December 21) "Sahafat al-watan ath-thani wa kadiyat al-'ilam fi lubnan" ["The Press of the Second Nation and the Media Problems in Lebanon"], No. 602.

Wehbe, Shada (2016, August 5) "Effect of Social Media in Lebanon: A Powerful Force for Change." www.socialmediatag.com/news/social-media-lebanon-effect-change/.

Wikipedia (2014) "Telecommunications in Lebanon." Retrieved on January 12, 2014
    from https://en.wikipedia.org/wiki/Telecommunications_in_Lebanon, Lebanon
    ranks 80th on the netindex.com.

Yamak, Labib Zuwiyya (1966) "Party Politics in the Lebanese Political System." In
    Leonard Binder (ed.), *Politics in Lebanon*. New York: John Willey.

Yazbek, Yusuf Ibrahim (1969) *Tarikh as-Sahafa al-Lubnaniyah* [*History of the
    Lebanese Press*]. In *Al-I'lam fil Hayat al-Hadirah* [*Information in the Present*].
    Beirut: Institute of the Press, Lebanese University.

Zayadin, H. (2014, March 28) "Lebanese Government Moves to Control Expression
    in the Online Realm." *Ifex*. Retrieved in July 2016 from www.ifex.org/
    lebanon/2014/03/28/bloggers_facing_threats/.

Index

Page numbers followed by f and n indicate figures and notes, respectively.